VOLUME 510　　　　　　　　　　　　　　　　　　　　JULY 1990

THE ANNALS

of The American Academy *of* Political
and Social Science

RICHARD D. LAMBERT, *Editor*
ALAN W. HESTON, *Associate Editor*

WORLD POPULATION:

APPROACHING THE YEAR 2000

Special Editor of this Volume

SAMUEL H. PRESTON

University of Pennsylvania
Philadelphia

Ⓢ SAGE PUBLICATIONS　*NEWBURY PARK　LONDON　NEW DELHI*

2.9.6.62

THE ANNALS

© 1990 *by* The American Academy *of* Political *and* Social Science

ERICA GINSBURG, *Assistant Editor*

Editorial Office: 3937 Chestnut Street, Philadelphia, PA 19104.
For information about membership* (individuals only) and subscriptions (institutions), address:

SAGE PUBLICATIONS, INC.
2111 West Hillcrest Drive
Newbury Park, CA 91320

HB
149.4+
A4 92-7
99°
v.5 10

From India and South Asia, write to:	*From the UK, Europe, the Middle East and Africa, write to:*
SAGE PUBLICATIONS INDIA Pvt. Ltd.	SAGE PUBLICATIONS LTD
P.O. Box 4215	28 Banner Street
New Delhi 110 048	London EC1Y 8QE
INDIA	ENGLAND

SAGE Production Editors: KITTY BEDNAR and LIANN LECH
*Please note that members of The Academy receive THE ANNALS with their membership.
Library of Congress Catalog Card Number 89-60870
International Standard Serial Number ISSN 0002-7162
International Standard Book Number ISBN 0-8039-3599-4 (Vol. 510, 1990 paper)
International Standard Book Number ISBN 0-8039-3598-6 (Vol. 510, 1990 cloth)
Manufactured in the United States of America. First printing, July 1990.

> The articles appearing in THE ANNALS are indexed in *Book Review Index, Public Affairs Information Service Bulletin, Social Sciences Index, Current Contents, General Periodicals Index, Academic Index, Pro-Views,* and *Combined Retrospective Index Sets.* They are also abstracted and indexed in *ABC Pol Sci, Historical Abstracts, Human Resources Abstracts, Social Sciences Citation Index, United States Political Science Documents, Social Work Research & Abstracts, Sage Urban Studies Abstracts, International Political Science Abstracts, America: History and Life, Sociological Abstracts, Managing Abstracts, Social Planning/Policy & Development Abstracts, Automatic Subject Citation Alert, Book Review Digest, Work Related Abstracts, and/or Family Resources Database.*

Information about membership rates, institutional subscriptions, and back issue prices may be found on the facing page.

Advertising. Current rates and specifications may be obtained by writing to THE ANNALS Advertising and Promotion Manager at the Newbury Park office (address above).

Claims. Claims for undelivered copies must be made no later than three months following month of publication. The publisher will supply missing copies when losses have been sustained in transit and when the reserve stock will permit.

Change of Address. Six weeks' advance notice must be given when notifying of change of address to ensure proper identification. Please specify name of journal. Send address changes to: THE ANNALS, c/o Sage Publications, Inc., 2111 West Hillcrest Drive, Newbury Park, CA 91320.

Origin and Purpose. The Academy was organized December 14, 1889, to promote the progress of political and social science, especially through publications and meetings. The Academy does not take sides in controverted questions, but seeks to gather and present reliable information to assist the public in forming an intelligent and accurate judgment.

Meetings. The Academy holds an annual meeting in the spring extending over two days.

Publications. THE ANNALS is the bimonthly publication of The Academy. Each issue contains articles on some prominent social or political problem, written at the invitation of the editors. Also, monographs are published from time to time, numbers of which are distributed to pertinent professional organizations. These volumes constitute important reference works on the topics with which they deal, and they are extensively cited by authorities throughout the United States and abroad. The papers presented at the meetings of The Academy are included in THE ANNALS.

Membership. Each member of The Academy receives THE ANNALS and may attend the meetings of The Academy. Membership is open only to individuals. Annual dues: $32.00 for the regular paperbound edition (clothbound, $45.00). Add $9.00 per year for membership outside the U.S.A. Members may also purchase single issues of THE ANNALS for $8.95 each (clothbound, $12.95).

Subscriptions. THE ANNALS (ISSN 0002-7162) is published six times annually — in January, March, May, July, September, and November. Institutions may subscribe to THE ANNALS at the annual rate: $72.00 (clothbound, $89.00). Add $9.00 per year for subscriptions outside the U.S.A. Institutional rates for single issues: $12.95 each (clothbound, $17.95).

Second class postage paid at Philadelphia, Pennsylvania, and at additional mailing offices.

Single issues of THE ANNALS may be obtained by individuals who are not members of The Academy for $8.95 each (clothbound, $17.00). Single issues of THE ANNALS have proven to be excellent supplementary texts for classroom use. Direct inquiries regarding adoptions to THE ANNALS c/o Sage Publications (address below).

All correspondence concerning membership in The Academy, dues renewals, inquiries about membership status, and/or purchase of single issues of THE ANNALS should be sent to THE ANNALS c/o Sage Publications, Inc., 2111 West Hillcrest Drive, Newbury Park, CA 91320. *Please note that orders under $25 must be prepaid.* Sage affiliates in London and India will assist institutional subscribers abroad with regard to orders, claims, and inquiries for both subscriptions and single issues.

THE ANNALS

of The American Academy *of* Political *and* Social Science

RICHARD D. LAMBERT, *Editor*
ALAN W. HESTON, *Associate Editor*

FORTHCOMING

LANGUAGE IN THE WORKPLACE
Special Editors: Richard D. Lambert
Sarah Jane Moore

Volume 511   September 1990

THE NORDIC REGION:
CHANGING PERSPECTIVES IN INTERNATIONAL RELATIONS
Special Editor: Martin O. Heisler

Volume 512   November 1990

JAPAN'S EXTERNAL ECONOMIC RELATIONS:
JAPANESE PERSPECTIVES
Special Editors: Solomon B. Levine
Koji Taira

Volume 513   January 1991

See page 3 for information on Academy membership and
purchase of single volumes of **The Annals.**

CONTENTS

BOOK DEPARTMENT CONTENTS

SOCIOLOGY

ECONOMICS

PREFACE

This volume is designed to introduce to a broad audience some of the best contemporary research on population issues in the world's major regions. The selections were chosen not because they were addressed to a specific problem or because they were united in approach or style. Instead, authors whose research on population change had demonstrated unusual distinction and insight were invited to describe and illustrate their research. In some cases their efforts take the form of reviews of research on major issues, but more often they present new information and analyses that elaborate upon themes that they had already addressed.

The most recent issue of *The Annals* dealing entirely with population matters was published in 1967.[1] In order to set the stage for what follows, it is useful to describe briefly some of the major demographic trends, as well as trends in population research, that have occurred in the interim.

Twenty years ago, most demographers were focusing their attention on what was widely acknowledged to be the "population problem." The number of humans was believed to be expanding too rapidly, especially in poor countries, where resources to support additional people were least abundant. This concern was reflected in both the title and the contents of an important National Academy of Sciences report, *Rapid Population Growth.*[2] But rapid growth was also a problem in the United States, where the President's Commission on Population Growth and the American Future was preparing its report addressing the environmental, economic, and social threats raised by sustained growth.[3] Both internationally and nationally, the preferred response to this problem was governmental sponsorship of family planning programs: subsidization of services that better enable individuals to act on their preferences for smaller families. Some argued that these programs did not go far enough because people wanted more children than were socially desirable.[4] Childbearing customs had evolved over centuries, and it appeared to many that they would change very slowly even though the conditions facing couples — especially the survival of their children — could change much more quickly.

This conception of the population problem is alive and well. It continues to motivate a great deal of international programmatic and research activity in the population field, including that of the largest donor, the U.S. Agency for International Development, as well as that of the United Nations, the World Bank, and many foundations. Along the way, reproductive rights and the health advantages of smaller families have been added

1. John D. Durand, ed., *The Annals* of the American Academy of Political and Social Science, vol. 369, *World Population* (Jan. 1967).

2. National Academy of Sciences, *Rapid Population Growth: Consequences and Policy Implications* (Baltimore, MD: Johns Hopkins University Press, 1971).

3. Commission on Population Growth and the American Future, *Population and the American Future* (Washington, DC: Government Printing Office, 1972).

4. Kingsley Davis, "Population Policy: Will Current Programs Succeed?" *Science,* 10 Nov. 1967, pp. 730-39.

to economic and environmental concerns as important justifications for family planning programs.

Yet much has changed in twenty years. In part because of the success of family planning programs themselves, birth rates in the world as a whole have declined by an average of 20 percent since 1965-69, while the total fertility rate — the average number of births to a woman who has completed childbearing — has declined by 30 percent (see Table 1). Only Africa fails to show widespread declines in birth rates. Fertility levels in every European and North American country, along with Japan and several other East Asian countries, have fallen below the replacement level — the level required in order to avoid a decline in size between successive generations. China's success in reducing fertility has been perhaps most spectacular in view of its size and low income level, but its program has raised troubling questions about human rights by violating the voluntaristic principles of family planning programs.

Despite the sizable declines that have occurred in fertility, the growth rate of the world's population has fallen by only 16 percent since 1965-70 because death rates have continued to fall rapidly. Furthermore, the base to which growth rates are applied continues to expand. About 438 million people were added to the world's population between 1985 and 1990, compared to the 362 million added between 1965 and 1970. The momentum of population growth ensures that a rapid expansion of the adult population will occur beyond the time when women achieve replacement-level fertility.[5]

Partly fueled by concern with the population problem and partly on its own internal dynamics, the field of population studies has flowered in the past two decades. The number of demographic surveys in developing countries has grown by an order of magnitude, shedding a great deal of light on quantitative dimensions of demographic parameters. At the same time, the limitations of such surveys have become increasingly apparent, leading some analysts to undertake much more intensive ethnographic studies. These studies suggest that the earlier view of fertility in developing countries as deeply encrusted in custom and convention needs modification. Childbearing motives appear to be most profitably treated as components of household strategies for survival and advancement. Since the institutional and economic context within which families operate varies dramatically from Bangladesh to China to Sierra Leone to Colombia, it is only through intensive inquiries at specific locations and involving specific groups that the demographic features of these strategies can be illuminated.

One of the major by-products of the many fertility surveys has been a much more precise mapping of the levels of and differences in child mortality in developing countries. Because of their ability to measure and interpret child-mortality variation, demographers have come to play a leading role in international health analysis. Meetings of major population associations now include nearly as many sessions on mortality as on fertility, a far cry from a decade ago. Yet the limitations of survey data are no less apparent in studies of mortality than of fertility, and a number of investigators are attempting to enrich the knowledge of mortality conditions through investigation of household-level processes in particular sites.

5. Nathan Keyfitz, "On the Momentum of Population Growth," *Demography,* 8:71-80 (1971); Samuel H. Preston, "The Relation between Actual and Intrinsic Growth Rates," *Population Studies,* 40:343-51 (1986).

TABLE 1
POPULATION SIZE AND COMPONENTS OF CHANGE IN MAJOR REGIONS OF THE WORLD, 1965-70 AND 1985-90

	Population Size (millions)		Annual Growth Rate (percentage)		Crude Birth Rate (per 1,000)		Crude Death Rate (per 1,000)		Total Fertility Rate		Life Expectancy at Birth	
	1970	1990	1965-70	1985-90	1965-70	1985-90	1965-70	1985-90	1965-70	1985-90	1965-70	1985-90
World	3,698	5,292	2.06	1.73	33.9	27.1	13.3	9.9	4.88	3.44	53.8	61.5
Africa	363	648	2.63	3.00	47.7	44.7	21.1	14.9	6.71	6.23	44.1	51.9
Latin America	285	448	2.60	2.09	37.9	29.1	10.9	7.5	5.50	3.61	58.7	66.0
North America	226	276	1.13	0.82	18.0	15.0	9.3	8.6	2.54	1.81	70.5	75.5
East Asia (including China)	986	1,334	2.42	1.31	34.6	19.7	10.4	6.7	5.39	2.31	60.2	69.9
South Asia	754	1,202	2.40	2.34	41.9	35.2	18.1	11.8	5.96	4.72	47.4	56.9
Europe	460	498	0.67	0.23	17.7	13.0	10.4	10.7	2.50	1.74	70.6	74.2

SOURCE: United Nations, *World Population Prospects, 1988* (New York: United Nations, 1989).

Birth and death are biological as well as social events, and population scientists have made great progress in understanding the biology of reproduction in the past several decades. Much of what is known has originated in a population laboratory in Bangladesh, where exceedingly detailed studies of reproductive cycles could be conducted. Less progress has been made in identifying key biological elements of mortality, in part because the process is much more complex. The important role of diarrheal diseases in child mortality in poor countries has been firmly established, however, and effective and inexpensive means have been developed to combat it.

The sharp reductions that have occurred in fertility in much of the world have produced rapid changes in age distributions: declining proportions of children and increasing proportions of the elderly. A substantial amount of demographic research is being addressed to the potential problems created by solutions to the problem of rapid growth. In particular, will the state be required to subsidize more heavily the growing elderly populations in developing countries, who will have fewer offspring on whom to rely? In developed countries, are the family changes that are associated with below-replacement fertility producing diminished well-being for children at the same time that social programs are increasingly being directed to the older population?

ORGANIZATION OF THIS VOLUME

As fertility rates have fallen, the bases for government intervention in childbearing have come under closer scrutiny. In deciding whether to have an additional birth, most families appear to go through some informal process of weighing the costs and benefits of such an action. But if it is in the parents' interest to have a birth, why is it not also in the government's interest? A conventional answer is that one couple's children reduce the well-being of other families; their childbearing creates negative externalities. But demonstrations of such an impact are nearly nonexistent. Because of the centrality of this issue to current discussions of the population problem, the volume begins with an article by Ronald Lee that attempts to quantify the externalities to childbearing in five countries.

Lee's results are surprising and challenge current justifications for fertility-reduction policies that go beyond provision of family planning services. The negative externalities to childbearing are extremely modest in Kenya, Bangladesh, and India and reach the level of annual per capita income only in Saudi Arabia, where additional births dilute ownership rights to the vast state-owned oil resources. In the United States, on the other hand, the externalities to childbearing are positive and very large at approximately $105,000. They result from the fact that an additional birth permits greater cost sharing for public goods such as defense, as well as easier repayment of the national debt. They also reflect the fact that public expenditures are heavily biased toward the elderly and hence more readily absorbed in a population with a younger age structure. Lee's estimates of the externalities to childbearing in the United States are not very different from recent estimates of the private cost to parents of raising a child to adulthood, implying that most of these expenditures are in a sense direct contributions by parents to the commonweal. Lee's article provides a clear justification for greater subsidization of childbearing and child rearing in the United States, where child costs are privatized to a greater extent than in Europe.

Externalities need not exist in order to justify family planning programs, although some of the enthusiasm for such programs is certainly predicated on their presumed existence. In their purest form, however, such programs simply allow couples to achieve their desired family size, without attempting to influence or constrain those desires. Family planning programs in something resembling their pure form have been the principal form of state action in the area of fertility.

Have they worked? One measure is whether couples have taken advantage of the services offered and reduced their rates of childbearing. The next article, by Ronald Freedman, reviews the evidence regarding the impact of family planning programs on aggregate fertility levels. The clearest evidence that programs can work is derived from well-designed studies in small geographic areas, especially the study in the Matlab area in Bangladesh, where an experimental design was rigorously implemented. China's program also seems principally responsible for the major fertility declines there in the 1970s. The Bangladesh and Chinese experiences are also considered in later chapters by Menken and Phillips and by Greenhalgh.

Extending these results to other areas is not straightforward. Freedman notes a close international correlation between the effectiveness of family planning programs and declines in fertility, but he discusses the inevitable reservations that correlational studies raise, including the possibility that a society's unmeasured desires to reduce fertility influence whether it mounts a family planning program. Some countries such as India, with a long-standing family planning program, have barely nudged the birth rate, while others like Brazil have had major declines in fertility without governmental programs. Such programs are clearly neither necessary nor sufficient to reduce fertility, and Freedman discusses some of the other influential macro-level conditions. But he cautiously concludes that family planning programs have probably played a major independent role in fertility declines in many places.

The next two articles deal with recent changes in patterns of, respectively, mortality and migration at a global level. John Caldwell offers a major synthesis of micro- and macro-level studies of mortality determinants during the twentieth century, based in part on fieldwork that he has conducted in West Africa, South India, and Sri Lanka. Caldwell has almost single-handedly moved mortality studies in developing countries into the realm of the social and behavioral sciences, and in this article he clearly demonstrates the value of this merger.

He argues that reductions in mortality have been principally a result of changes in social relations within the family, especially the greater sense of autonomy and efficacy among mothers, combined with improvements in the accessibility of modern health services. Improvements in education and greater exposure to Western ideas are the key factors that have transformed beliefs that illness is of divine or magical inspiration into recognition that modern medicine can prevent or treat major infectious diseases. In turn, these changes are part of the dismantling of subsistence production systems and the development of markets. While advances in education or Westernization and in health services can have a substantial impact on their own, Caldwell argues that it is the combination of the two that has the greatest payoff. His arguments are abundantly illustrated, and they add up to the most comprehensive statement currently available about the social origins of the mortality revolution.

Douglas Massey focuses on international migration, especially on the new streams from South to North that have emerged in the postwar period. But his explanations of these patterns are similar in many respects to Caldwell's. In summarizing and integrating recent research on factors driving migration, Massey assigns primacy to the destruction of the small-scale institutions typical of subsistence agrarian societies that results from industrialization and formation of markets. He notes the centrality of families as the decision-making units in responding to the new conditions. In particular, migration is an important strategy whereby families can reduce uncertainty in their future income prospects through spreading their risks across widely varying circumstances. Once begun, migration streams endure because of the family linkages established between areas of origin and destination. Policymakers cannot fine-tune migration streams as they would the money supply, in his apt analogy, because of the momentum that they acquire. Since international migration is now responsible for about one-third of the population growth in the United States and is likely to increase as a component of growth in most of the developed world, his conclusions are timely and important.

The remaining articles focus on demographic processes in more narrowly defined regions of the world. Asia accounts for 59 percent of the human population and much of its diversity as well. The first three selections focus on different regions of Asia.

Susan Greenhalgh considers the forces underlying recent fertility change in China. She argues that, while the Chinese population-control policies were pivotal in the birth-rate reduction that occurred during the 1970s, they would not have succeeded to the same extent without very tight state control of jobs, housing, and other major sectors of the economy. The extension of this control to very local levels was essential to the enforcement of targets. As economic liberalization policies in the countryside were introduced in the 1980s, rural birth rates began to climb. She also suggests that other socialist policies had reduced the benefits of children to parents by the early 1970s in a way that facilitated the fertility decline. Her powerful interpretation of these events suggests that little of China's experience with population policies is transferable to other countries and raises the possibility that China — which alone accounted for 51 percent of the birth-rate decline in developing countries between 1965-70 and 1985-90 — may be on the verge of a sizable increase in fertility.

Bangladesh is one of the world's poorest countries. Because of its population density, slow technical progress, high birth rates, and limited resources, it raises the Malthusian specter more vividly than any other region. In contrast to most poor countries, however, Bangladesh has superb demographic data by virtue of the Demographic Surveillance System in Matlab, a reasonably representative area.

Jane Menken and James Phillips review the lessons that have been learned from this unique resource. Most of them are of a biomedical nature, befitting a population where biological imperatives are paramount. It is in Matlab that the linkages between nutritional status of both mother and child, breast-feeding, and fecundity have been most clearly established. Demonstrating how these have combined to produce the sharp seasonality of births is demographic detective work at its best. Matlab has also taught us much about the consequences of unfortunate natural experiments such as the famine of 1974-75. Yet not all of its lessons are biomedical. As noted earlier, it has been the scene of the most carefully conducted experiment in the delivery of family planning services to a poor rural population. That this experiment produced a sharp reduction in fertility is a decisive indication that there were preexisting but unrealized desires to reduce fertility and that supply factors can influence fertility outcomes.

The changes in fertility and mortality that most of the developing world has experienced have been sharpest in East Asia. They are both causes and consequences of radical changes in family relations between generations and sexes. Linda Martin offers a wide-ranging assessment of these changes in China, Japan, Korea, and Taiwan, based primarily on the good survey data available in these countries. She notes a decline of arranged marriages and of coresidence of the elderly and their children. The balance of power in generational relations between women is shifting toward younger women, who are better educated and more likely to be working outside the home. At the same time, the pressure for care of the elderly expands as more survive and fewer offspring are available to share the task. Although change is evident, the intergenerational coresidential family remains a far more prominent and cohesive entity than in the West. Economic and demographic change is transforming the lives of individuals through a distinctive Confucian filter.

Africa has its own distinctions. Family systems in parts of sub-Saharan Africa appear more fluid than in any other major region, although they are echoed in areas of overseas African settlement and increasingly imitated in the West. Not infrequently, men have multiple wives, and with increasing frequency women have alliances with several men. Unions vary in intensity and obligations and often progress from one state to another. Children are often exchanged between families seeking to establish ties with each other. The relationships are poorly captured by conventional demographic surveys, whose categories typically reflect Western norms.

Based largely upon her fieldwork in Sierra Leone, Caroline Bledsoe describes the complexity of sexual and marital unions in West Africa. She argues that the unstructured nature of union formation and childbearing allows wide play for self-interested behavior and rapid adjustment to broad economic and social change. Her discussion of how the increased educational levels of young women have disturbed previous patterns, in a setting where Christian ideals are often embraced by the better-educated, is especially vivid. Understanding the nature of family relations in Africa, she points out, is a necessary prelude to constructing sound policies for improving child health, reducing rates of childbearing, and blunting the spread of the epidemic of acquired immune deficiency syndrome.

Alberto Palloni then summarizes his major efforts to document demographic changes in Latin America during the twentieth century and to explicate their sources. Since vital registration systems are incomplete in most of Latin America, he has undertaken a large project of demographic reconstruction. The effort is not limited to classic measures of vital rates but extends to indicators of the roles of marriage, marital fertility, contraception, and breast-feeding. The results demonstrate a diversity of patterns around several common themes: mortality declines that in the early stages appeared to be independent of levels of economic development but that at later stages became more closely associated with them; and a rapid fertility decline during recent decades in a number of countries that is clearly attributable to increased use of contraception but less obviously associated with government-sponsored family planning programs. Palloni's careful documentation of these changes in individual Latin American countries shows the futility of treating the continent as a single entity and lays a sound basis for any appreciation of its complex demography.

The final two articles in the volume deal with the major demographic issues in the two largest industrialized countries: family change in the United States and ethnicity in the Soviet Union. Andrew Cherlin describes the convulsive changes in the American family over the past several decades: reduced marriage and fertility, increased divorce and cohabitation. Only now are data systems coming to grips with the increased informality of American sexual unions, and they reveal that about half of American couples now cohabit before marriage. Cohabitation with new partners after marriages end has also risen, accounting for some of the decline in rates of remarriage. Cherlin suggests that these changes have both an economic and an ideational basis: an increased cultural emphasis on autonomy and personal growth that was facilitated by an economy that allowed basic material needs to be more readily satisfied. There is no obvious reason to regret that adults now have a wider range of options available in their quest for self-fulfillment, but there are clear indications that family changes have left some damaging marks on children. Cherlin suggests that concern with child quality, partly provoked by anxieties about the future performance of the labor force, are likely to be more prominent in the next few years than concern with below-replacement fertility.

Barbara Anderson and Brian Silver are among the first analysts to have access to results from the Soviet Union's census of 1989. They take the opportunity to describe the extraordinary ethnic heterogeneity of the Soviet Union and changes therein. Muslim ethnic groups, which constitute only a sixth of the population, have accounted for half of the recent population growth. In the next few years, Russians will no longer constitute a majority of the population. Official policies designed to induce greater residential mixing of ethnic groups have been retracted because they exacerbated ethnic tensions and threatened ethnic distinctiveness. Reflecting this change, there has been net out-migration of Russians from regions that are traditionally non-Russian. The ethnic divisions of the Soviet Union, which map quite closely onto regional divisions, loom portentously over the path to full democracy.

Each of the authors was invited to speculate about what might happen over the next decade in his or her particular area of expertise. Most declined the invitation, and those who accepted were exceedingly cautious. Their reserve probably reflects an appreciation of the enormous demographic changes that have occurred in the past two decades. It also reflects the fact that, as demographers have peered more closely into the institutions from which demographic change originates, the world seems more and more complex and differentiated. Family, state, market, culture, media, and schools are not unidimensional entities, nor are their salient dimensions readily measured. Fuzzy sets are replacing some of the mechanistic formulations that earlier characterized the field. Yet the demographic variables themselves are among the most precisely measured and concrete social indicators, even in developing countries. This confrontation between demographic clarities and the indistinct topology of social life is producing some of the most interesting research in the social sciences today. Even if we may not know much about the year 2000 until we get there, we can be grateful for the considerable light that has been shed on recent events.

SAMUEL H. PRESTON

ANNALS, *AAPSS*, **510,** July 1990

Population Policy and Externalities to Childbearing

By RONALD LEE
with the assistance of
TIM MILLER

ABSTRACT: When individual couples make informed fertility decisions that reflect a concern for the future well-being of their own children, the aggregate demographic outcome should be both socially and individually optimal. This result depends on several assumptions, including the absence of externalities to childbearing — costs and benefits of children that fall on society at large without impinging on their parents directly or passing through markets. Four categories of externalities are here evaluated: reproductive dilution of collective wealth; cost spreading for public goods; public-sector intergenerational transfers — health, education, and pensions; and other governmental expenditures. Intergenerational transfers are found to create large positive externalities in industrial welfare states but small negative ones in Third World countries. Public goods lead to sizable positive externalities in both groups of countries. Other governmental expenditures lead to considerable negative externalities. Collective wealth in the form of publicly owned mineral reserves leads in some cases to enormous negative externalities, while in other cases it is of little importance. No evaluation is attempted for collective environmental wealth, scale returns, or induced technological change.

Ronald Lee has been, since 1979, professor of demography and economics at the University of California, Berkeley, following eight years at the University of Michigan. He holds graduate degrees from Harvard and Berkeley.

Tim Miller is a graduate student in demography and economics at the University of California, Berkeley. He holds a B.A. in economics from Princeton.

A young couple is delighted at the birth of their child. If it is a typical couple, the mother may reduce her work outside the home while the father increases his, leaving total family income roughly unchanged. But the per capita income of the household drops, since the denominator has increased by one person. Similarly, national per capita income drops because total income is unchanged while the denominator increases. Every birth has these effects, in the short run at least. Should the national government, for this reason, seek to reduce fertility and thereby raise per capita income? Most people, I am sure, would not think so. Why, then, would many people view possible aggregate-level evidence that more rapid population growth leads to slower growth in per capita income as providing grounds for governmental intervention in family-building decisions?

There is, in fact, a potentially sound reason: perhaps not all the costs and benefits of bearing and rearing the child, and of the child's eventual adult roles, are borne by the parents. Costs and benefits passed on to society at large are called externalities to childbearing. Many possible examples come readily to mind. The child receives subsidized health and education services; it will enter the labor market and claim a job that uses capital, and by doing so it will reduce the wages of all other workers while raising rents and profits of owners; it will pay taxes and share the burden of costly social investments; it will marry and bear children; it will contribute to the congestion of sidewalks, roadways, airports, and parks; its noise will disturb some, as its company will gladden others; it will save and accumulate assets that may raise the productivity of other workers; it will eventually retire and receive a costly pension; its activities will release carbon dioxide and contribute to global warming;

it will finally receive costly medical care that is highly subsidized. In these and many other ways, positive and negative effects of the birth of the child and all its descendants will ripple through the society and the economy affecting not only its parents but all others for ever after. It may be as misleading to view the birth of a child as a purely private matter as it is to view it as a purely public one.

Yet such pervasive consequences of childbearing do not in themselves justify public intervention in reproductive decision making. Most of our actions have far-flung consequences, but most do not warrant intervention. Modern economic theory confirms Adam Smith's insight that the actions of self-serving individuals are knit by competitive markets into socially optimal outcomes. So long as the consequences of our actions are mediated by competitive markets, laissez-faire is an efficient policy. Recent theoretical analysis of fertility decision making has confirmed that the theorem applies here as well.[1] It is only the costs and benefits of fertility that are not transmitted through the market, that is, externalities to childbearing, that lead to divergences of private and social interests. Not all the consequences previously listed are externalities; nonetheless, many are, and these may justify public intervention in family-building decisions.

Indeed, arguments for and against governmental intervention are frequently based on assertions about reproductive ex-

1. M. Nerlove, A. Razin, and E. Sadka, "Socially Optimal Population Size and Individual Choice," in *Economic Theory of Optimal Population*, ed. Klaus F. Zimmerman (Berlin: Springer-Verlag, 1989), pp. 19-38; Robert Willis, "Externalities and Population," in *Population Growth and Economic Development: Issues and Evidence*, ed. D. Gale Johnson and Ronald D. Lee (Madison: Wisconsin University Press, 1987), pp. 661-700.

ternalities, as illustrated by the following quote from the World Bank: "Each individual family's decision to have another child seems rational. Yet added together, these separate decisions make all families, and especially children, worse off in the end. There is a gap between the private and social gains to large families."[2]

To sharpen the discussion, it is useful to draw the somewhat artificial distinction between the classical family planning program, on the one hand, and programs going beyond family planning, on the other. Family planning programs assist families to attain the family size they desire through subsidies for contraceptive research, information, and distribution. Policies going beyond family planning seek to alter the desired number of children through propaganda or incentives or to alter fertility independent of desires, perhaps through coercive means.[3] Family planning programs can be justified in many ways, since they merely increase the options open to individual couples and seek to remedy deficiencies in the provision of such services by the private market. Programs going beyond family planning can be justified only by an appeal to large reproductive externalities. Assessment of reproductive externalities must therefore be central to the entire debate over population policy.

The distinction between those costs and benefits of childbearing borne by the parents and those spilling over to others can-

not be drawn without reference to the institutional arrangements of each particular society, and the relative importance of different kinds of externalities will likewise depend on economic circumstances that may depend in part on the density of the population. For example, the modern welfare state, with its extensive taxes, subsidies, and income transfers, is particularly subject to certain kinds of reproductive externalities. In a society of autonomous family farms with no public sector, most actions, including childbearing, would have fewer spillover consequences. In a society in which property rights were largely undefined and rights of resource use were communal, reproductive externalities might be pervasive but of trivial value. Generally, long-run population growth makes an increasing range of natural resources sufficiently valuable to induce the emergence of property rights governing their use.

It should be no surprise, therefore, that there is a striking disjuncture between governmental perceptions of the balance of positive versus negative externalities in more developed countries (MDCs) versus less developed countries (LDCs). Among MDCs, many believe that birth rates are too low, and these countries have policies designed to raise them. Among LDCs, the vast majority believe their birth rates are too high, and they have policies to reduce them. This disjuncture arises in part from their respective levels of fertility and rates of population growth. The average total fertility rate in MDCs is only 1.9 children per woman, while in LDCs it is twice as high, at 4.0. The corresponding rates of annual natural increase are 0.6 percent and 2.1 percent, respectively. Proportions in the older age groups are also far higher in MDCs—11.3 percent age 65 and over versus 4.0—and proportions of children far lower—23.1 percent under age 15 versus 39.1. This is

---

2. World Bank, *World Development Report 1984* (New York: Oxford University Press, 1984), p. 184.

3. The distinction is somewhat artificial because in reality most programs mix elements of both and because, even in theory, increasing availability and affordability of contraception leads to changes in desired family size. See, for example, the striking discussion in Gary Becker, *A Treatise on the Family* (Cambridge, MA: Harvard University Press, 1981).

far from the whole story, however; broad differences in the state's responsibility for intergenerational income transfers also play an important part. Specifically, LDCs are committed to public education and health programs, directed primarily at children. Support for the aged is largely a family matter, one that provides a strong motive for childbearing and one that has been largely undermined by transfer programs in MDCs. In MDCs the balance of transfers is reversed; while public expenditures for education are certainly costly, they are dwarfed by the combined costs of income transfers and health-care subsidies for the elderly, which are several times higher on a per capita basis. MDCs, therefore, often strive for higher fertility to reduce the burden of old-age dependency, while LDCs strive for lower fertility to reduce the burden of public costs of children.

Despite the widely acknowledged importance of externalities for the formation of population policy, research on the topic is strangely meager. Instead, research aiming at policy relevance generally addresses aggregate-level relations between population processes and such indicators as per capita income, saving, agricultural output, or educational attainment, with no attempt to distinguish between internalized costs and benefits, on the one hand, and externalities, on the other. Fortunately, the past few years have seen a number of important theoretical contributions on reproductive externalities.[4] Based in part on these, and

particularly on the work of Nerlove et al.,[5] I have attempted to evaluate externalities arising from a number of sources in the United States and several LDCs: India, Bangladesh, Saudi Arabia, and Kenya. This research, which I will discuss at greater length later in this article, represents a first step toward firmer empirical knowledge in this important area but still leaves much to be desired. One deficiency is that the analysis remains essentially static, shedding little light on the dynamic processes of economic growth. Another arises from the difficulty of evaluating externalities in the context of market imperfections and my inability to value collective environmental resources. A third is the necessity of taking the structure of government budgets as given and immutable. Nonetheless, I believe that the calculations are quite informative and revealing.

CONCEPTUALIZING EXTERNALITIES

The market as an institution governing decentralized decision making may, in the presence of externalities, fail to bring about an optimal outcome from the point of view

---

4. Garret Hardin first raised the central issue in his classic paper "The Tragedy of the Commons," *Science,* 162:1243-48 (1968). Nerlove and his collaborators make a very important contribution, summarized in Nerlove, Razin, and Sadka, "Optimal Population Size." Other important recent contributions include Willis, "Externalities and Population"; Zvi Eckstein and Kenneth I. Wolpin, "Endogenous Fertility and Optimal Population Size," *Journal of Public*

Economics, 27:93-106 (June 1985); Paul Demeny, "Population and the Invisible Hand," *Demography,* 23(4):473-88 (Nov. 1986); Yew-Kwang Ng, "The Welfare Economics of Population Control," *Population and Development Review,* 12(2):247-66 (June 1986); Samuel Preston, "Are the Economic Consequences of Population Growth a Sound Basis for Policy?" in *World Population and U.S. Policy: The Choices Ahead,* ed. Jane Menken (New York: W. W. Norton, 1986), pp. 67-95; Gary Becker, "Family Economics and Macro Behavior," *American Economic Review,* 78(1):1-13 (Mar. 1988). The present article builds on two earlier papers of mine: Ronald D. Lee, "Evaluating Externalities to Childbearing in Developing Countries: The Case of India"; idem, "Population Growth and the Environment: Cows and Babies in the 'Tragedy of the Commons,' " forthcoming.

5. Nerlove, Razin, and Sadka, "Optimal Population Size."

of participating individuals. For example, couples might prefer to have fewer children, living under happier conditions, but find themselves individually powerless to achieve such an outcome. In this case, couples would choose a lower level of fertility through cooperative collective choice — say, a binding vote on family size — than they would under laissez-faire. This logic leads directly to the conclusion that governments should in such cases intervene in reproductive decision making so as to bring about an outcome that most couples would find preferable. If reproductive externalities are on net insignificant, then the collective choice would not differ from the laissez-faire outcome, and governmental intervention could not be justified in this way. We can imagine a series of generations choosing optimal fertility through collective choice. Without externalities, the outcome would be socially efficient in the sense that no change in the fertility of any generation could make some generation better off without making some other generation worse off.[6] With externalities, the well-being of all subsequent generations could be improved by altering fertility. This is a minimal criterion for a socially desirable outcome, but nonetheless it will prove a useful one in viewing the population problem.[7]

In this section I will illustrate diagrammatically how a series of collective fertility choices would lead eventually to an equilibrium and how reproductive externalities lead to over- or underpopulation. This analysis is more technical than the rest of the article and is not essential to understanding what follows, so the reader is invited to skip ahead to the next section, on "specific sources of reproductive externalities."

To put the issue in starkest relief, let us set aside all differences in tastes, wealth, and other circumstance and suppose that all couples in a generation are identical. Further suppose that couples enjoy having many children but are concerned that high fertility will diminish the future well-being of their children, about which they also care.[8] Now consider an optimal choice between numbers of children per family and future well-being for each child. Such a choice for one generation is shown in Figure 1.

The longer, downward-sloping line depicts the relationship between the size of the next generation and its average well-being. Also shown is an indifference curve depicting the trade-off between a couple's satisfaction from the number of children they have and the well-being they anticipate for their children as adults.[9] This par-

---

6. "Better off" and "worse off" must be understood in a purely per capita sense here, since the numbers of individuals in subsequent generations would be altered. For a discussion of the difficult issues involving actual versus potential lives, see Partha Dasgupta, "The Ethical Foundations of Population Policy," in *Population Growth and Economic Development,* ed. Johnson and Lee, pp. 631-60.

7. Note, however, that as is explained more fully later in this article, parents are assumed to care about the well-being of their own grown children and therefore to moderate their own fertility. It is quite possible, nonetheless, that each generation will choose fertility above replacement and consequently will choose a lower standard of living for the next generation than

for itself. Unless a government has values transcending the collective wishes of its citizens, it is not clear why it should care more about intergenerational equity than they do — realizing, of course, that if there are negative externalities, collective choice will appear to express greater concern for the next generation than will individual choice.

8. More children would inherit a smaller piece of the family farm, for example. See Nerlove, Razin, and Sadka, "Optimal Population Size."

9. Note that for a given size of the first generation, N_1, choosing a size for the next generation, N_2, is equivalent to choosing a collective net reproduction rate (*NRR*). This equivalence makes it possible to draw the indifference curve. But the set of indifference curves will move every time the initial popula-

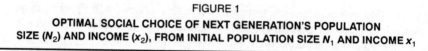

FIGURE 1

OPTIMAL SOCIAL CHOICE OF NEXT GENERATION'S POPULATION
SIZE (N_2) AND INCOME (x_2), FROM INITIAL POPULATION SIZE N_1 AND INCOME x_1

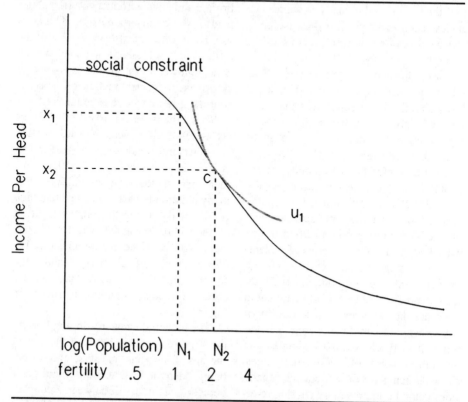

NOTE: From initial population N_1, fertility, measured as the net reproductive rate (*NRR*), is given by N_2/N_1. Thus the horizontal scale of fertility depends on N_1, as does the location of the indifference curves, of which u_1, the highest attainable from N_1, is one. The optimal choice is point *c*, with *NRR* = 2.

ticular indifference curve is tangent to the first line, indicating the optimal collective choice. In this case, the choice is for fertility above replacement level and an increase in population size from one generation to the next, with a consequent reduction in per capita well-being for the next generation.

tion size is changed, always remaining centered at an *NRR* = 1 for $N_1 = N_2$. When the log of N is on the horizontal axis, only the location but not the shapes of the indifference curve will change when N_1 changes.

Figure 2 shows the long-run equilibrium outcome of a sequence of similar collective choices over many generations. Eventually a population size and level of well-being are reached at which the satisfaction from above-replacement fertility is just offset by the dissatisfaction from the expected consequent poverty of their children, so they choose a stationary population and fertility at replacement level. Contemplating the outcome, one might wonder why the choice was not for a smaller and happier

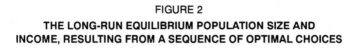

FIGURE 2
THE LONG-RUN EQUILIBRIUM POPULATION SIZE AND
INCOME, RESULTING FROM A SEQUENCE OF OPTIMAL CHOICES

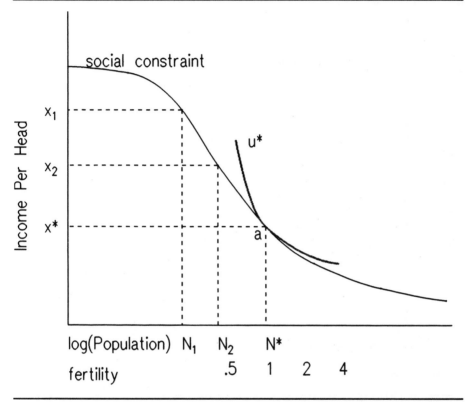

NOTE: See note to Figure 1. Note the shift in fertility scale and indifference map. At N^*, the optimal choice at a is for net reproductive rate = 1, so that the next generation's size is again N^*. Point u^* represents lower individual utility than u_1, since population growth has reduced per capita income.

population, but only by appeal to values transcending the individual could one impose a different outcome. Put differently, this outcome is efficient in terms of individual goals.

Now suppose that there is some sort of externality to childbearing. In that case, individual choices will not be efficient, and the laissez-faire outcome will be inferior to the outcome that would result from collective choice. This will be true for every generational step in the process, and it will also be true for the eventual equilibrium. Figure 3 shows how the laissez-faire equilibrium differs from collective choice in the case of negative externalities. With a negative externality to childbearing, some part of the cost of a child is not borne by the parents, so the slope of the parental budget constraint is less steep than that of the society as a whole. At the same time, in laissez-faire equilibrium expectations must

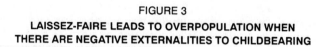

FIGURE 3
**LAISSEZ-FAIRE LEADS TO OVERPOPULATION WHEN
THERE ARE NEGATIVE EXTERNALITIES TO CHILDBEARING**

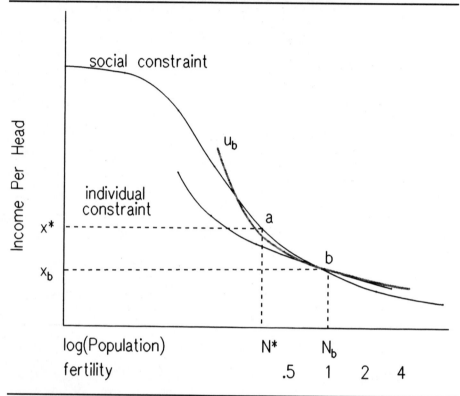

NOTE: See notes to Figures 1 and 2. The individual budget constraint is sloped less steeply than the social budget constraint, reflecting negative externalities. The laissez-faire equilibrium outcome is at *b,* where an indifference curve, u_b, is tangent to the individual constraint where it intersects the social constraint. Point *a* is the collective equilibrium, with smaller population and higher income.

be realized, so the social and individual constraints must intersect at *NRR* = 1.[10] It is readily seen that in this case, the collective-

10. In the laissez-faire equilibrium, the expectations of parents about the future welfare of their children must be realized, for otherwise expectations would change from generation to generation, and this would not be an equilibrium. Away from equilibrium, we do not know without further assumptions about expectations what the couple's budget constraint would look like. The simplest additional assumption would be that parents expect current per capita availability of the nonprivate good to persist and only the

choice equilibrium will be at a smaller population with a higher per capita level of well-being than under laissez-faire. The laissez-faire outcome fails to maximize the well-being of each generation of parents, given the population size bequeathed it by the preceding generations. It is inefficient.

internalized costs to affect their budget constraint. Then at every step the couple's budget constraint would intersect the collective budget constraint where the NRR is unity.

One solution to the failure of laissez-faire would be for a central planner to impose coercively an appropriate level of fertility. But a decentralized approach is also possible, whereby a set of taxes and subsidies relating to children is introduced to confront the parents with the social cost of their reproductive decisions.

Later in this article, I will introduce estimates of externalities that in principle tell us the size of the tax or subsidy on each birth that would be necessary to internalize the social costs arising from a variety of sources. The estimates I will give refer to the externalities to a birth in the current generation, under current conditions. One could also ask about the taxes or subsidies necessary to achieve the long-run optimum equilibrium. This question, however, would be impossible to answer without a great deal more information and, furthermore, given the fluid state of the real world, would be less informative than an estimate based on contemporary conditions.

SPECIFIC SOURCES OF REPRODUCTIVE EXTERNALITIES

There are several kinds of reproductive externality. The most basic and most pervasive occurs whenever there is any form of public or collective wealth to which all people have right of free access and which is diminished in per capita value by sharing. This kind comes closest to Hardin's metaphor of the tragedy of the commons. There are many examples. Some are environmental, including air shed, watershed, the ozone layer, silence, and solitude. There are other forms of collective wealth to which governments make specific claims: public lands, publicly owned mineral rights, parks, coastal fisheries, potential hydroelectric energy sources, and publicly owned capital stock. Public debt is a

negative form of public wealth, leading to a positive externality. Each birth dilutes the value of the rights of others to use or share such collective wealth, yet because property rights are not defined for such wealth, or the rights are held collectively by the government, parents do not view this dilution as a cost of childbearing through which their own fertility affects the future well-being of their own particular children. In contrast, they view their own private wealth as subject to greater division when their fertility is higher, and they reduce their fertility accordingly.

A second kind of externality arises through public provision of so-called public goods, that is, goods and services that can be enjoyed by any number of people without congestion or diminution of individual satisfaction. Classic examples include national defense, weather forecasting, and radio and television broadcasting. Support for the arts, for research and development, for the space program—all these are examples as well. There are also many quasi-public goods such as transportation and communication systems, public utilities, waterworks, harbors, and costs of government and foreign embassies; these are subject to congestion, but provision is much cheaper per capita when the population is larger or denser.[11] Public goods lead to positive externalities because each additional birth eventually increases the tax base over which the costs of public goods can be spread, thereby reducing the tax burden on others. We might consider inducements to privately funded research and development, and whatever other influence there might be of population size

11. Larger, denser populations generally consume more of these public goods, but that is to be expected, since for such populations they are far cheaper and the optimal level of provision is higher.

and growth on technological progress, under this heading as well.

A third kind of externality arises through intergenerational transfers — that is, when one age group consumes more or less than it produces, with the difference made up by some sort of transfer to or from other age groups. Those intergenerational transfers that take place within families do not lead to externalities, but those taking place through the public sector, and possibly even through the credit market, may. The most prominent age-related public-sector transfers are for health, education, and public pensions — the latter are social security in the United States. To a first approximation, the average individual over the life cycle will pay taxes — including social-security contributions — equal in survival-weighted present value to the health, education, and social-security benefits they receive, so it might seem that no externality arises. On closer analysis, however, we see that sustained higher fertility tilts the age distribution toward the younger ages, changing the relative sizes of the age groups at any instant.[12] This is far from a trivial matter. It underlies the pronatalist policies of many industrial nations that seek to raise fertility so that there will be a more favorable old-age dependency ratio in the future.

A fourth kind is similar to the last, arising from the demand for other governmental services created by an additional member of the population. On average, the demand created is likely to precede the age of paying taxes, so that once again a younger age distribution may prove socially costly, even if for each child the present value of governmental services received equals the present value of taxes paid over the life cycle.

EVALUATING EXTERNALITIES

These, then, appear to be the principal sources of externalities to childbearing that could provide a rationale for governmental policy. In what follows I shall attempt to quantify some of these, at least roughly, for the United States, India, Saudi Arabia, Bangladesh, and Kenya. Estimation is based largely on examination of government budgets and other aggregate statistics at the national and state or district level, with occasional resort to survey data for details on age profiles of earnings, consumption, education, and health-care usage. Certain important categories of externalities are omitted for want of even approximate data, most notably negative environmental externalities and positive externalities arising from stimulus to technological progress and economies of scale.

Collective wealth

Table 1 presents the estimates for these countries, with the results grouped under three headings: public assets, public goods, and intergenerational transfers. Consider public assets.[13] The first line shows dramatic differences: Saudi Arabia, not surprisingly, dominates with mineral rights —

12. Another way of looking at this is that higher fertility raises the population growth rate, which raises the interest rate, which enhances life-cycle welfare if the initial average age of receiving benefits exceeds the average age of paying taxes, and reduces life-cycle welfare otherwise. See Eckstein and Wolpin, "Endogenous Fertility"; Ronald D. Lee and Shelley Lapkoff, "Intergenerational Flows of Time and Goods: Consequences of Slowing Population Growth," *Journal of Political Economy*, 96(3):618-51 (June 1988).

13. These are evaluated as the product of expected current reserves and the difference between current pithead value and costs of extraction. See Merton H. Miller and Charles W. Upton, "A Test of the Hotelling Valuation Principle," *Journal of Political Economy*, 93(1):1-25 (Feb. 1985).

TABLE 1

ESTIMATED EXTERNALITIES TO CHILDBEARING IN SELECTED COUNTRIES

Item	United States (1985)	India (1981)	Bangladesh (1980)	Saudi Arabia (1986)	Kenya (1986)
Public assets					
Mineral rights	−3,798	−(0 to 13,000)	−289	−189,554	−168
Government debt	+10,013	+107	+41	0	+151
Government capital	0	−27	−1	−19,340	0
Government land	−813	−(10 to 200)	−11	?	−180
Fisheries	?	−50	−29	?	−33
Foreign aid	0	−35	−346	0	−929
Subtotal	+5,402	+20 to −13,205	−634	−208,894	−1159
Public goods	+74,950	+710	+615	+81,100	+1,484
Intergenerational transfers					
Health, education, pensions	+35,713	−25	−6	−1,358	−48
Other public expenditures	−11,025	−34	−8	−1,330	−22
Subtotal	+24,688	−59	−22	−2,688	−70
Total externality	105,040	+655 to −12,554	−33	−130,482	+255
Gross national product per capita	16,757	260	140	6,950	300
Ratio to gross national product per capita	+6.3	+2.5 to −48.3	−.2	−18.8	+.9

SOURCES: Ansley J. Coale and Paul Demeny, *Regional Model Lifetables and Stable Populations* (New York: Academic Press, 1983); International Labour Office, *The Cost of Social Security* (Geneva: International Labour Office, 1985); International Monetary Fund, *Government Finance Statistics Yearbook* (Washington, DC: International Monetary Fund, 1988); United Nations, *Demographic Yearbook, 1986* (New York: United Nations, 1988); U.S. Department of the Interior, Bureau of Mines, *Minerals Yearbook, 1987* (Washington, DC: Government Printing Office, 1989); various publications of the Bangladesh Bureau of Statistics, including its *1982 Statistical Yearbook of Bangladesh* (Dhaka: Bangladesh Bureau of Statistics, 1985); various Indian government publications and surveys, including India, Ministry of Planning, Department of Statistics, *Statistical Abstract of India, 1984* (Delhi: Indian Department of Statistics, 1984); various statistical publications of Kenya's Central Bureau of Statistics, including its *Statistical Abstract, 1987* (Nairobi: Central Bureau of Statistics, 1988); various statistical publications of Saudi Arabia's National Central Department of Statistics, including Saudi Arabia, Ministry of Finance and National Central Department of Statistics, *Statistical Yearbook, 1987* (Riyadh: National Central Department of Statistics, 1988); various statistical publications of the U.S. Census Bureau, including U.S. Department of Commerce, Bureau of the Census, *Statistical Abstract of the United States, 1988* (Washington, DC: Government Printing Office, 1988).

NOTE: All figures pertain to the reference year, which differs from country to country and is indicated at the top of the table. "Other public expenditures" includes half of the value of quasi-public goods—most infrastructural expenditures—plus all other expenditures not counted elsewhere. These are allocated by age midway between the average age of the population and the average age of the labor force. The value for public land in Kenya includes both total estimated value of forests, which are assumed to be publicly owned, and the profits of restaurants and hotels, which are believed to be largely attributable to the tourist attraction of the national game parks. For details on the method of calculation, see Ronald D. Lee, "Evaluating Externalities to Childbearing in Developing Countries: The Case of India."

largely petroleum, of course — worth about $190,000 per citizen, which is the share claimed, in some sense, by each newborn, which is a negative externality. India also shows a relatively high value here, at up to $13,000, due largely to its extensive coal reserves, although depending on method this could actually be near zero.[14] The figure for the United States is notably lower, at $3000, followed by much lower figures for Bangladesh and Kenya. I expect that the Kenyan figure reflects a lack of exploration more than a true absence of reserves.

If government debt can simply grow in proportion to the population and need never be repaid, then it does not give rise to childbearing externalities. Here I assume, instead, that it must eventually be repaid. In this case, the burden of repayment would be spread more thinly over a larger population, leading to a positive externality to childbearing — or, in the case of a net creditor nation, a negative one. Foreign debt and internal debt count equally here, for although the asset created by internal debt is private, its repayment is a public burden. The United States is champion in this category, although relative to per capita gross national product (GNP), its situation is similar to the other countries', except for Saudi Arabia, which has no debt.

Only certain categories of publicly owned capital stock lead to externalities. If the capital has been purchased through an issue of equity or bonds, then it is no different from private capital. If it is accumulated out of tax revenues, and there is reason to expect such cumulation to continue in the future, then there is no externality. When the capital stock comes from re-

tained earnings, foreign aid, or some other source, however, then it does lead to a negative externality, since the per capita value is diminished by a birth. On this basis, public capital is an important category only for Saudi Arabia, where it has been financed from oil revenues.[15] Also included here is an estimated per capita value of $7500 for government-held financial assets.

Publicly owned land is very difficult to identify and evaluate, since there is a spectrum of public-use rights, particularly in more traditional economies, and because the quality or market value of the land is seldom documented. In none of the countries does public land appear to be a very important category, however. Likewise, coastal fishing rights, though difficult to evaluate, do not appear to be a large item for any of these countries.

Public goods

A scan of government budgets yields totals of public-good-type expenditures. Relatively pure public goods receive full weight, while quasi-public goods receive a half weight. These figures may be expressed per capita and then converted to the present value of a perpetual stream.[16] Results are shown in the second panel of Table 1. Expressed as a multiple of per capita income, these are fairly similar except for Saudi Arabia: United States, 4.5; India, 2.7; Bangladesh, 4.4; Kenya, 4.9; but Saudi

---

14. Note, however, that the publicly run coal industry has operated at a loss in recent years, making evaluation of this resource difficult. For a more extensive discussion, see Lee, "Evaluating Externalities."

15. We assume that 40 percent of government oil revenues have been invested in physical capital, which depreciates at 10 percent per year. The estimate is obviously very rough.

16. As with collective resources, the impact of a birth is not limited to its lifetime but extends infinitely forward. Reproductive value can be used to fine-tune the estimate. See Lee, "Evaluating Externalities."

Arabia, 11.7![17] These all generate quite hefty positive externalities to childbearing. For the United States, 70 percent of public-good expenditures is for defense; for Saudi Arabia, 60 percent; for India, 46 percent; for Kenya, 25 percent; and for Bangladesh, only 16 percent. There are also great variations in the share in public-good expenditures of economic services and infrastructure, from 70 percent for Bangladesh to only 9 percent for the United States.[18]

Intergenerational transfers:
Health, education, and pensions

Not surprisingly, the industrial welfare states devote a substantially greater proportion of national income to transfers, both cash and in kind, than do typical Third World countries. For example, India in recent years has devoted about 4 percent of GNP to public expenditures on health, education, and pensions, of which nearly two-thirds has gone for education and only 10 percent for pensions. The United States, by contrast, has spent about 15 percent of GNP, or four times India's share, on such transfers, of which 36 percent was for education, while about 35 percent was for pensions.

The difference, of course, is not just in the scale of transfers but also in their allocation by age. The MDCs have far higher

proportions of elderly in their populations than do the LDCs. In the United States, for example, at the current vital rates, the stable population would have a ratio of children to the elderly about one-twentieth as high as Kenya's. This purely demographic difference would, in itself, make MDCs more concerned with the economic burden of supporting the elderly. But this is only half the story. In LDCs, care and support for both children and the elderly are largely family matters and therefore private. In MDCs, by contrast, while the rearing of children remains primarily a family obligation, the elderly are increasingly supported by the public sector through in-kind transfers of health services and through income transfers, or pensions. In the United States, an average elderly person receives net transfers costing roughly 3.7 times as much as does a child — about $9900 versus $2700, in 1985 dollars. In India, Bangladesh, Kenya, and Saudi Arabia, the same ratio is between 0.6 and 0.8. Taking into account these differences in age distribution and in the scale of transfers, we find that in the United States an elderly person receives annual transfers equal to 59 percent of per capita GNP, while in Bangladesh, the corresponding percentage is 1.8. In the hypothetical U.S. stable population, more than 10.6 percent of GNP would be transferred to the elderly, while in none of the four LDCs would more than 0.5 percent, and in Kenya and Bangladesh, less than 0.2 percent would be.

Not surprisingly, these differences in the magnitude and age distribution of transfers have important consequences for differences in childbearing externalities between MDCs and LDCs. These externalities depend on the average age of receipt of transfers minus the average age of payment of taxes, on the one hand, and on the present value of expected lifetime receipts

---

17. The figure for Saudi Arabia may appear mistaken, since public goods are financed from oil revenues, not taxes. Nonetheless, it is correct, because the dilution of oil revenues has already been counted as a negative externality, while, to the extent that public-good-type expenditures were included in the figure, it overstates the negative externality and must be adjusted through this positive entry.

18. These are counted as quasi-public goods in the calculation, receiving a weight of 0.5. Public administration and public order and safety are treated similarly.

of transfers, on the other. In the United States, the average age of receipt of age-related public transfers is 10 years greater than the average age of payment of taxes. In India, Bangladesh, Saudi Arabia, and Kenya, it was less by 11, 11, 13, and 14 years, respectively. Consequently, each birth in the United States was subject to a positive externality of about $36,000, or 2.1 times per capita income. In the four LDCs examined, each birth was subject to a negative externality falling in the range of 0.04 times per capita income for Kenya to 0.2 for Saudi Arabia.

There are two striking lessons here. First, the great concern in MDCs for the impact of demographic aging on public-sector transfer programs is entirely understandable, whether or not one views pro-natalist policies as a wise response. This general conclusion is reinforced if we also take account of transfers through the market.[19] Second, reproductive externalities arising through public-sector transfers in LDCs are of surprisingly little consequence, although they have been repeatedly emphasized in the literature.[20]

Other governmental expenditures

Finally, there are other government services that are not specifically age related but that must be increased roughly in proportion to the population. These include the balance of the quasi-public goods,

19. See Lee and Lapkoff, "Intergenerational Flows."

20. Note, however, that these calculations assumed a real rate of interest of 2 percent, that is, the difference between the nominal rate of interest and the rate of inflation. This was the average real rate of return on long-term Indian government bonds issued in the preceding decade. Taking a higher opportunity cost for capital funds would place a higher value on the negative externality.

plus all other governmental activities. If these are congested—and therefore demanded—in proportion to the size of the labor force, then they are offset by taxes, and no externality arises. If, however, they are provided in proportion to the total population size, independent of age, then an externality arises through the difference between the average age of the stable population and that of paying taxes, which is typically about −10 years in all countries except Kenya, in which it was −18. I have assumed a result halfway between these poles, which yields a further negative externality to child-bearing that sometimes exceeds that arising from health, education, and pensions. The commonsense logic here is that high fertility generates a demand for government services and infrastructure before it generates the taxes to pay for these, imposing a heavier burden of taxation on the working population.

Combining all these estimates yields the following results, for the total childbearing externality expressed as a multiple of per capita GNP: United States, +6; India, +3 to −48; Bangladesh, zero; Saudi Arabia, −19; and Kenya, +1. Inspection reveals that externalities become quantitatively important either when old-age support is the responsibility of the state or when publicly owned natural resources are a major form of collective wealth. I expect that many readers will dismiss the latter source of externalities as too fanciful, leaving only the first.

CONCLUSION

We have considered estimates of reproductive externalities falling into four categories: reproductive dilution of collective wealth; cost spreading for public goods; public-sector intergenerational transfers—health, education, and pensions; and other governmental expenditures. Taking our results at face value, we have found that intergenerational transfers create large positive externalities in the United States and probably in other industrial welfare states but small negative ones or none at all in the Third World countries examined. Public goods lead to sizable positive externalities in all countries considered. Collective wealth in the form of publicly owned mineral reserves leads in some cases to enormous negative externalities, while in other cases it is of little importance. Other forms of collective wealth, such as public capital stock, public debt, or public lands, give rise only to small negative externalities. No evaluation was attempted for collective environmental wealth or of induced technological change. These omitted items are potentially of considerable importance, and the net evaluation may be quite misleading without them. Recall also that a number of specific assumptions went into the calculation: for example, that populations were homogeneous with respect to wealth and tastes, that parental expectations were accurate, and that social goals were only the aggregation of individual preferences.

Setting aside these reservations, the literal policy implications of the results are clear: a tax or subsidy should be imposed on each birth, equal to the net externality. Such a policy would not change the wealth of the average couple of the current generation, since revenues raised by the policy would be redistributed equally to all couples. It would, however, alter the fertility incentives and fertility decisions and thereby the size and per capita wealth of the next generation.

Would such a policy be appropriate, supposing that a convincing evaluation of the external costs and benefits were achieved? Surely, skepticism is warranted. The case that laissez-faire fertility outcomes are both individually and socially optimal in the absence of externalities rests on the assumption that couples make well-informed decisions about their fertility, reflecting accurate individual expectations concerning life for the next generation. Some may question the degree of conscious decision making about fertility, particularly in more traditional societies. In any event, individuals may fail to anticipate the extent of future changes in the economic and health environment. Technological progress and capital accumulation, both largely due to outside forces, tend to raise systematically the well-being of the next generation, or at least they have done so over the post-World War II decades for most populations. Medical and public-health progress, again occurring largely outside the range of family decision making, have brought about dramatic gains in survival in LDCs. Parents who believed they were having many children merely to ensure that two or three would survive may find that instead four or five have survived. Such failures of expectations seriously weaken the argument that actual fertility in LDCs represents a privately optimal trade-off between the size of the next generation and its economic well-being. When expectations fail in this way, the long-run equilibrium may nonetheless be optimal even if the path taken to it is not. But if there is reason to believe that the actual path would involve painful surprises and adjustments, then surely government intervention would be justified even in the absence of externalities and could lead to a welfare improvement. To summarize, public interventions based upon externalities would also need to account for the possibility that private childbearing decisions may not be optimal even for those making them.

Furthermore, a government that estimated large negative childbearing externalities using the method of this article could solve its population problem by doubling military spending, a pure public good, thereby offsetting the negative externality. This, of course, is nonsense, but it illustrates the flaw in taking all other governmental policies and allocations as fixed, while trying to fine-tune fertility incentives. An impractical but more appealing approach would be to evaluate childbearing externalities in the context of policies that are optimal in all other respects.

Tempering the numerical results with skepticism, while adhering to the spirit of this analysis, I offer some general policy recommendations. First, disseminate information to enable parents to form more accurate expectations about child survival and nonfamilial influences on income growth, particularly in LDCs. Second, vigorously pursue family planning programs because of the familial welfare gains these promote but also because, in some LDCs at least, negative externalities provide an additional macrosocietal payoff to such programs. At the same time, in MDCs positive externalities detract from the familial gains. Third, reproductive externalities resulting from dilution of our collective global environmental wealth — air shed, watershed, ozone layer — may be extremely important but have not been evaluated. If we ignore them, a case can be made for pronatalist incentives in MDCs, and perhaps mild antinatalist incentives in some LDCs.

In MDCs, positive externalities to childbearing created by public provision of old-age support may well be an important reason for low fertility; that is, fertility would likely be higher if the full benefits and costs of childbearing fell on parents alone. In many LDCs, however, I suspect that childbearing externalities have little to do with the high fertility observed. In both Bangladesh and Kenya, two countries generally viewed as having severe population problems, childbearing externalities appear close to zero. It is more likely that high fertility is an individually rational but exceedingly inefficient solution to problems faced by parents in the absence of social institutions for spreading risks, saving for old age, providing physical security, and obtaining labor. The inefficiency is both individual and societal, and the remedy is institutional development.

ANNALS, *AAPSS,* **510,** July 1990

Family Planning Programs in the Third World

By RONALD FREEDMAN

ABSTRACT: Most of the population of less developed countries (LDCs) now lives in countries with national family planning programs to reduce fertility and improve family welfare. Such programs are a new phenomenon. In some LDCs increasing birth-control practice and fertility declines occurred along with considerable social and economic development, but even there rapid changes among the disadvantaged masses are generally associated with strong family planning programs. Fertility has also fallen in some countries with only some development but with vigorous family planning programs. China, Indonesia, Sri Lanka, and Thailand are such cases. In such places as sub-Saharan Africa and South Asia, fertility generally remains quite high, apparently because of little development and traditional familial institutions. Even in these situations, however, there are examples of significant fertility declines, in some cases nationally and in other cases in intensive, high-quality pilot projects that have established the latent demand for family planning.

Ronald Freedman is professor emeritus of sociology at the University of Michigan, where he received B.A. and M.A. degrees, followed by a Ph.D. at the University of Chicago. During 41 years at Michigan he founded the Population Studies Center. His career has involved teaching, research, and consultation about fertility and family planning in both developed and less developed countries, including Taiwan, China, Hong Kong, Indonesia, and Malaysia. He is past president of the Population Association of America.

B Y 1983, 76 percent of the population of less developed countries (LDCs) lived in countries with official policies and national family planning programs to reduce their population growth by reducing fertility.[1] An additional 17 percent lived in countries that officially supported family planning programs to improve the health and welfare of their mothers and children.

Such national policies and family planning programs are a new phenomenon. In 1960 only one country, India, had such a program and that was ineffectual. At that time probably less than 10 percent of the married women of childbearing age in LDCs were using contraception and much of that practice was ineffective. By 1985 an estimated 45 percent — about 400 million women — were using contraception, and 80 percent of that practice involved such effective methods as the contraceptive pill, the intrauterine device (IUD), and sterilization. The most widely used method in LDCs, as in the world as a whole, is now sterilization.[2]

These massive increases in contraceptive prevalence in just a few decades are remarkable, because they have required profound changes in reproductive behavior deeply rooted in traditional familial institutions and in values about intimate sexual relationships. Although these changes are impressive, further large increases in contraceptive use in LDCs are necessary if LDC fertility is to reach the low levels required by the population policies of most

LDC countries and the population projections of the United Nations.

While the contraceptive prevalence rates were rising in LDCs between 1960-65 and 1980-85, the fertility rates were falling, partly because of rising age at marriage but mainly because of deliberate fertility limitation within marriage. The total fertility rate fell from 6.1 to 4.2, a 31 percent decline.[3]

Despite the decline in fertility, the decline in the rate of population growth in LDCs as a whole has been small, because there was a simultaneous decline in mortality, which largely offset the fertility decline.

The contraceptive prevalence rates cited for all LDCs are weighted averages of widely varying country rates. The rates are moderately to very high in all of East Asia and in parts of Southeast Asia — over 65 percent in China, Hong Kong, Singapore, Korea, and Taiwan and close to 50 percent in Indonesia. In Latin America the overall rate is 54 percent, with especially high rates in Brazil, Mexico, Colombia, and Costa Rica, moderate rates — 40 to 60 percent — in most other countries, but a rate as low as 7 percent in Haiti. The prevalence rates are almost uniformly low and fertility rates very high in sub-Saharan Africa and in much of the Islamic population of the Near East and Southwest Asia. Even in these regions, where conditions for fertility decline are believed to be very unfavorable, exceptions are beginning to appear. There have been significant increases in contraceptive use and declines in fertility

1. Dorothy L. Nortman, *Population and Family Planning Programs: A Compendium of Data through 1983* (New York: Population Council, 1985), p. 32.

2. United Nations, *Levels and Trends of Contraceptive Use as Assessed in 1988* (New York: United Nations, 1989). Unless otherwise indicated, contraceptive prevalence rates are from this source.

3. United Nations, *World Population Prospects, 1988* (New York: United Nations, 1989), p. 150. The total fertility rate estimates the number of children each woman would have if she lived through the childbearing years, subject to fertility rates at each childbearing age for the specified year.

in Zimbabwe, Botswana, and Kenya recently.[4] In the Muslim world there are similar examples in Tunisia, Algeria, Egypt,[5] and in some fundamentalist Islamic regions of Indonesia.

CAUSES OF THE RISE IN CONTRACEPTIVE PREVALENCE

The causes of such variability in contraceptive use and fertility levels are matters of controversy.

Twenty-five years ago, based on the rapid fertility decline in the West between about 1870 and World War II, most scholars believed that the answer was simple. Social and economic development, urbanization, higher educational levels, work in the modern, nonfamilial economy, and lower mortality increased the cost and decreased the benefits of children. They also increased the value of investing more in a smaller number of children, so that small families planned with the use of contraception became the norm. There is an important element of truth in these ideas. When social and economic development levels are high, small families and birth control are widely prevalent.

In recent decades, however, empirical studies have indicated that explaining the causes of the transition from high to low fertility is not so simple. Historical studies have demonstrated that fertility decline began in various parts of Europe under widely varying social and economic conditions and without modern contraceptives or family planning programs.[6] Whether fertility did decline was also considerably influenced by such cultural factors as secularism, language, and ethnicity.

A growing body of evidence from the experience of LDCs since 1960 also indicates that the adoption of birth control and fertility declines occur under a variety of conditions. Massive changes in reproductive behavior appear to be influenced not only by the changing demand for children and for family planning methods but also in some cases by the supply of birth-control services and information, by both organized programs and the private sector.

The World Fertility Survey in 42 LDCs found that such structural variables as education, labor force activity, and urbanization have only modest relations to contraceptive use and fertility across Third World countries. Further, the relationships that do exist vary greatly between the regions of the world.[7]

A hypothesis receiving increasing attention is that diffusion of ideas about the concept, means, prevalence, and legitimacy of birth control plays an important role in fertility decline. This ideational factor may be particularly important for present-day LDCs, because the earlier development and practice of these ideas in the West is part of world history and is carried by the international mass-media network. Spreading this set of ideas is an essential function of family planning programs.

4. Data about recent levels of contraceptive practice and fertility in this article for the following countries are from the ongoing surveys of the Demographic and Health Surveys, Institute for Resource Development, Columbia, MD: Botswana, Burundi, Indonesia, Kenya, Liberia, Mali, Senegal, Thailand, Togo, and Zimbabwe.

5. Philippe Fargues, "La baisse de la fécondité arabe," *Population,* 43(6):987 (Nov.-Dec. 1988).

6. For example, Ansley J. Coale and Susan C. Watkins, eds., *The Decline of Fertility in Europe* (Princeton, NJ: Princeton University Press, 1986).

7. German Rodriguez and John Cleland, "Socio-Economic Determinants of Marital Fertility in 20 Countries: A Multivariate Analysis," in *World Fertility Survey Conference, 1980: Record of Proceedings* (London: World Fertility Survey, 1981), 2:337-403.

Fertility declines in LDCs do not always involve organized national family planning programs. Notable fertility declines in Latin America — for example, in Brazil — have occurred with the assistance of private organizations or individual contacts with pharmacies and doctors.

A variety of studies have attempted to determine the extent to which family planning programs have produced fertility declines in addition to what would have happened anyway as a result of social and economic development. For example, Lapham and Mauldin, in a study of 93 LDCs, reported that socioeconomic development and family planning program effort each had an independent effect on contraceptive use and fertility decline. But the major reported effect was a joint product of the two forces.[8]

It is illustrative of the problems in such attempts at a comprehensive answer that this one has been criticized on the grounds, among others, that countries that already have declining fertility mount strong programs that are, then, more the effect than the cause of the fertility decline.

The issue is complicated by the fact that countries with little social and economic development generally have very weak family planning programs, presumably because they do not have the infrastructure required for this or other development programs. All the 22 countries ranked lowest on socioeconomic development indices in the Lapham-Mauldin study are also ranked as having weak or very weak family planning programs.

8. Robert J. Lapham and W. Parker Mauldin, "The Effects of Family Planning on Fertility: Research Findings," in *Organizing for Effective Family Planning Programs*, ed. R. J. Lapham and G. B. Simmons (Washington, DC: National Academy Press, 1987), pp. 647-80.

I believe that, on balance, the evidence is that family planning programs can have an effect that is interdependent with, but not merely reflective of, social and economic development. There is, however, no firm consensus among scholars in the population field on this important issue.

Since a simple cross-cultural explanation of all LDCs still escapes us, it may be the better part of wisdom to consider groups of countries with common elements.

I will be referring to effective family planning programs — those that are successful in enabling large numbers of couples to have the number of children they want when they want them. For countries that have a policy to reduce the rate of population growth, an effective program also motivates enough couples to limit family size so that national fertility rates fall. This may involve education, mass-media programs, various types of incentives, and social and political pressure. Such activist programs to change values and behavior are sometimes controversial both within the countries and in the world arena.

LDCs WITH RAPID DEVELOPMENT

Fertility rates certainly have fallen especially rapidly in countries with considerable social and economic development as well as effective family planning programs — Korea, Taiwan, Singapore, and Mexico are examples. It is probable that in the long run fertility would have fallen in such countries with or without family planning programs. It is doubtful, however, that the decline would have been as rapid without the family planning programs, especially among the disadvantaged masses — the poor, the uneducated, and the rural.

For example, consider the case of Taiwan, a pioneer in both family planning and other development programs.[9] In 1960, just before the program was begun, the total fertility rate was about 6 and contraceptive use was still at low levels. By 1986, only 26 years later, the fertility rate had fallen by 70 percent to 1.7 — below replacement levels — and virtually all women were using contraception before the end of their childbearing years. The level of contraceptive use doubled from 28 to 56 percent between 1965 and 1970. More important, among illiterate women contraceptive use during this period increased from 19 to 51 percent. By 1975, the differentials in contraceptive use between strata defined by education, urbanization, or income had virtually disappeared. No doubt the success of Taiwan's program was interdependent with its rapid social and economic development, but it is unlikely that the disadvantaged masses — the poor, rural, and illiterate — would have adopted family planning so rapidly without the family planning program. Even in 1985, 60 percent of Taiwanese couples were getting their contraceptive services through the government programs.

Taiwan also illustrates the fact that a rapid change in reproductive behavior can occur despite persistence of traditional familial institutions. Even in 1985, when fertility was very low and contraceptive prevalence very high, a large majority of older Taiwanese were living with married sons and about two-thirds of recently married couples began married life living with the husbands' parents.[10]

The sharp fertility reduction in the West before World War II, without either modern contraceptives or organized programs, often is cited as evidence that those are unnecessary for fertility decline if development is sufficient. It is plausible, however, that, had organized programs with modern contraceptives been available in Europe, fertility might have fallen more rapidly, more equally among social groups, and with less suffering from unwanted births and abortions.

COUNTRIES WITH
MODERATE DEVELOPMENT

There is another group of countries in which some social and economic conditions were considered to be unfavorable prior to their programs and fertility declines.

The most conspicuous example is China, where fertility declines of unprecedented magnitude and speed have occurred under presumably unfavorable social and economic conditions but with a massive family planning program of awesome effectiveness. Between 1970, when the rural family planning program began in earnest, and 1980 the fertility rate of rural China fell from 6.3 to 2.9, a 53 percent decline. For rural illiterate women, fertility fell by 50 percent, from 6.6 for the years 1967-70 to 3.3 for 1979-82. China's fertility program is unprecedented for its massive apparatus and effectiveness. It depends on the ability of the government to mobilize and control the behavior of the masses at the village

9. Ming-Cheng Chang, Ronald Freedman, and Te-Hsiung Sun, "Trends in Fertility, Family Size Preferences and Family Planning Practice: Taiwan, 1961-85," *Studies in Family Planning*, 18(6):320-37 (Nov.-Dec. 1987).

10. Maxine Weinstein et al., "Household Composition, Extended Kinship, and Reproduction in Taiwan: 1965-1985," *Population Studies*, in press.

level, all the more remarkable because of the hundreds of thousands of villages involved, with 800 million rural people distributed over a vast area. No doubt, remarkable preceding reductions in mortality and more modest but significant gains in education and other social changes are relevant. The close connection in the timing of the sharp fertility decline and the onset of the rural program and its simultaneous occurrence in all major sectors of the population make it highly probable, however, that the program was a major force in the rapid decline.

Questions can be raised about degrees of coercion in the Chinese program. Nevertheless, it is important and unexpected that a program could mobilize the infrastructure, bureaucratic apparatus, and the masses of the population to produce such a large and rapid fertility decline. The absence of such capacity in such countries as India, Bangladesh, and Pakistan may account in part for the ineffectiveness of their family planning programs.

Indonesia's fertility decline and its rise in contraceptive prevalence also has occurred under initially rather unfavorable social and economic conditions. Contraceptive prevalence rates have risen from about 2 percent, when the program began in 1970, to 48 percent in 1987. During the same period, fertility fell from an estimated 5.5, during the years 1967-70, to 3.3. Like China, Indonesia has utilized its long-standing institutional capacity to mobilize the village masses for its family planning programs, where the traditional authority of the village leader and organized peer pressure have played an important role. Warwick, in an intensive study of Indonesia's program, has made a convincing case that its distinctive program strategy

and aggressive implementation have had a major independent effect that cannot be accounted for by the significant social and economic development gains that have also occurred there since 1970.[11]

Thailand is another country whose rapid fertility decline to very low levels and increasing contraceptive prevalence to high levels have occurred with a very strong program and only moderately favorable socioeconomic conditions.[12]

In the Indian state of Kerala and in Sri Lanka, improvements in health, education, and minimal subsistence supports have been associated with lower fertility levels and moderately high contraceptive prevalence, despite low and lagging levels of economic development. In both cases increasing age at marriage has had a role in fertility decline.

COUNTRIES WITH RELATIVELY LITTLE DEVELOPMENT

Finally, we consider places with little socioeconomic development and weak infrastructure, where individuals still receive most of their physical and emotional support from familial institutions and where children are perceived to yield significant benefits as compared to their costs. The status of women is poor and often depends on their fertility. Most of the countries of sub-Saharan Africa are in this category, along with India, Pakistan, Bangladesh,

11. Donald P. Warwick, "The Indonesian Family Planning Program: Government Influence and Client Choice," *Population and Development Review*, 12(3):453-90 (Sept. 1986).

12. John Knodel, Aphichat Chamratrithirong, and Nibhon Debavalya, *Thailand's Reproductive Revolution: Rapid Fertility Decline in a Third-World Setting* (Madison: University of Wisconsin Press, 1987).

and smaller countries of Southwest Asia. The countries in this group that have family planning programs have not been very successful in increasing contraceptive prevalence enough to decrease fertility very much.

Low contraceptive prevalence and high fertility in such countries are generally explained on the ground that having many children, and especially sons, is regarded as a positive good. The question of demand for fertility control simply does not arise for most families. According to this view, family planning programs are inevitably ineffective in these places, because there is no significant demand for their services.

On the other hand, advocates of the potential of family planning programs argue that in many such countries there is at least some latent demand for family planning services, but that it does not become manifest because the family planning system is weak, with poor-quality services provided in ways that are inappropriate for the local culture.

The largest among these countries, India, with more than 800 million people, is important not only because of its size but also because it has had a family planning program for decades and has given it high priority at least since 1966. Although neither its fertility nor family planning data are of good quality, a probable consensus among informed observers is that there has been a modest rise in contraceptive prevalence and a comparably modest fall in fertility, especially in the last 15 years. According to estimates of the Indian Department of Family Planning, contraceptive prevalence rose from 4 percent in 1967 to 38 percent in 1987. Variation in such contraceptive prevalence rates between 352 districts, including most of India's population, has been shown to be modestly correlated to female literacy and rural electrification, but its relation to family planning program effort is unknown.

India's program has gone through many permutations in the last twenty years. This, together with the great variation in cultural, caste, economic, and social strata in this vast country, makes it difficult to summarize the program's problems. Nevertheless, there probably is a consensus among most Indian and foreign observers that the program has been poorly executed.[13] One Indian official some years ago told me, "The Indian program hasn't failed. It hasn't been carried out."

The program has been criticized for:

— an obsession with targets for the program and for each worker set at such high levels and so obviously unattainable as to demoralize personnel;
— too much concentration on one drastic method — sterilization — linked to a controversial incentive program;
— rotating its district family planning and other officers among posts so often as to impede continuity in a long-run program; and
— the fact that officials at central and state and even district levels are not in touch with the realities of life at the village level, unlike the cases of Indonesia and China, which countries use ties to those grass-roots levels very effectively.

On the positive side is the fact that 72 districts are reported to have contraceptive prevalence rates of 50 percent or higher and 18 have rates of 60 percent or more.

13. In an address to a meeting of the International Union for the Scientific Study of Population in New Delhi in September 1989, Prime Minister Rajiv Gandhi admitted that the Indian program has fallen far short of aspirations because of bureaucratic bungling and inflexibility in the face of large local variations in the social situation.

Even if discounted for overreporting, these data suggest that some combination of favorable conditions and possibly better program implementation are found in some districts, which might provide models for other districts.

Unfortunately, despite India's considerable intellectual and scientific resources, there has been no sustained effort to learn what combination of specific developmental and cultural conditions, program design, and program implementation can account for these successes or for India's failure to be more generally successful in attaining its own goals for its population program.

Pakistan, with 115 million people, has a very low contraceptive rate, recently estimated at only 9 percent, and a fertility rate of about 6. Although it has had a family planning program for several decades, it has been a low-priority, poorly implemented program. The combination of low levels of social and economic development, a patriarchal, familistic culture, religious barriers, and an ineffective family planning program makes its lack of progress toward its professed lower-fertility goals understandable.

Bangladesh, with more than 100 million people, has the low developmental levels and the cultural barriers that characterize Pakistan. While its contraceptive prevalence rate of 25 percent is significantly higher than Pakistan's and many women report wanting no more children on fertility surveys, respected observers have asserted that familial institutional supports for high fertility make early fertility declines unlikely. In Bangladesh, however, a carefully monitored pilot project in Matlab seems to have demonstrated that an intensive, high-quality family planning service program can make a significant difference even in such unfavorable circumstances.[14] The project brought contraceptive prevalence up from very little to 45 percent, with a commensurate fall in fertility. Attempts are now being made to extend into new areas the essentials of what was learned in Matlab. Initial results are encouraging but not conclusive.

At Chogoria, in Kenya, a medical missionary hospital mounted a family planning program with some similarities to the project in Matlab.[15] There, too, contraceptive prevalence has been brought up to the 40 percent level. Statements indicating a potential demand have been tested with a good-quality service program and found to be real.

Skeptical evaluations of the prospects for fertility decline in sub-Saharan Africa have been applied to Kenya as well.[16] A recent survey in Kenya has, however, shown a significant 50 percent rise in contraceptive prevalence between 1984 and 1989, with an accompanying fall in fertility from 7.7 to 6.7. By 1989, 40 percent of married women as young as 25-29 years old said they wanted no more children and 36 percent said that they wanted to postpone the next child for at least two years. The Chogoria test and the recent survey suggest that these statements are meaningful.

14. Michael A. Koenig et al., "Trends in Family Size Preferences and Contraceptive Use in Matlab, Bangladesh," *Studies in Family Planning*, 18(3):117-27 (May-June 1987).

15. Howard I. Goldberg, Malcolm McNeil, and Alison Spitz, "Contraceptive Use and Fertility Decline in Chogoria, Kenya," *Studies in Family Planning*, 20(1):17-25 (Jan.-Feb. 1989).

16. Odile Frank and Geoffrey McNicoll, "An Interpretation of Fertility and Population Policy," *Population and Development Review*, 13(2):209-43 (June 1987).

In many sub-Saharan countries the basic infrastructure is weak, and there is a severe shortage of professional personnel. Small-scale investigations, often less intensive and rigorous than the cited pilot projects, have been used to develop and test provisionally the feasibility of locally appropriate service programs. In one such program in the Sudan, contraceptive prevalence rates were reported as rising from 9 to 25 percent in eight years, and replication yielded similar results in four years.[17]

In many poor, high-fertility LDCs, including Bangladesh and Kenya, lower mortality means higher child survival, so that many LDC women, by the time they are about 30, already have alive the number of children they want. The increasing number of living children in each family creates pressure on traditional institutions developed on the implicit assumption that many children would die.

At the same time, increasing numbers of Third World citizens are getting new ideas from the expanding world network of communication, transportation, and economic interdependence, whose influence increasingly reaches into even LDC villages. These ideas include new facts and models about reproductive behavior but, just as important, about health, the value of education, new consumption goods, and political power. Such new ideas generate rising aspirations among parents, both for themselves and for their children, although the pace of such changes varies enormously from place to place. The conventional wisdom has been that poor, illiterate LDC peasants are unlikely to be interested in birth control, but under the changing conditions induced by the greater survival of children and the impact of new ideas, that wisdom may be less generally valid than in earlier days. A national survey in Indonesia in 1976 found unexpectedly that new contraceptive practice was considerable among the rural, the poor, the uneducated, and the residents of backward villages.[18]

It is in such situations that increasing numbers of women with years of childbearing still ahead are saying on surveys that they want no more children. This does not mean that they have all made definite, unambiguous decisions. Some have, but much larger numbers are under crosspressures between traditional values and institutions and new realities and ideas. A good family planning information and service program helps to crystallize latent demand for contraception by emphasizing the usefulness and legitimacy of family planning as a partial solution for the problems of families.

The pilot studies at Matlab and Chogoria and declining fertility in several African countries are indications of the potential for successes in at least some places where success is believed, a priori, to be very unlikely. This does not mean, however, that high contraceptive prevalence and lower fertility can be achieved everywhere where social and cultural conditions apparently are unfavorable.

PROSPECTS AND POLICIES IN
POORLY DEVELOPED COUNTRIES

There is, in fact, little doubt that traditional familial institutions, low develop-

17. Operations Research Program, *Africa: A New Frontier in Family Planning* (New York: Columbia University, Center for Population and Family Health, 1988). The term "operations research," designating rigorous quantitative work in some other fields, is less appropriate for some of these projects.

18. Ronald Freedman, S. E. Khoo, and B. Supraptilah, "Use of Modern Contraceptives in Indonesia: A Challenge to the Conventional Wisdom," *International Family Planning Perspectives*, 7(1):3-15 (Mar. 1981).

ment levels, poor infrastructure, and shortages of indigenous professional personnel and of other resources make early rapid fertility declines unlikely in places like Pakistan and much of sub-Saharan Africa. For example, surveys in 1986 and 1987 in Mali, Burundi, Liberia, Senegal, and Togo found that the number of children women wanted were, on average, similar to the number they were having—six to seven.

Under these difficult circumstances, it is particularly unpromising to attempt to implement national plans for uniform programs across a country without regard to local readiness, ethnic and tribal differences, trained personnel locally acceptable, and adequate supplies of appropriate contraceptives and other resources. It seems to be more rational to begin with selective program initiatives in promising local areas and population strata and for purposes meeting manifest local needs.

Pilot projects, such as that in Matlab, Bangladesh, or the one in Chogoria, Kenya, have the potential of testing for latent demand in local areas, identifying the subgroups that are interested, and developing culturally relevant programs to meet the demand, if demand is found. Such projects with intensive inputs may appear to be expensive, but given the poor investment return from ineffective national programs in many poor LDCs, the investment in pilot projects appears to be worthwhile. Such pilot projects should be mounted in situations where a success is likely. If the possibility of an effective program is gravely in question, it is plausible to begin under favorable conditions with later expansion to more difficult places as confidence, legitimation, and program models develop.

In surveys in sub-Saharan Africa a considerable number of women who are not interested in restricting the number of their children before having a large number say that they would like to postpone their next birth for at least two years. This suggests that the initial use of contraception for spacing rather than limiting births might find significant numbers accepting contraception, especially in the many African countries in which prolonged sexual abstinence after a birth has been customary. Some family planning programs in such countries already are moving in that direction in combination with maternal and child health services. Even if the total number of births women have remains unchanged, lengthening the intervals between births has the effect of decreasing annual fertility rates and the rate of population growth.

EXTERNAL SUPPORT FROM DEVELOPED COUNTRIES

LDCs get considerable support from developed countries and from the United Nations, the World Bank, and other private and public agencies.[19] In 1985, about $512 million in such external support was committed. While the United States Agency for International Development has made the largest bilateral commitments, at least 16 other countries in 1985 made contributions, several of them giving more than the United States when computed as a percentage of gross national product.

In most LDCs with family planning programs, such external financial assistance has been important in providing foreign exchange for purchasing contraceptives and other supplies and equipment and has also financed such infrastructure as clinics and motor vehicles. To varying degrees

19. Dorothy L. Nortman, "External Funding for Population Programs in Developing Countries, 1982-1985," *International Family Planning Perspectives*, 14(1):2-8 (Mar. 1988).

such support also pays for operating costs of the programs. The value of technical assistance from advisers provided by external agencies is more controversial, but there is little doubt that the external agencies have played an important role in legitimating family planning programs through dialogues with political leaders and in other ways. External assistance has sometimes been attacked or even rejected on ideological grounds.

THE ROLE OF
UNFORESEEN SOCIAL CHANGE

One purpose of both pilot studies and other soundings of latent demand in high-fertility countries is early detection of the effects of social changes. Traditional cultural and institutional forces supporting high fertility are not immune to the rapid social changes sweeping the world. Social scientists do much better at analyzing what societies have been than what they are becoming.

Recent rises in contraceptive prevalence and declines in fertility in places like Kenya, Zimbabwe, Botswana, and Algeria were not foreseen by most observers a few years ago. Once fertility in LDCs has declined by about 10 percent with more birth control, in most cases the decline continues. This also was the earlier experience in the West.

Most observers also did not foresee in the 1960s the rapid demographic transformations of places like Taiwan, Korea, Indonesia, China, and some Latin American countries. That is because they did not foresee the scope and rapidity of the following changes, which variously affected major fertility and mortality decline: rapid social and economic development, creation of family planning programs effective in reaching large parts of the population, legitimation of the idea of birth-control methods and of organized family planning programs, and development of new birth-control methods.

The prospects of effective family planning programs and fertility declines in specific high-fertility countries will depend on the future scale of such changes in each country as well as on other changes not presently foreseen.

ANNALS, *AAPSS,* **510,** July 1990

Cultural and Social Factors Influencing Mortality Levels in Developing Countries

By JOHN C. CALDWELL

ABSTRACT: Recent analyses of Third World data, both at the level of national or other large aggregates and at that of individuals studied in sample surveys, have revealed the surprising fact that social characteristics, such as the level of schooling or fertility control, or cultural characteristics, such as ethnic group, are usually more influential in determining mortality levels than is access to medical services, income, or nutritional levels. Evidence from the United States at the beginning of the century suggests that this was not the case earlier in the West. This article examines the evidence, shows why developing countries are currently in an unusual situation, and presents anthropological evidence on how cultural, social, and behavioral factors achieve their impact. An attempt is made to begin the construction of a more general theory of mortality transition.

John Caldwell received his Ph.D. degree in demography at the Australian National University, Canberra. He and his wife, Pat Caldwell, have researched population change via anthropological and demographic field-research techniques in Thailand, Malaysia, sub-Saharan Africa, India, and Sri Lanka. From 1970 to 1988 he was head of the Australian National University's Department of Demography and now is director of its Health Transition Centre. He is author of Theory of Fertility Decline; *and coauthor of* The Causes of Demographic Change: Experimental Research in South India.

OVER the last 100 years, the history of mortality in the West has given all the appearances of supporting a common-sense and economic-determinist interpretation of health change. During that period, life expectancy in the most developed countries increased by more than 50 percent, from under 50 years to around 75 years. Nothing like this had happened before in human history. But no one was very surprised, because other changes of fundamental importance had also occurred: with the full flowering of the Industrial Revolution, real incomes in the most economically advanced countries had multiplied almost tenfold over that period. This allowed people to be better fed and clad, permitted the construction of improved hospitals that the populace could increasingly afford to use, and provided the resources to treat drinking water and sewage. At the same time, the interrelated scientific revolution first made safer medical procedures possible and ultimately produced sulfa drugs, antibiotics, new vaccines, and powerful insecticides.

Material improvement and scientific advance seemed to have been the main engines driving down mortality, an interpretation that this article will argue was not, for the West, far wrong. Furthermore, for most of this period, the interpretation was largely confined to the West, partly because most analysts lived there but largely because there was little in the way of health statistics elsewhere. This fact was to cloud our interpretation of the forces behind the global mortality transition when it began to gather momentum in the present century.

Certainly, it was known that these advances were not equally shared. As early as 1852 William Farr had demonstrated major mortality differentials in England by socioeconomic class,[1] but these were assumed to reflect real differences in the means to bring minimum comfort and to pay for treatment and little else. Not everyone agreed that individual behavior played no significant role in determining the level of mortality, as was shown by the aims and activities of the Infant Welfare Movement in English-speaking countries before World War I or by the Maternal and Child Welfare Movements of the 1920s and 1930s.[2] A revisionist approach to the history of medicine has been developed in recent decades by Thomas McKeown and colleagues,[3] but the thrust of this work has been to emphasize the impact of economic change at the expense of scientific medicine.

NEW EVIDENCE FROM DEVELOPING COUNTRIES

A major shift in our interpretation of the mortality transition has been made possible by a change of focus to the development problems of the Third World, where life expectancy in sub-Saharan Africa is still below 50 years and in South Asia below 55 years. These are populations largely lack-

1. William Farr, *Vital Statistics: A Memorial Volume of Selections from the Reports and Writings of William Farr* (Metuchen, NJ: Scarecrow Press, 1975).

2. Ellen Ross, "Mothers and the State in Britain, 1904-1914" (Paper delivered at the Conference on the Historical Context and Consequences of Declining Fertility in Europe, Cambridge Meeting, July 1989); Philippa Mein Smith, "Infant Survival, the Infant Welfare Movement and Mothers' Behaviour, Australia with Reference to New Zealand, 1900-1945" (Ph.D. thesis, Australian National University, Canberra, 1989).

3. Thomas McKeown, *The Role of Medicine: Dream, Mirage or Nemesis* (London: Nuffield Hospitals Trust, 1967).

ing adequate death registration systems and medical identification of the cause of death, so adequate data banks on mortality and social and economic conditions have been amassed by the United Nations and the World Bank only in recent years.

This evidence shows that levels of income and health services are weak predictors of mortality levels and that social determinants apparently play a major role in determining mortality. This article summarizes that evidence, attempts to employ it to explain global mortality transition, and analyzes the available information on how social factors affect death rates.

It has become increasingly clear that Third World national mortality levels exhibit a very different pattern from what their income levels would imply. Some poor developing countries have largely escaped the Malthusian shackles. A 1985 Rockefeller Foundation Conference[4] selected for investigatory study four Third World societies that had achieved low levels of mortality "at low cost": certainly, when compared with developed countries with similar mortality levels, at absolute low cost, but not always at relatively low cost if the measure is the proportion of national income spent on health and social services likely to assist the maintenance of health. The societies chosen—Sri Lanka; Kerala State, in southwest India; China; and Costa Rica—all had life expectancies in the 66- to 70-year range. In the case of the first three societies, this was at least 15 years higher than the average for countries with similar incomes, about 3 years lower than Eastern Europe, and only 7 years below Western Europe and North America. This level of mortality had been achieved

by these three societies with per capita incomes in the $300-400 range, or one-fortieth that of Western Europe and one-fiftieth of North America.[5] Considerable attention was paid to the nature of their health and social services.

Part of the explanation for the high life expectancies probably lies in the social-service net that Sri Lanka, China, and Costa Rica provide. It should be noted, however that Sri Lanka spends only 1.2 percent of its gross national product on health, slightly above the average for its income level, compared with 3.7 percent for Western industrialized countries, which spend, in absolute terms, about 140 times as much per person.[6] In terms of the number of inhabitants per physician, Sri Lanka, with 7500 persons per doctor, or 15 times as many as in the West, is typical of its income level;[7] Kerala probably presents a similar picture, although the identification for statistical purposes of doctors in both India and China includes many persons whom other countries would exclude and so makes comparisons impossible. The conclusion is inescapable that neither income nor the levels of health services and interventions are the primary explanation for the remarkable health achievements of these societies.

The new data banks provided valuable clues. Multivariate analysis allowed the level of a range of socioeconomic factors and health inputs in developing countries to be related to mortality levels. Flegg

4. Scott B. Halstead, Julia A. Walsh, and Kenneth S. Warren, *Good Health at Low Cost* (New York: Rockefeller Foundation, 1985).

5. Cf. World Bank, *World Development Report, 1988* (New York: Oxford University Press, 1988), pp. 222-23, tab. 1.

6. Ibid., pp. 266-67, tab. 23. There are no figures for Kerala, which probably spends less, or China, while Costa Rica spends a proportion of the gross national product in the range of the proportion spent by the industrialized countries.

7. Ibid., pp. 278-79, tab. 29.

showed that the level of literacy was the best indicator of low infant mortality, although the degree of equality in income and the level of medical care also played important roles.[8] Caldwell demonstrated that low national mortality was most highly correlated with the proportion of females in school a generation earlier, and that the levels of family planning practice and male school attendance were also important indicators of low mortality.[9] Lower correlations were found with the ratio of doctors to population and nutritional levels, and a still lower correlation with income levels. Recently, Rogers and Wofford have confirmed the prime role of literacy and the proportion of the population working outside agriculture and, of lesser importance, the safety of the water supply.[10] Health inputs, as measured by the ratio of physicians to population, showed a lower level of correlation, while nutrition was not found to be significant. The importance of schooling a generation earlier lies in the fact that it determines the current level of parental education, especially important in the case of mothers. The marked differential in the survival of children according to the level of mother's education had been noted in Ghana in the 1960s by Gaisie[11] and in a range of Latin American countries in the 1970s by Behm.[12] The importance of child survival for determining mortality levels lies in the fact that, in high-mortality countries, typically at least one-quarter of all births result in deaths before 5 years of age, and because of the age structure of the population, half of all deaths in the society occur to persons under 5 years.

Meanwhile, these macro observations were being increasingly supported by individual-level data collected by national and subnational representative surveys in the Third World. A major opportunity was presented by the organization of surveys of good scientific quality in 45 developing countries by the World Fertility Survey program in the decade after 1975. Two different analyses[13] largely supported each other in their finding that parental education is the most important influence on child survival, with mother's schooling usually having the greater impact. Income, evidenced by father's occupation, is also important. Child mortality declines with every additional year of mother's education with no lower threshold, so that even one or two years of schooling in a rural school has some impact. Furthermore, social influences are of greater importance, as evidenced by wider differential mortality between groups, for children aged 1-4 years than for infants, presumably because

8. A. T. Flegg, "Inequality of Income, Illiteracy and Medical Care as Determinants of Infant Mortality in Underdeveloped Countries," *Population Studies*, 36(3):441-58 (Nov. 1982).

9. John C. Caldwell, "Routes to Low Mortality in Poor Countries," *Population and Development Review*, 12(2):179, tab. 3 (June 1986).

10. Richard G. Rogers and Sharon Wofford, "Life Expectancy in Less Developed Countries: Socioeconomic Development or Public Health?" *Journal of Biosocial Science*, 21:245-52 (1989).

11. S. K. Gaisie, *Dynamics of Population Growth in Ghana*, Ghana Population Studies no. 1 (Legon, Accra: University of Ghana, Demographic Unit, 1969).

12. Hugo Behm, *Final Report on the Research Project on Infant and Childhood Mortality in the Third World* (Paris: Comité international de coopération dans les recherches nationales en démographie, 1983).

13. John C. Caldwell and Peter F. McDonald, "Influence of Maternal Education on Infant and Child Mortality: Levels and Causes," in *International Population Conference, Manila, 1981*, (Liège: International Union for the Scientific Study of Population, 1981), 2:79-96; J. N. Hobcraft, J. W. McDonald, and S. O. Rutstein, "Socioeconomic Factors in Infant and Child Mortality: A Cross-National Comparison," *Population Studies*, 38(2):193-223 (July 1984).

of the leveling effect on the latter of nearly universal breast-feeding.

Mensch, Lentzner, and Preston analyzed 15 surveys in Africa, Asia, and Latin America, only 6 of which were from the World Fertility Survey program. They explored the impact of 12 groups of social, economic, and health-care variables, both uncontrolled and then controlled for the influence of the other variables. They concluded that the major influences on child survival were mother's education, ethnicity, and, largely in urban areas, father's education.[14]

The extent to which maternal education has been identified as a major — or even the major — factor in determining child mortality is astonishing, although even this finding merely provides clues to the forces at work rather than a simple answer. When two socioeconomically similar areas in Nigeria's Ekiti district were compared in order to discover the mortality impact of different levels of health services, it was discovered that, even where there was no access to modern health services, mother's schooling was an important determinant of child survival.[15] Research in southwest Nigeria, especially in Ibadan, for the Changing African Family Project, showed that the importance of maternal education remained after controlling for the occupations of both mother and father, the urban-rural division and the residential location within urban areas, whether the marriage was monogamous or polygynous, and whether the parents practiced family planning or not.[16] Mensch, Lentzner, and Preston concluded:

When examined by itself, an additional year of mother's schooling reduces child mortality by an average across our 15 countries of 6.8 percent, with the majority of countries falling in the range of 5.0 to 9.0 percent. After all other variables are entered into the estimation equation, the effect is still a reduction of 3.4 percent in mortality per year of schooling. This latter is the "direct" effect of schooling and is biased downward as an estimate of the "total" effect by the inclusion of variables whose value is partly determined by mother's schooling itself.[17]

Maternal education and child survival were the focus of two papers, the first by Cleland and van Ginneken[18] and the second by Cleland alone. The latter concluded:

The most important features of the maternal education-childhood mortality association may be summarized thus: there is no threshold; the association is found in all major developing regions; the linkage is stronger in childhood than in infancy; only about half of the gross association can be accounted for by material advantages associated with education; reproductive risk factors play a minor intermediate role in the relationship; greater equity of treatment between sons and daughters is no part of the explanation; the association between mother's education and child mortality is slightly greater than for father's education and mortality.[19]

14. United Nations, *Socio-Economic Differentials in Child Mortality in Developing Countries,* by Barbara Mensch, Harold Lentzner, and Samuel Preston, ST/ESA/SER.A/97 (New York: United Nations, 1985).

15. I. O. Orubuloye and John C. Caldwell, "The Impact of Public Health Services on Mortality: A Study of Mortality Differentials in a Rural Area of Nigeria," *Population Studies,* 29(2):259-72 (July 1975); Caldwell, "Routes to Low Mortality."

16. John C. Caldwell, "Education as a Factor in Mortality Decline: An Examination of Nigerian Data," *Population Studies,* 33(3):395-413 (Nov. 1979).

17. United Nations, *Socio-Economic Differentials,* p. 287.

18. John Cleland and Jeroen van Ginneken, "Maternal Education and Child Survival in Developing Countries: The Search for Pathways of Influence," *Social Science and Medicine,* 27(12):1357-68 (1988).

19. John Cleland, "Maternal Education and Child Survival: Further Evidence and Explanations," in

The point that may not have been sufficiently stressed is that education has two separate but multiplicative impacts, one on individuals whose behavior is changed relative to their society and one that changes the whole society. An examination of the World Fertility Surveys concluded:

There is as close a correlation between child survival and general levels of [female] education in a community as there is between child survival and maternal education. An educated woman may feel more deprived in a country where most other women are educated than in one where they are not; nevertheless, her children stand a much greater chance of survival. If we take these two factors together, the contrasts are enormous. In Latin America, the death rate among the children of uneducated Peruvian women is almost 7 times greater than among Venezuelan women with seven years of education. In Asia, the mortality among children of uneducated Nepalese women is almost 15 times greater than it is among those of Malaysian women with seven or more years of schooling.[20]

One persistent, but underresearched, finding is that there are major ethnic or cultural differentials in mortality, especially child mortality, even in the same country and with the same access to health services — differences that survive controlling for income and education. This has been shown between Chinese and Malays in Malaysia[21] and between the different peoples of the West African savanna in rural Mali.[22] Mensch, Lentzner, and Preston examined 60 ethnic groups in 11 countries of Africa, Asia, and Latin America and almost invariably found significant ethnic differentials in child survival in each country, with the mortality level in one group sometimes being twice or more that of another. They noted that Chinese populations in Southeast Asia are characterized by unusually low mortality.[23]

One aspect of the impact on child mortality of different cultural attitudes and practices is that of preference for sons over daughters. This preference, where it is found, almost certainly keeps child mortality higher than it might otherwise be in that the preferential treatment is unlikely to force male mortality down by as great an additional increment as it unnecessarily keeps female mortality high. The World Fertility Surveys provided for the first time, by the use of a life-history approach, substantially accurate data on child mortality by age and sex. This showed that in the sensitive age range of 1-4 years there is excess female over male mortality throughout nearly all North Africa, the Middle East, South Asia, and East Asia, with greater diversity in Southeast Asia and Latin America, and little or no additional danger for females only in sub-Saharan Africa.[24] Data on differential sex mortality from the Indian Sample Registration Survey and the International Diarrhoeal Dis-

What We Know about Health Transition: The Proceedings of an International Workshop, Canberra, May 1989, ed. John C. Caldwell et al. (Canberra: Australian National University, Health Transition Centre, 1990).

20. John C. Caldwell, "Mass Education as a Determinant of Mortality Decline" (CASID Lecture, Michigan State University, 25 Oct. 1988), reprinted in Selected Readings in Cultural, Social and Bhavioural Determinants of Health, ed. John C. Caldwell and Gigi Santow (Canberra: Australian National University, Health Transition Centre, 1989), pp. 103-11.

21. Julie DaVanzo, William P. Butz, and Jean-Pierre Habicht, "How Biological and Behavioural

Influences on Mortality in Malaysia Vary during the First Year of Life," Population Studies, 37(3):381-402 (Nov. 1983).

22. Allan G. Hill, ed., Population Health and Nutrition in the Sahel: Issues in the Welfare of Selected West African Communities (London: Kegan Paul International, 1985).

23. United Nations, Socio-Economic Differentials, pp. 77-111.

24. Shea O. Rutstein, "Infant and Child Mortality: Levels, Trends and Demographic Differentials," Comparative Studies: Cross-National Summaries, no.

eases Research Centre's Bangladesh population laboratory in the Matlab district demonstrate how culturally specific behavior can affect mortality. Female mortality is not above that of males during the first year of life, when breast-feeding provides equal nourishment and protective antibodies; it is relatively high in the 1- to 4-year age range, when that protection has dwindled but children are still highly dependent on others; it falls toward parity between 5 years and marriage as girls become more capable of fending for themselves; and it rises above that of males again during the reproductive years, largely because of high maternal mortality in the poor obstetric conditions of much of South Asia. Thereafter it falls below male levels.[25]

There is convincing evidence that the achievement of a small family, or even the intention of having one by employing birth control, is associated with declines in child mortality. There is a correlation between national levels of child mortality and family planning practice that compares only with that between maternal education and ethnicity.[26] The Nigerian segment of the Changing African Family Project found in Ibadan city child-mortality levels that were far lower among those women who had achieved relatively small families than among those who had not.[27] The One-per-

Thousand Survey of China found extraordinarily low mortality among only children whose parents had completed the documentation opting for that status.[28] The interrelations here are complex and are discussed in the next section.

I continued further with the approach adopted in the "Good Health at Low Cost" conference.[29] A comparison of the mortality and per capita income rankings of the 99 Third World countries reported fully by the World Bank because their populations exceed 1 million showed that, in terms of their income, 11 did exceptionally well with regard to health, being 25 to 62 places higher in their health rankings than their incomes would have predicted, while another 11 did exceptionally badly, falling 25 to 70 places below prediction. Armed with this information and that from correlation analysis, together with anthropological, sociological, and historical information on the societies that had been most successful in driving down mortality within their income constraints, the study came to a number of conclusions. Parental education is of great importance, especially that of mothers. So is the control of fertility or even the attempt to control it. Female autonomy is important, and its relative lack was the main reason that 9 of the 11 countries less successful in converting their incomes into low mortality were found in the western branch of Islam stretching from Senegal to Iran. Grass-roots radicalism, egalitarianism, and democracy were important in both creating a successful popular demand for health and educational services and ensuring that they worked. Neither female autonomy nor radicalism has as yet been as successfully researched as education,

43, rev. ed. (London: World Fertility Survey, Dec. 1984); Pat Caldwell and John C. Caldwell, "Where There Is a Narrower Gap between Female and Male Situations: Lessons from South India and Sri Lanka" (Paper delivered at the Social Science Research Council Workshop on Gender Differentials in Mortality in South Asia, Dhaka, Bangladesh, Jan. 1987).

25. Caldwell and Caldwell, "Where There Is a Narrower Gap."

26. Caldwell, "Routes to Low Mortality," p. 179, tab. 3.

27. John C. Caldwell and Pat Caldwell, "The Achieved Small Family: Early Fertility Transition in an African City," Studies in Family Planning, 9(1):2-18, app. B (Jan. 1978).

28. John C. Caldwell and K. Srinivasan, "New Data on Nuptiality and Fertility in China," Population and Development Review, 10(1):71-79 (Mar. 1984).

29. Caldwell, "Routes to Low Mortality."

partly because there are no simple measures equivalent to years of schooling.[30] Clearly, as is discussed in the next section, these characteristics are interrelated. The study went far toward suggesting that societies are largely prisoners of their cultures and histories and that the roots of contemporary health successes lie far back in those histories. The exceptions were the successes achieved by Communist revolutions in China and Vietnam and, less certainly — because it earlier was marked by some of the other characteristics — by Cuba.

Where the greatest successes over mortality have been gained, this achievement has been the product of an interaction between certain cultural and social characteristics on the one hand and the easy accessibility of basic modern health services on the other. In spite of the fact that parental education and the practice of fertility control correlate so much more highly with mortality levels than do medical interventions in the contemporary Third World, the evidence strongly suggests that alone they cannot make dramatic reductions in mortality levels. They may, in fact, correlate more highly because health investment has been running ahead of social investment in terms of the optimum mix.

Sri Lanka had experienced massive social change by the 1920s. The 1921 census had found 56 percent of males and 21 percent of females to be literate, a level that Pakistan was not to reach for another half century. Yet life expectancy was little over 30 years.[31] It was the provision of health services, first in urban areas and then, from 1945 onward, rapidly in rural areas, that allowed the subsequent dramatic fall in death rates. Yet earlier the country had been highly sensitive to the need to combat sickness and possessed one of the most extensive and developed systems of traditional medicine in the world. Traditional medical systems may provide solace and reduce pain and even symptoms in chronic or other conditions, but the evidence seems clear that modern medicine is needed to drive down mortality rates.

France had reduced its fertility level to the equivalent of 3.5 births per woman by 1850, but its life expectancy was only 39 years.[32] Three societies that had experienced a great deal of social change — Sri Lanka, Kerala, and Costa Rica — enjoyed periods of intensive activity when health services were spread much more widely to the rural populations and the urban poor during the years 1946-53, 1956-71, and 1970-80, respectively; in each case mortality fell much more rapidly than in earlier or later years.[33] There are also societies where lack of specific types of social change, often female autonomy or female education, means that major infusions of modern health services do not achieve their anticipated impact. By 1980 Libya employed more doctors per capita than Japan or Ireland and was reaching the levels of the United Kingdom and New Zealand, but life expectancy there was 16 years shorter and the infant mortality rate seven times as high.

There is, then, some kind of symbiosis between social change and modern medi-

30. John C. Caldwell and Pat Caldwell, "Women's Position and Child Mortality and Morbidity in LDCs," in *Conference on Women's Position and Demographic Change in the Course of Development, Asker (Oslo) 1988* (Liège: International Union for the Scientific Study of Population, 1988), pp. 213-36.

31. Caldwell, "Routes to Low Mortality"; T. Nadarajah, "Trends and Differentials in Mortality," in *Population of Sri Lanka* (Bangkok: Economic and Social Commission for Asia and the Pacific, 1976), p. 148.

32. Nathan Keyfitz, *World Population: An Analysis of Vital Data* (Chicago: University of Chicago Press, 1968).

33. Caldwell, "Routes to Low Mortality," p. 181.

cine, the latter measured more by its accessibility to a wide population than by its level of technology. A comparison of two socioeconomically similar populations in Nigeria, one with access to a hospital and doctors and the other isolated from such interventions, suggests that the gain in life expectancy — equivalent to the more easily measured changes in child mortality — was 20 percent when the sole intervention was easy access to adequate health facilities for illiterate mothers, 33 percent when it was education without health facilities, and 87 percent with both.[34]

Cleland and van Ginneken summarized data from a wide range of countries showing that the use of modern health services increased with duration of education.[35] They believed that most evidence showed the interaction between education and health services to be less spectacular than that found in Nigeria.[36] They reached the conclusion that about one-half of the very great differentials found across the Third World in child survival by education of mother are probably explained by "economic advantages associated with education (income, water and latrine facilities, clothing, housing quality, etc.)."[37] They were more cautious about how the "pure" impact of mother's education was to be divided between interaction with modern medicine and behavioral and care factors that prevent children from becoming sick or having an accident in the first place, but they emphasized that both were likely to be important. Income also interacts with health-service provision, and this interaction is especially strong when there is little attempt to provide a free health service.

A range of researchers attribute most of the pure effect of maternal education to the better use of modern health services, but a significant number also attribute an important role to family health management independent of curative services.[38] In a Nigerian village that was so far from modern health services that very few children had ever been taken to doctors or nurses, mothers with some schooling experienced only one-third the child loss of mothers with no schooling. Only some of this can be explained by greater use of modern pharmaceuticals such as the malaria suppressants brought by a cyclist who ran an itinerant pharmacy service.[39] It might also be noted that the skills in health management that can prevent children from becoming sick or dying in the absence of modern health services are the same ones that allow health services to be exploited more successfully. Further convincing evidence of cultural and social differentials in child mortality in the pre-modern-medicine era has been provided by research among societies in rural Mali where the modern era has not yet begun. The substantial difference in child mortality between adjacent cultural groups was explained by different styles of child care.[40] In contemporary societies, some families are much more prone to experience sickness and to lose children than others, as was shown forty years ago

34. Ibid., p. 204; cf. Orubuloye and Caldwell, "Impact of Public Health Services."

35. Cleland and van Ginneken, "Maternal Education," pp. 1361-62.

36. Ibid., pp. 1362-63.

37. Ibid., p. 1360.

38. For detailed references, see Caldwell and Caldwell, "Women's Position," pp. 222-23.

39. Orubuloye and Caldwell, "Impact of Public Health Services," p. 268.

40. Katherine Hilderbrand et al., "Child Mortality and Care of Children in Rural Mali" (Paper delivered at the National Institute for Research Advancement and IUSSP Seminar on Social and Biological Correlates of Mortality, Tokyo, 24-27 Nov. 1984).

for Newcastle-upon-Tyne, England,[41] and recently in India.[42]

INTERPRETING THE EVIDENCE TO FORMULATE A THEORY OF HEALTH TRANSITION

The first proposition is that there have always been socioeconomic differentials in mortality levels and that they predated the impact of modern medicine. This situation was partly a function of income and the ability to eat better and enjoy other material comforts, as Malthus noted.[43] But the evidence on social differentials by ethnic group, and of greater propensity for child loss in some households than others, even in rather homogeneous contemporary English urban areas or Indian villages, suggests that social differentials were also important. It is unlikely that research will ever identify pre-modern-medicine populations with no social differentials in mortality, especially child mortality, but it is highly probable that the differentials will be smaller than those in the era of modern medicine. It should be noted that this era did not suddenly begin. Moreover, modern

41. J. Spence et al., *A Thousand Families in Newcastle-upon-Tyne: An Approach to the Study of Health and Illness in Children* (New York: Oxford University Press, 1954).

42. Monica Das Gupta, "Death Clustering, Maternal Education and the Determinants of Child Mortality in Rural Punjab, India," in *What We Know about Health Transition,* ed. Caldwell et al.

43. Cf. John C. Caldwell, "Family Change and Demographic Change: The Reversal of the Veneration Flow," in *Dynamics of Population and Family Welfare 1987,* ed. K. Srinivasan and S. Mukerji (Bombay: Himalaya, 1988), pp. 71-96; John C. Caldwell and Pat Caldwell, "Family Systems: Their Viability and Vulnerability: A Study of Intergenerational Transactions and Their Demographic Implications" (Paper delivered at IUSSP Seminar on Changing Family Structures and Life Courses in LDC's, East-West Population Institute, Honolulu, HI, 5-7 Jan. 1987).

medicine has become ever more effective, so that social differentials in mortality arising out of interaction with modern medicine are likely to have increased in the present century.

The second proposition is that a substantial part, probably the majority, of the explanation for social differentials in mortality in the contemporary Third World lies in the interaction with modern medicine. Evidence for the mechanics of this interaction is presented at the end of this article. The interface between society and modern medicine is broader than the proponents of scientific medicine usually like to admit. It includes not only doctors, nurses, midwives, and pharmacists but also pharmaceuticals distributed through traditional markets, by wandering untrained salesmen, and, on a massive scale, through both traditional medical practitioners and nontraditional untrained practitioners or quacks. This informal system helps to change beliefs and practices with regard to illness and its treatment and increasingly acts as a referral system to the more formal health sector. It is also probable that this uncontrolled spread of modern medicine saves more lives rather than causes additional deaths, although the whole matter has hardly been researched at all. This informal sector is the only channel of modern medicine to much of rural South Asia and sub-Saharan Africa and almost certainly plays a role in the continuing decline in mortality in both regions. The impact of modern medicine in the formal sector is a function less of its scientific levels than of its accessibility through rural clinics and national health schemes reducing the cost to the patient. The breakthrough periods in reducing mortality levels in different Third World countries have been associated with the democratization of services, not with an increase in the quality of medical technology.

The third proposition is that the various social mechanisms identified as playing a role in reducing mortality are really different facets of the same phenomenon, which might be called social modernization, or the rise of individualism or Westernization. It is really something broader and in many ways is the social counterpart of the transition from subsistence production to the market economy. It is the move toward a system where individuals have options and can exercise choices — and realize that they can do so and act on that realization. The findings with regard to maternal education, female autonomy, and grass-roots radicalism are all part of this picture. It is also why sudden social shocks can accelerate demographic processes, as the French Revolution and the Japanese defeat in World War II did in the case of the fertility decline and as the Chinese Revolution did with regard to mortality even if its stated aim was far from the promotion of individualism. It is the dismantling of the subsistence-production organization and the control and belief systems that was necessary to ensure survival.

Underlying these changes were profound economic changes. It was economic growth that produced the full market economy and ultimately allowed individuals a degree of independence from the unified family economy. Nevertheless, in terms of demographic behavior, the shifts in belief systems were very important. In the area of health the important changes were toward a belief that sickness and death were the result of nondivine and nonmagical forces of this world, that there was something that could be done about them in the form of either careful behavior or seeking the best help, and eventually that modern medicine was usually the most effective help that

could be obtained. In a study area in rural India, we called the process the secularization of health behavior.[44] That secularization does not necessarily involve a diminution of religion, but it does involve its retreat from intervention in causing the everyday disasters of this world. In the Indian village the decline of the so-called little tradition and its village goddesses and profusion of evil spirits, in the face of the great tradition of mainstream Hinduism, associated with literacy, courts, and cities, is an example of this, as was the Puritan movement in England, which eventually moved ordinary people toward the view that most earthly phenomena in their day-to-day lives were a matter of material cause and effect and that to think otherwise could be blasphemous. It might be noted that earlier behavior was not irrational in that much less could at that time be done to avert sickness and death.

The West experienced these changes first because of unparalleled economic growth from at least the sixteenth century. It was eventually to export some of this growth as the world moved toward a global economy, but in the process it exported its behavioral beliefs and social attitudes and ultimately its medical technology and accompanying health philosophy. This export was achieved by colonial administrators, missionaries, the media, and, most powerfully, by the modern education systems that are laden with Western, market, so-called rational values with regard to behavior and family relationships and systems. These conduits were so effective because they were hardly conscious of their proselytizing role but usually believed they

44. John C. Caldwell, P. H. Reddy, and Pat Caldwell, "The Social Component of Mortality Decline: An Investigation in South India Employing Alternative Methodologies," *Population Studies*, 37(2):185-205 (July 1983).

were propagating either objective truth or objectively desirable behavior. The impact of such ideological exports has probably played a central role in the near-global fertility transition that is occurring.[45]

There is compelling evidence that the impact of maternal education on child survival is not merely a case of learning more about health. The most important evidence is that it occurs everywhere: in good schools with good teachers who do teach about health and in poor schools with underqualified teachers who devote no time to the subject, as well as in every part of the Third World. Even stronger evidence is provided by the linear impact of education so that even a little elementary schooling has a proportional impact. Clearly, we are witnessing the general impact of ideas, ideologies, and behavioral models. In rural Bangladesh, Lindenbaum found that mothers who had been to school were cleaner and raised their children more hygienically and carefully, not because they had learned that this would save the children's lives but because they assumed that those with education behaved in such a superior way.[46] In a south Indian rural area, we found that mothers with schooling associated themselves and their schooling much more closely with "modern" institutions — independence and five-year plans as well as health centers and the case for using

them — than did illiterate mothers who felt that they were not part of this new world. The educated also felt this about the uneducated, thus reinforcing the latter's mental set.[47]

A corollary of this argument is that maternal education is likely to produce much greater differentials in child mortality in the contemporary Third World than in the West, even the historical West, because the market-attuned behavioral system had already evolved in the West. This bald statement might be modified by noting that education in the West did accelerate the working classes' adoption of middle-class values and that "rational individualistic" behavior has continued to develop in the West. Preston has produced evidence from the U.S. census of 1900 to show that the gap between educated professional classes and the rest of the society in child survival was much smaller than in the contemporary Third World and evidence from Baltimore in 1915 to show only small differentials between literate and illiterate mothers once father's income had been controlled.[48] He argued that this was because the level of health ignorance of the middle class in America of that time was high and closer to that of the working class than is the case in the contemporary Third World. I subsequently contested this view, partly on the basis of a social-historical study of health behavior in nineteenth-century Australia,

45. John C. Caldwell, *Theory of Fertility Decline* (London: Academic Press, 1982), esp. chap. 9, "The Failure of Theories of Social and Economic Change to Explain Demographic Change: Puzzles of Modernization or Westernization," pp. 269-300.

46. Shirley Lindenbaum, Manisha Chakraborty, and Mohammed Elias, "The Influence of Maternal Education on Infant and Child Mortality in Bangladesh" (Report for the International Centre for Diarrhoeal Disease Research, Bangladesh, 1983), reprinted in *Selected Readings*, ed. Caldwell and Santow, pp. 112-31.

47. John C. Caldwell, P. H. Reddy, and Pat Caldwell, *The Causes of Demographic Change: Experimental Research in South India* (Madison: University of Wisconsin Press, 1988), esp. chap. 6, pp. 132-60 and chap. 7, pp. 161-86.

48. Samuel H. Preston, "Resources, Knowledge and Child Mortality: A Comparison of the U.S. in the Late Nineteenth Century and Developing Countries Today," in *International Population Conference, Florence 1985* (Liège: International Union for the Scientific Study of Population, 1985), 4:373-86.

and maintained that the lesser differential was due to the fact that modern medicine was much less developed and had relatively little to offer.[49] I now believe that my interpretation was only part of the explanation and that the other part was that, as Western education's message was so much closer to the Western behavioral pattern of the time, its impact on changing attitudes and behavior with health implications was much less than in the contemporary Third World. It might be noted that Preston and Ewbank have produced a study showing U.S. child-mortality rates by social class widening between 1895 and 1925, "consistent," they argue "with the faster adoption of behavioral innovations by the upper class groups."[50] Among the behavioral innovations that they document is the growing resort to modern and increasingly effective medicine by professional classes.

One further point should be made with regard to education. All contemporary Third World data show a significant impact on child mortality from fathers' education as well as that of mothers and that much of this effect survives controlling for income. Discussion has centered unduly on the maternal effect, even though the existence of such an effect is good evidence that education probably affects both a father's attitude and behavior with regard to his children's health and also his relationship with his wife, with a resultant secondary impact on his children's health and treatment.

There is a related but distinct matter with regard to children's health. That is the

matter of the intrafamilial emotional and resource-allocation priorities. These change as the market develops and with Westernization but are better treated as a separate strand in social change likely to be accelerated or retarded according to the nature of family structures. I have called the intrafamilial flow of resources wealth flows and the change that directs more of them toward children than parents or fathers the reversal of the intergenerational wealth flows to a downward direction.[51] The fourth proposition is that child mortality will fall more rapidly as the intergenerational wealth flow turns downward. This almost inevitably happens as fertility declines. Indeed, not only does parental concern for child survival increase, as has happened in contemporary China, but so does community and national interest in encouraging parents to care for these increasingly rare and precious commodities, as happened in the case of the infant-welfare movement in the West from around 1900 as the full extent of the recent fertility decline became clear. Families are willing to spend more effort and a greater proportion of income on child care and survival. The situation is even more complex than this because there is a correlation in the Third World between the level of family planning practice and child survival even before fertility decisively declines. The reason appears to be that the wealth flow has begun to turn; the families are already placing more emphasis on children relative to the old, are planning for their future, are finding that the adequate allocation of resources to each child for the successes of those plans can be attained only with fewer children, and are trying harder to ensure their survival.

49. Caldwell, "Routes," p. 206.

50. Douglas C. Ewbank and Samuel H. Preston, "Personal Health Behaviour and the Decline in Infant and Child Mortality: The United States, 1900-1930," in *What We Know about Health Transition*, ed. Caldwell et al.

51. Caldwell, *Theory of Fertility Decline.*

ELABORATIONS

Two modifications need to be introduced to this picture of social and family change. The first is that the rate of family change depends to a considerable extent on its preexisting structure. In sub-Saharan Africa, partly because of the lineage system and partly because of widespread polygyny, wives usually have separate budgets from those of their husbands and are themselves responsible for many of the resources needed by their children.[52] This gives mothers a great deal of autonomy with regard to health decisions affecting both their own and their children's health, but it often severely limits the resources available. In these circumstances, a strengthening of the spousal emotional and economic bond, as well as any movement toward monogamy, is likely to accelerate child-mortality decline. Similarly in South Asia and elsewhere, nuclear-family residence in contrast to extended-family residence is likely to give the young mother greater control over her children's health treatment. In south India, education can produce a degree of emotional nucleation even within the extended family and can give a mother greater control over health decisions affecting her children.

The second modification is that a strong cultural tradition limiting women's autonomy, especially when reinforced by a religion that regards the seclusion of women as a prime moral objective, can have a deleterious effect both on female health in general and on all child health because of the limitation in mothers' taking quick and effective action. This is the major reason why the Arab world does conspicuously badly relative to income in attaining low mortality. Such traditions can limit the education of women and can limit the health effectiveness of that education. This is why in the World Fertility Survey program the differentials in child survival by mother's education were so small in Bangladesh and why in Syria and Jordan, although they were considerable between mothers who had never been to school and those who had — possibly a cultural or ethnic effect — they were very small by duration of schooling.

The final proposition is that cultural, social, and behavioral factors have an impact both on an individual's mortality and on the mortality of an individual's dependents. So much analysis has been carried out on child survival because demographers' techniques for estimating mortality levels from most Third World data are much better at the youngest ages. This has also allowed the specific study of the impact of the mother's social characteristics, because of the particularly important role she usually plays in the treatment of young children. It would be unwise, however, to believe that parents played the sole role in ensuring the survival of children. In much of the Third World, grandparents and siblings play important roles. The improved relative survival chance of girls after 5 years of age in South Asia shows that increasingly children play a role in their own survival and presumably, then, that their own social characteristics are increasingly important. There are data now for Europe showing that mortality rates for adult males are much lower among the more educated,[53]

52. John C. Caldwell and Pat Caldwell, "The Cultural Context of High Fertility in Sub-Saharan Africa," *Population and Development Review*, 13(3): 409-37 (Sept. 1987); John C. Caldwell, Pat Caldwell, and Pat Quiggin, "The Social Context of AIDS in Africa," *Population and Development Review*, 15(2) (June 1989).

53. T. Valkonen, "Social Inequality in the Face of Death," in *European Population Conference: Plenaries*, ed. International Union for the Scientific Study of

evidence probably of a firmer decision to control their own lives and fate. The determinants of dependent children's mortality are a point of prime importance in high-mortality societies, for where life expectancy is below 50 years and the population is growing at 3 percent per annum, as in sub-Saharan Africa, the majority of deaths are likely to be to persons under 5 years of age. With a life expectancy of 60 years and a growth rate of 2 percent, however, as is now found in Southeast Asia, that proportion drops to around one-quarter; and with a life expectancy of 75 years and a growth rate of 0.5 percent, as now characterizes the West, the proportion falls to one-fortieth. Hence, as mortality falls, the emphasis on health behavior shifts from parenthood to how the middle-aged look after themselves.

THE TRANSLATION OF BEHAVIOR INTO SURVIVAL

This section documents the fact that behavior, especially mother's behavior, can, in Third World societies, be translated into lower child mortality. It focuses on rural south India, with a life expectancy around 50 years, and Sri Lanka, nearing 70 years, areas where I have undertaken anthropological studies of demographic behavior.[54]

The term "health management" describes behavior that prevents sickness from occurring or limits the damage once it does occur. Greater female autonomy or education increases a woman's capacity in health management in two ways: first, by giving her greater determination and self-confidence and, second, by reducing the family and other constraints placed upon her. In traditional society, child care is often a diffused responsibility. Galal el Din showed how in a Sudanese village children were rather casually looked after by the whole village, as well as by their siblings, but, as mothers became more educated, they took greater control and responsibility themselves.[55] A research program in a north Indian village showed how women in semiseclusion had little confidence in their ability to identify sickness or to take the appropriate steps.[56] In rural south India, we found that more educated mothers gave greater emphasis to cleanliness, hygiene, nutrition, and the need for rest and sleep when children were sick. They were more effective in demanding from their husbands a greater share of available resources for their children rather than for their husband's relatives. When sickness did occur, they were more likely to adopt effective home action. This is an important point, for home care is reported to constitute at least half of all treatment in the Third World.[57]

Population and the European Association for Population Studies, for the Finnish Central Statistical Office (Helsinki: Central Statistical Office, 1987), pp. 201-61.

54. Caldwell, Reddy, and Caldwell, *Causes of Demographic Change;* John C. Caldwell et al., "Sensitization to Illness and the Risk of Death: An Explanation for Sri Lanka's Approach to Good Health for All," *Social Science and Medicine,* 28(4):365-79 (1989); John C. Caldwell et al., "Cultural, Social and Behavioural Determinants of Health and Their Mechanisms: A Report on Related Research Programs," in *What We Know about Health Transition,* ed. Caldwell et al.

55. Mohamed el Awad Galal el Din, "The Economic Value of Children in Rural Sudan," in *The Persistence of High Fertility: Population Prospects in the Third World,* ed. John C. Caldwell (Canberra: Australian National University, 1977), 2:617-32; idem, "The Rationality of High Fertility in Urban Sudan," in ibid., 2:633-58.

56. M. E. Khan et al., *Inequalities between Men and Women in Nutrition and Family Welfare Services: An In-Depth Enquiry in an Indian Village,* Population and Labour Policies Program Working Paper no. 158 (Geneva: International Labour Office, 1987).

57. N. A. Christakis and A. M. Kleinman, *Illness Behavior and Health Transition in the Developing World,* mimeograph (Cambridge, MA: Harvard University, School of Public Health, 1989).

In south India, we studied in detail the various interrelations between sick children and their families on the one hand and the medical service on the other in a situation where one village in a rural area had a government health center with a resident doctor. The person who first detected child sickness was in 80 percent of the cases the mother; however, illiterate mothers were unlikely to take action or even draw attention to the sickness, waiting for their mothers-in-law or husbands to take note and action. One reason that mortality was higher in the south Indian research area than in the Sri Lankan one was that only 10 percent of mothers in the former took treatment action on their own responsibility, compared with 50 percent in the latter. As a mother's education increased, she was more likely to be the chief proponent of action when her children were sick and more likely to ensure that they were treated by the doctor.

In the same study, one of the steepest differentials by maternal education was in the time spent by the mother with the doctor. Given the absence of backup laboratory testing, diagnosis depends to a very large extent on case histories as presented by mothers. Doctors think that illiterate women cannot adequately present such evidence and make relatively little effort to listen to them. Partly because of their lack of education and partly because doctors say less to them, illiterate women are less likely to carry out the doctor's instructions properly and less likely to persist with the treatment. A very steep and significant differential by education is found with regard to the mother's reaction when the child's condition does not improve. With more schooling a mother is increasingly likely to return to the health center to report the problem to the doctor, while an uneducated mother frequently fails to do so partly on the grounds that the doctor has already done his best and partly on the grounds that she cannot tell an important man he has failed.

When we contrasted this situation with Sri Lanka, with its much higher levels of female education, we found in the Sri Lankan household an almost competitive attitude to the quick detection of sickness and the seeking of treatment. The strongest contrast, however, was in the Sri Lankan impatience with treatment that was not resulting in improvement and the consequent changing of doctors or from doctors to hospitals after only a few days. The low mortality levels suggest that this is an effective treatment strategy.

THE DIRECTION OF CHANGE

In most of the Third World, with its limited and only slowly spreading modern health services, mortality levels can be dramatically reduced by behavioral changes. Those changes are not easily achieved, as they affect not only mortality levels but the structure of society and all social relations. Nevertheless, there is a potential for rapid change that did not exist in the West because Western social patterns are spread, largely without that aim in mind, by education, the media, and religious proselytizing. Education has had a major impact, and this is now being supplemented by the women's movement. Underlying it all is the development of the market economy and accompanying movements away from the family control patterns and resource priorities characteristic of subsistence agriculture.

The Social and Economic Origins
of Immigration

By DOUGLAS S. MASSEY

ABSTRACT: Contemporary immigration patterns represent a sharp break from the past, when international movements were dominated by flows out of Europe to a few key destination areas. Europe has now become a region of immigration, and, like other developed regions, it draws migrants from a variety of Third World countries. The large-scale movement of immigrants from developing to developed regions has both economic and social foundations. Economically, immigration originates not from simple wage differentials between poor and rich countries but from the spread of economic development to rapidly growing Third World populations and from a persistent demand for low-wage workers in developed nations. Immigration has many social foundations, but the formation of migrant networks is probably the most important. Networks build into the migration process a self-perpetuating momentum that leads to its growth over time, in spite of fluctuating wage differentials, recessions, and increasingly restrictive immigration policies in developed countries.

Douglas S. Massey received a Ph.D. in sociology from Princeton University in 1978 and is currently professor of sociology at the University of Chicago and director of its Population Research Center. He has published a variety of articles on international migration and has coauthored a book on Mexican migration to the United States, Return to Aztlan *(1987).*

IN the years since the end of World War II, international migration has emerged as a major demographic force throughout the world. This globalization represents a significant break from the past, when international migration was dominated by movements between Europe and a few select non-European countries. At present, virtually all developed nations receive immigrants from a variety of less developed countries, and immigration is rapidly transforming the social and economic composition of sending and receiving societies alike.

The modern history of international migration can be divided into four periods. From 1500 to 1800, world immigration patterns were dominated by Europe and stemmed from processes of colonization and economic growth under mercantilism. Over the course of 300 years, Europeans colonized large portions of the New World, Africa, and Asia. Although the exact number of European emigrants is unknown, the outflow was sufficient to establish colonial rule over a large part of the world. The emigrants generally fell into three classes: a relatively large number of agrarian settlers; a smaller number of administrators and artisans, who established colonial towns and cities; and an even smaller number of entrepreneurs, who founded plantations to produce raw materials for Europe's growing mercantilist economy.

Although the number of Europeans involved in plantation production was small, this sector had a profound impact on the size and composition of colonial populations, especially in the Americas. Plantations require large amounts of inexpensive labor, a demand met partially by indentured labor from Asia.[1] The most important source for plantation labor, however, was the forced migration of African slaves. Over three centuries of colonial rule, some 9.6 million Africans were imported into the Americas as slaves.[2] Together with European colonists, they radically transformed the racial and ethnic composition of the New World.

The second period of emigration begins in the early nineteenth century and stems from the industrialization of Europe, the achievement of independence by several New World colonies, and the spread of economic development to these newly formed countries. Industrialization is a revolutionary and destructive process that transforms rural, agrarian societies of small-scale institutions, stable social structures, and limited markets into urbanized nations of large bureaucratic institutions, fluid social organizations, and extensive markets. In densely settled Europe, this revolution inevitably displaced large numbers of people from traditional lands and livelihoods; in sparsely settled frontier societies such as the United States and Argentina, it created conditions of high labor demand.

Thus the period from 1800 to 1915 was characterized by a massive transfer of people from the industrializing countries of Europe to a few former colonies that were themselves in the throes of rapid development. Of the more than 48 million emigrants who left Europe from 1800 to 1925, 85 percent went to Argentina, Australia, Canada, New Zealand, or the United States, with the latter receiving 60 percent by itself.[3] Important sending nations were Britain, Italy, Norway, Portugal, Spain, and

---

1. Hugh Tinker, *The Banyan Tree: Overseas Emigrants from India, Pakistan, and Bangladesh* (New York: Oxford University Press, 1977).

2. Philip D. Curtin, *The Atlantic Slave Trade: A Census* (Madison: University of Wisconsin Press, 1969).

3. Imre Ferenczi, *International Migrations*, vol. 1, *Statistics* (New York: National Bureau of Economic Research, 1929).

Sweden.[4] Ebbs and flows in the volume of European emigration were closely related to cycles of economic expansion and recession and to the spread of industrialism across the European continent.[5]

This period of large-scale international migration from Europe ended with the outbreak of World War I, which brought European emigration to a halt and ushered in four decades of limited international movement. By 1920, several important receiving countries had passed restrictive immigration laws, and the onset of the Great Depression in 1929 stopped virtually all international movement. Except for a small amount of return migration, there was little movement during the 1930s; and during the 1940s, international migration was checked by World War II. What movement there was consisted largely of refugees and was not tied to conditions of economic growth or development.

The contemporary period of international migration begins about 1950 and represents a sharp break with the past. Rather than being dominated by flows between Europe and a handful of former colonies, immigration became a truly global phenomenon, as the number and variety of both sending and receiving nations increased. This greater variety is indicated by Table 1, which lists major sources and destinations for contemporary immigration. As can be seen, the global supply of immigrants has now shifted from Europe to the Third World. Whereas 85 percent of international migrants before 1925 originated in Europe,[6] since 1950 Europeans have become an increasingly minor part of the flow. Meanwhile, the number of immigrants from Africa, Asia, and Latin America has steadily grown.[7]

The variety of destination countries has also increased. In addition to such traditional immigrant nations as Canada, the United States, Australia, New Zealand, and Argentina, countries throughout Western Europe — notably Germany, France, Switzerland, Sweden, and the Netherlands — now also attract migrants; and for the first time, Europe has become an area of immigration rather than emigration.[8] By the 1980s even such long-time sending nations as Italy had become destinations for immigrants from poorer countries in the Near East and Africa.[9] Moreover, during the 1970s several less developed but capital-rich nations also began to attract immigrants, notably oil-exporting nations such

4. Douglas S. Massey, "Economic Development and International Migration in Comparative Perspective," *Population and Development Review,* 14:383-414 (1988).

5. Gino Germani, "Mass Immigration and Modernization in Argentina," *Studies in Comparative International Development,* 2(11):165-82 (St. Louis, MO: Washington University, Social Science Institute, 1966); Brinley Thomas, *Migration and Economic Growth* (New York: Cambridge University Press, 1954); Dorothy S. Thomas, *Social and Economic Aspects of Swedish Population Movements: 1750-1933* (New York: Macmillan, 1941).

6. Ferenczi, *International Migrations.*

7. Mary M. Kritz, Charles B. Keely, and Silvano M. Tomasi, *Global Trends in Migration: Theory and Research on International Population Movements* (Staten Island, NY: Center for Migration Studies, 1981).

8. Demetrios G. Papademetriou, "International Migration in North America and Western Europe: Trends and Consequences," in *International Migration Today,* vol. 1, *Trends and Prospects,* ed. Reginald Appleyard (Paris: United Nations Educational, Scientific, and Cultural Organization, 1988), pp. 311-80; John Salt, "Europe's Foreign Labour Migrants in Transition," *Geography,* 70:151-58 (1985).

9. Russell King, "Italian Migration: The Clotting of the Haemorrhage," *Geography,* 70:171-75 (1985).

TABLE 1

SOURCE COUNTRIES OF IMMIGRANTS FOR MAJOR
MIGRANT-RECEIVING COUNTRIES DURING THE POSTWAR PERIOD

Destination Country	Major Migrant-Sending Countries, in Rough Order of Importance
North America	
United States	Mexico, Philippines, Korea, China, Dominican Republic, India, Vietnam
Canada	Britain, United States, China, Vietnam, India, Portugal, Italy, Jamaica
Western Europe	
Britain	West Indies, India, Pakistan
France	Portugal, Algeria, Morocco, Italy, Spain, Tunisia, Turkey
Germany	Turkey, Yugoslavia, Italy, Greece
Sweden	Finland, Yugoslavia, Turkey, Greece
Switzerland	Italy, Spain, Germany, Yugoslavia, Turkey, Austria
South Pacific	
Australia	Britain, Italy, New Zealand, Yugoslavia, Greece
New Zealand	China, Hong Kong, Cook Islands, Netherlands, Britain, Hungary, Poland, Singapore, India
Latin America	
Argentina	Paraguay, Chile, Bolivia, Uruguay
Venezuela	Colombia, Italy, Spain
Africa	
Ivory Coast	Togo, Burkina Faso, Nigeria
South Africa	Lesotho, Mozambique, Malawi, Botswana
Middle East	
Saudi Arabia	Yemen, Egypt, Jordan, Sudan, Pakistan, India, North Korea, Indonesia
Kuwait	Egypt, Jordan, Syria, Iraq, India, Pakistan
Bahrain	Pakistan, India, North Korea

SOURCES: John Salt, "Europe's Foreign Labour Migrants in Transition," *Geography,* 70:151-58 (1985); Reginald Appleyard, ed., *International Migration Today,* vol. 1, *Trends and Prospects* (Paris: United Nations Educational, Scientific, and Cultural Organization, 1988); U.S. Department of Justice, Immigration and Naturalization Service, *Statistical Yearbook 1988* (Washington, DC: Government Printing Office, 1989).

as Saudi Arabia, Bahrain, Kuwait, Nigeria, and Venezuela.[10]

The source of migrants for any receiving nation depends on a variety of factors: geography, colonial history, trade, and politics. In general, countries are likely to

10. Aderant Adepoju, "International Migration in Africa South of the Sahara," in *International Migration Today,* vol. 1, *Trends and Prospects,* ed. Appleyard, pp. 17-88; Jorge Balán, "International Migration in Latin America: Trends and Prospects," in ibid., pp. 210-63; Ian J. Seccombe, "International Migration in the Middle East: Historical Trends, Contemporary Patterns, and Consequences," in ibid., pp. 180-209.

receive immigrants from Third World nations that are geographically close, important trading partners, political allies, or former colonies. The vast majority of immigrants to the United States, for example, come from Asia, Latin America, or the Caribbean—only 10 percent are currently from Europe—and the most important source countries are Mexico, the closest developing country; the Philippines, a former colony; Korea, which has a large U.S. military presence and extensive trade relations with the United States; Vietnam, where a failed U.S.-backed regime generated large numbers of refugees; and Cuba, the location of another failed U.S.-backed regime that generated refugees and immigrants. In contrast, major source countries for France are Italy, Spain, and Portugal, which are the poorest and closest European countries; but the importance of these European sources has greatly diminished in recent years. Increasingly, French immigrants have come from Algeria, Morocco, and Tunisia, former colonies and geographically among the closest developing nations.[11]

Thus, in the years since World War II, there has been a remarkable shift in the structure and composition of international migration. The massive transatlantic movement that stemmed from the industrialization of Europe and the rapid development of the New World has given way to a very different transfer of migrants, one between relatively poor Third World countries and more developed postindustrial societies in Europe, North America, and the South Pacific, as well as several oil-rich countries in the Middle East, Africa, and South America.

THE ECONOMIC FOUNDATIONS OF IMMIGRATION

Although international migration is widely recognized as an economic process, the economic foundations of immigration are frequently misunderstood and rest on two common misconceptions. The first is that immigration is caused by wage differentials between sending and receiving nations, and the second is that pressures for emigration stem from a lack of economic development in sending regions. Both views are well entrenched in the thinking

of social scientists and policymakers alike and appear to follow logically from the application of economic theory.

Macroeconomic theory holds that wages are determined by the balance of labor supply and demand within regional markets. If there is a relative scarcity of workers in one market and a relative abundance in another, wages will be high in the former and low in the latter. Migration represents an equilibrating mechanism between the two regions. If the high wages are sufficient to cover the costs of interregional movement and adjustment, workers from the low-wage area will move to the high-wage area. The increased supply of workers in the high-wage area puts downward pressure on wages there while the loss of workers from the low-wage area creates upward wage pressure there. The process continues until, at equilibrium, the wage differential between the two areas equals the costs of interregional movement and adjustment.[12]

The corresponding microeconomics of this larger process have been developed in classic articles by Sjastaad and Todaro, which conceptualize migration as a cost-benefit decision.[13] Potential migrants figure the total future increase in earnings they can expect as a result of migrating to a higher-paying job, weighted by the probability of obtaining that job and discounted by a factor reflecting the lower utility of earnings in the future. From this expected gain they subtract expected costs. If the bal-

11. Philip Ogden, "France: Recession, Politics, and Migration Policy," Geography, 70:158-62 (1985); Salt, "Europe's Foreign Labor Migrants."

12. Michael J. Greenwood, Migration and Economic Growth in the United States (New York: Academic Press, 1981).

13. Larry A. Sjastaad, "The Costs and Returns of Human Migration," Journal of Political Economy, 70S:80-93 (1962); Michael P. Todaro, "A Model of Labor Migration and Urban Unemployment in Less-Developed Countries," American Economic Review, 59:138-48 (1969).

ance between anticipated gains and costs is positive, a person decides to migrate.

Although a large wage differential is clearly an incentive to movement, it is neither a necessary nor a sufficient condition. Oded Stark and his associates have argued theoretically, and demonstrated empirically, that migration decisions in developing countries are typically made by families, not individuals, and that families migrate not only to maximize earnings but also to minimize risks.[14] Economic conditions in developing countries are volatile, and families face serious risks to their wellbeing from many sources — natural disasters, political upheavals, economic recessions. Sending different family members to geographically distinct labor markets represents a strategy to diversify and reduce the risks to household income.

This strategy requires only that earnings at points of origin and destination be uncorrelated or inversely correlated. With a zero or negative association between business cycles in sending and receiving areas, a household may not be greatly harmed by economic dislocations at home if one or more family members are abroad earning steady wages. If the place of destination has higher wages, so much the better, but higher wages are not a necessary condition for economic improvements to result from migration.

Higher wages also are not a sufficient condition for international migration. Research by Greenwood indicates that, within the United States, labor demand — that is, the availability of jobs — is far more impor-

tant in attracting migrants than are high wages.[15] Other researchers have found that secular trends in migration between Mexico and the United States are uncorrelated with wage differentials between the two countries;[16] and Böhning's analysis of international migration within Europe suggests that wage rates are a minor predictor of labor mobility.[17] Thus the relative importance of wage differentials in causing international migration has often been overstated. Higher wages represent one of several possible incentives for international migration and not necessarily the most important.

Related to this overemphasis on wage differentials is a second misconception, that international migration is caused by a lack of development and that, by promoting economic development in poor nations, the pressure for international movement can be reduced. This view misinterprets the nature of the development process, which is inherently destructive and destabilizing and in the short run enhances the pressures for emigration rather than reduces them.

14. Oded Stark and D. Levhari, "On Migration and Risk in LDCs," *Economic Development and Cultural Change,* 31:191-96 (1982); E. Katz and Oded Stark, "Labor Migration and Risk Aversion in Less Developed Countries," *Journal of Labor Economics,* 4:131-49 (1984).

15. Greenwood, *Migration and Economic Growth;* Michael J. Greenwood and G. L. Hunt, "Migration and Interregional Employment Redistribution in the United States," *American Economic Review,* 74:957-69 (1984).

16. W. Parker Frisbie, "Illegal Migration from Mexico to the United States: A Longitudinal Analysis," *International Migration Review,* 9:3-13 (1975); Mario I. Blejer, Harry G. Johnson, and Arturo C. Prozecanski, "An Analysis of the Economic Determinants of Legal and Illegal Mexican Migration to the United States," *Research in Population Economics,* 1:217-31 (1978); J. Craig Jenkins, "Push/Pull in Recent Mexican Migration to the U.S.," *International Migration Review,* 11:178-89 (1977).

17. W. R. Böhning, "The Differential Strength of Demand and Wage Factors in Intra-European Labour Mobility: With Special Reference to West Germany, 1957-1968," *International Migration,* 8:193-202 (1970).

Industrial societies develop out of peasant economies characterized by an economic orientation that emphasizes sustenance and full employment rather than output maximization and profit.[18] In peasant economies, output is determined not by markets but by the size and composition of households, and economic and social relations are predicated on assumptions of stability and continuity. Economic development necessarily destroys this stable social and economic system through three mutually reinforcing processes: the substitution of capital for labor, the privatization and consolidation of landholding, and the creation of markets. The destruction of the peasant political economy creates a pool of socially and economically displaced people with weakened ties to the land, the community, and past ways of life. These displaced rural dwellers provide the source for both internal and international migrants.

The intrusion of capital into peasant agriculture is extremely destabilizing because it is labor saving rather than labor generating. Investments in machines, new crops, improved seeds, insecticides, and irrigation all reduce the number of workers needed to produce a given unit of agricultural output. Although the investment of capital greatly increases the food surplus and makes high levels of urbanization possible, within rural villages capitalization reduces the demand for labor, often quite dramatically, and makes peasant farmworkers increasingly underemployed and redundant to agricultural production.

Processes of agricultural enclosure and land consolidation generally accompany capitalization. Peasant landholdings are

18. Alexander V. Chayanov, *The Theory of Peasant Economy* (Madison: University of Wisconsin Press, 1986).

typically organized on a communal or kinship basis. Land either is held in common by all members of an agricultural community, with families receiving customary rights of usufruct, or is held directly in small plots by specific family groups. These land-tenure arrangements are not well suited to capital-intensive agriculture, however. Machines and mass-production techniques are most effectively applied to large private tracts, creating incentives for elites to consolidate landholding under private auspices, thereby destroying another foundation of peasant social and economic organization.

The enclosure of peasant land and its use for the capital-intensive production of cash crops contributes to a third process by which peasant communities are effaced: the creation of markets. Without access to communal lands, peasant farmers are forced to sell their labor, either as sharecroppers or as wage workers. The selling of labor undermines the peasant social and economic system, which views work as part of a complex system of rights and reciprocal obligations. Over time, rigid social and economic relationships that would normally preclude participation in the more fluid social order of the industrial world are attenuated.

With the emergence of markets, social relationships are increasingly separated from economic relationships, and the rational pursuit of self-interest and personal gain gradually supplant adherence to well-defined social norms as the basis for human action. In this process of social transformation, households shift their orientation from subsistence agriculture to market production, and family workers increasingly sell their labor to others rather than donate it to household production. With the emergence of widespread market behavior, the peasant political economy is gradually, but irrevocably, effaced.

The processes of capitalization, enclosure, and market creation are inherently revolutionary, and many people are displaced from traditional livelihoods and past ways of life. These displaced people constitute the source for the mass population movements that inevitably accompany development. Most become internal migrants, responding to prospects for economic betterment and enhanced productivity in emerging urban areas. But newly emerging cities historically have not been able to absorb all of the rural migrants displaced by development and, inevitably, some of the displaced have migrated abroad.

Among European countries, there was a close historical correlation between the onset of industrial development and the beginning of mass emigration.[19] This association is created by the cyclical nature of economic growth. No matter how rapid or dynamic a country's transformation in the course of development, economic growth is never monotonic. No country has followed a steady upward growth path; rather, economic growth is characterized by short-term cycles of expansion and contraction that only in the long run yield a rising curve.[20] The periodic nature of urban industrial expansion, combined with a constant pressure for out-migration from rural areas, creates a potential for emigration that is structurally built into the development process.

Historical data from Europe show that rates of emigration are inversely correlated with upswings and downswings in the domestic business cycle, whereas rates of rural-urban migration are positively correlated. In contrast, European emigration historically was positively related to the American business cycle. During periods when European industries were expanding, rural out-migration was directed primarily to European cities, but when the urban industrial economy was in recession, peasants were drawn to opportunities overseas.[21] If we define cycles of recession in Europe as push periods and cycles of American growth as pull periods, then emigration was greatest when periods of push and pull coincided and was least when there was neither a push nor a pull. A pull from America was generally ineffective in promoting emigration during periods of European prosperity, suggesting that population movements were dominated by conditions in the European urban-industrial sector.[22]

The historical experience of Europe is not wholly generalizable to contemporary developing countries, however. Significant differences in demographic and technological conditions make the pressures for emigration from developing countries today much greater than they were for European nations in the past. In Europe, the transition from high to low mortality rates occurred slowly and fertility levels were modest because of a distinctly European pattern of late marriage and widespread celibacy. After a relatively short lag, fertility rates began to fall because the desire for family limitation stemmed from the same social and economic changes that produced the mortality decline. As a result, the gap between birth and death rates was not large and it closed rapidly, yielding modest and

19. Massey, "Economic Development and International Migration."

20. Simon Kuznets, *Modern Economic Growth: Rate, Structure, and Spread* (New Haven, CT: Yale University Press, 1966).

21. Thomas, *Migration and Economic Growth.*

22. Thomas, *Social and Economic Aspects.*

progressively declining rates of natural increase.

In the developing world, however, the decline in mortality occurred rapidly in a few years after 1945, but fertility remained high because of universal early marriage and a lack of desire for family limitation. The resulting large gap between birth and death rates persisted for decades because the declines in mortality stemmed from imported technologies and public-health measures rather than from socioeconomic changes that simultaneously reduced birth rates. As a consequence, during its period of dynamic population growth, the Third World displayed very high rates of natural increase that were far in excess of those experienced by European countries during the nineteenth century. These higher population growth rates have exacerbated the pressures for emigration in contemporary developing countries by increasing the ratio of population to land and driving down agrarian wages.

At the same time, the technology of production has become increasingly capital intensive. During the nineteenth century, gains in productivity were achieved largely through the reorganization of production and the division of labor; the machines themselves were crude by modern standards. The number of peasants displaced by agricultural mechanization was limited while the demand for unskilled labor in urban factories was high. Over the course of the twentieth century, however, technology has become increasingly capital intensive. Agricultural mechanization now has the potential to displace far more people from rural employment, while factories need fewer workers to produce the same output. Technological improvements have also reduced substantially the time and money required to travel internation-

ally, and modern mass communications have made inhabitants of the Third World more aware of opportunities and conditions abroad than were European peasants of the past.

Thus the economic foundations for modern international migration lie not simply in low wages or a lack of economic development in poor countries but in the spread of increasingly capital-intensive economic development to rapidly growing Third World populations that are linked to the developed world by modern systems of transportation and communication. Although the high wages in developing countries provide an incentive to migrate, the uncertainty created by economic development also makes emigration an attractive strategy for risk diversification.

THE SOCIAL FOUNDATIONS OF IMMIGRATION

International migration also has important social foundations that must be taken into account to achieve a complete understanding of contemporary immigration patterns. The social structure of migration explains such apparently anomalous outcomes as the growth of immigration rates during periods of stable or falling wage differentials and the continuation of immigration despite the implementation of restrictive immigration policies. Immigration is far more dynamic than standard economic analyses suggest because it tends to feed back on itself through social channels. As a result, immigration becomes progressively independent of the economic conditions that originally caused it. Once a critical takeoff stage is reached, migration alters social structures in ways that increase the likelihood of subsequent migration. This feedback process has been called "the circular and cumulative causation of migration" by Myrdal,[23] and it relies on a variety of social-structural mechanisms, the most important of which is network formation.

Migrant networks are sets of interpersonal ties that link together migrants, former migrants, and nonmigrants in origin and destination areas through the bonds of kinship, friendship, and shared community origin.[24] They increase the likelihood of migration because they lower the costs of movement and therefore increase the expected net returns to migration.[25] Migrant costs include the direct monetary costs of making a trip, the information and search costs paid to obtain a new job, the opportunity costs of income forgone while searching for work, and the psychic costs of leaving a familiar environment and moving to a strange setting. All of these costs are reduced when a prospective migrant has a personal tie to someone with prior experience in a particular destination area.

The first migrants who leave for a new destination have no social ties to draw upon, and for them migration is costly, particularly if it involves entering another country without documents. After the first migrants have left, however, the costs of migration are substantially lower for their friends and relatives living in the community of origin. Because of the nature of kinship and friendship structures, each new migrant creates a set of people with social ties to the destination area. Migrants are inevitably linked to nonmigrants through bonds of kinship and friendship, and the latter draw upon obligations implicit in these relationships to gain access to employment and assistance at the point of destination, substantially reducing their migrant costs.

Once the number of network connections in an origin area reaches a certain threshold, migration becomes self-perpetuating because migration itself creates the social structure needed to sustain it. Every new migrant reduces the costs of subsequent migration for a set of friends and relatives, and some of these people are thereby induced to migrate, which further expands the set of people with ties abroad and, in turn, reduces costs for a new set of people, causing some of them to migrate, and so on.

Networks also make international migration extremely attractive as a strategy for risk diversification.[26] When migrant networks are well developed, they put a destination job within easy reach of most community members, making emigration a reliable and very secure source of income. In other words, the self-feeding growth of networks that occurs through the progressive reduction of costs may also be explained theoretically by the progressive reduction of risks. Every new migrant expands the network and reduces the risks of movement for all those to whom he or she is related, eventually making it virtually risk free and costless to diversify house-

23. Gunnar Myrdal, *Rich Lands and Poor* (New York: Harper & Row, 1957).

24. Charles Tilly and C. H. Brown, "On Uprooting, Kinship, and the Auspices of Migration," *International Journal of Comparative Sociology*, 8:139-64 (1967); John S. MacDonald and Leatrice D. MacDonald, "Chain Migration, Ethnic Neighborhood Formation, and Social Networks," in *An Urban World*, ed. Charles Tilly (Boston: Little, Brown, 1974).

25. Douglas S. Massey and Felipe García España, "The Social Process of International Migration," *Science*, 237:733-38 (1987).

26. J. Edward Taylor, "Differential Migration, Networks, Information and Risk," in *Research in Human Capital and Development*, vol. 4, *Migration, Human Capital, and Development*, ed. Oded Stark (Greenwich, CT: JAI Press, 1986), pp. 147-71.

hold labor allocations through emigration.

Thus, from either a cost-benefit or a risk-aversion perspective, migration generates a social structure that leads to its cumulative causation over time. Migration may begin for a variety of reasons, but once the number of migrants reaches a critical threshold, expanding networks cause the costs and risks of movement to fall and the probability of migration to rise. These trends feed off one another, and over time migration spreads outward to encompass all segments of society, giving immigration a strong momentum that persists in spite of changes in economic conditions or the implementation of restrictive immigration policies in destination countries.

THE FOUNDATIONS OF IMMIGRATION POLICY

The overemphasis on wages as determinants of immigration and the failure to appreciate the social dimensions of the migration process have led to immigration policies that often yield outcomes opposite those desired. Thus the recruitment of temporary foreign workers usually ends up generating a large, permanent minority population; and policies designed to ration immigrant visas end up reinforcing the process of network formation and generating still more migrants, both legal and illegal.

Viewing immigration as an economic phenomenon, governments in developed countries naively assume that the flow of immigrants can be managed and regulated like other economic processes, much as the money supply is managed through budgetary and fiscal policies. In the postwar period, therefore, many Western governments attempted to recruit foreign guest workers to fill short-term economic needs, assuming that

when the needs ended, the flow of immigrants could be turned off as easily as it was turned on. In all cases, however, this assumption proved to be unfounded.

In Western Europe, large-scale labor recruitment began during the 1950s, when rapid economic growth created an intense demand for unskilled workers in many sectors of the European economy.[27] Foreign labor was imported to meet this demand, and it allowed European economic growth to occur faster and to be sustained longer than would have been possible without it.[28] With the advent of the 1973 oil boycott and the ensuing recession, however, recruitment ended and foreign workers were encouraged to return home. But the number of foreign workers declined in only a few countries, and everywhere the size of foreign populations increased.[29] Faced with the prospect of being denied reentry, guest workers opted to remain in Western Europe and sent abroad for family members. As a result, the demographic composition of Western Europe's foreign population shifted — from temporary migrants to permanent residents, from males to females, from workers to dependents, and, increasingly, from immigrants to a second generation born or reared in Europe.[30]

America's guest-worker program began in 1942 as an emergency measure to ease

27. W. R. Böhning, *The Migration of Workers in the United Kingdom and the European Community* (New York: Oxford University Press, 1972).

28. Charles P. Kindleberger, *Europe's Postwar Growth: The Role of Labor Supply* (New York: Oxford University Press, 1967).

29. Philip L. Martin and Mark J. Miller, "Guestworkers: Lessons from Western Europe," *Industrial and Labor Relations Review*, 33:315-30 (1980).

30. Stephen Castles et al., *Here for Good: Western Europe's New Ethnic Minorities* (New York: Longwood, 1984).

labor shortages caused by World War II.[31] Although intended as a temporary wartime measure, the program was extended for 22 years. When the program was finally phased out in 1964, however, Mexican migration did not stop. Both legal and undocumented migration began a long, sustained rise in the early 1960s. In fact, Bracero migrants were not at all temporary; they were very likely to make additional trips without documents, were likely to introduce other family members into the migration process, and ultimately went on to settle permanently in the United States in large numbers.[32]

Another area where governments often work at cross-purposes with stated policy objectives is in attempting to limit and ration immigrant visas. Most countries employ a rationing system that relies on the principle of family reunification, where immigrants are admitted if they already have a relative living in the country. Family-reunification systems work at cross-purposes with the limitation of immigration because they reinforce the process of network formation and over time actually encourage further immigration.

All countries base their immigration laws on the principle of family reunification to some degree, but in the United States the principle predominates. U.S. immigrant visas are allocated by a system that assigns priorities to classes of people defined by kinship to citizens and resident aliens. This system codifies the process of network migration, since each person given legal residence creates another set of people — spouses and unmarried children — with the right to apply for legal entry themselves. If the immigrant goes on to become a U.S. citizen, additional entry slots within the system open up to an even larger set of relatives, including sons, daughters, brothers, and sisters, along with all of their spouses and children. Moreover, some relatives of citizens — spouses, children, and parents — are exempt from numerical limitation and may be admitted outside the preference system entirely. These newly admitted relatives may, in turn, sponsor the immigration of other relatives, especially in-laws of the original immigrant, thereby perpetuating the chain. Jasso and Rosenzweig estimate that, because of family reunification, every new immigrant admitted for work in the United States generates 0.6 to 0.7 extra adult immigrants and another 0.5 immigrant children within 10 years of entry.[33]

In the long run, therefore, immigration tends to breed more immigration, and if there is one prediction for the future it is that the current period of global immigration will continue. The economic foundations of migration lie in the spread of capital-intensive economic development to rapidly growing Third World populations that are linked to the developed world by modern systems of transportation and communication. Developed countries display a strong and persistent demand for low-wage workers, and the availability of jobs has been shown to be the strongest determinant of immigration. Once immigration has begun,

31. Joshua S. Reichert and Douglas S. Massey, "Guestworker Programs: Evidence from Europe and the United States and Some Implications for U.S. Policy," *Population Research and Policy Review*, 1:1-17 (1982).

32. Douglas S. Massey and Zai Liang, "The Long-Term Consequences of a Temporary Worker Program: The U.S. Bracero Experience," *Population Research Policy Review*, 8:199-226 (1989).

33. Guillermina Jasso and Mark R. Rosenzweig, "Family Reunification and the Immigration Multiplier: U.S. Immigration Law, Origin-Country Conditions, and the Reproduction of Immigrants," *Demography*, 23:291-312 (1984).

the social foundations of migration build a self-perpetuating momentum into the process. The growth and expansion of migrant networks progressively reduce the costs of international movement and make emigration a very attractive strategy for risk diversification among poor families in developing countries. Once a stage of mass migration has been reached, migration will tend to continue regardless of changes in wages, employment, or government immigration policies.

ANNALS, *AAPSS,* **510,** July 1990

Socialism and Fertility in China

By SUSAN GREENHALGH

ABSTRACT: Current figures indicate that China's 1990 population is in the area of 1.1 billion, 200 million less than the 1.3 billion predicted in the early 1970s. What will happen to fertility in China in the 1990s? To answer this question this article looks closely at the forces underlying the fertility decline of the 1970s and early 1980s. It argues that the success of the later-longer-fewer policy of the 1970s and of the one-child policy of the 1980s can only be explained by reference to the larger socioeconomic and sociopolitical context in which the policies were carried out. The construction of a socialist society in the first decade of Communist rule restructured social institutions and state-society relations in ways that fundamentally altered both the economics of childbearing, reducing the attractiveness of children to parents, and the politics of fertility decision making, giving parents little choice but to comply with restrictive fertility policies after they were introduced. The direction of fertility change in the 1990s is likely to hinge on developments in rural economic policies, whose future, the past has taught, is hazardous to predict.

After receiving her doctorate from Columbia University in 1982, Susan Greenhalgh joined the Population Council, where she is now a senior associate in the Research Division. An anthropologist and sinologist by training, she writes frequently on population policy and demographic trends in China, focusing generally on the interactions between population change and social, cultural, and political organization. She has conducted long-term field research in both Taiwan and the People's Republic, most recently spending six months in Xi'an studying the demographic transition in rural north China.

I N the early 1970s, when the population of mainland China numbered 830 million, specialists projected that by 1990 it would top 1.3 billion.[1] Like most predictions about China, this one turned out to be wrong. In April 1989, the population reached the 1.1 billion mark, and, if current growth rates continue, in 1990 it should be in the 1.12-1.13 billion range. Rather than rising and falling in a gentle curve, the rate of natural increase of the population dropped from 26 to 11 per thousand population before inching upward again to 14, registering an overall decline of 45 percent between 1970 and 1988 (see Table 1).

Will China's population growth rates continue to decline in the 1990s? Given its low and stable mortality levels and negligible rates of international migration, the key question is whether the low level of fertility achieved in the 1980s can be sustained to the end of the century. To answer this question we need to understand the forces that underlay the dramatic fertility decline of the 1970s and early 1980s.

Application of conventional demographic transition theory to China's fertility transition is unlikely to yield satisfying results, given the distinctive nature of China's developmental strategy and the apparently crucial role of the planned-birth program in reducing fertility in the absence of substantial socioeconomic modernization. Accordingly, students of China have proposed three types of explanations for its rapid fertility decline. From less to more complex, these stress the heavy-handed birth-planning program, interactions between birth planning and certain facets of socioeconomic modernization, and the transformation of community institutions.[2]

While birth planning, modernization, and community change all played crucial roles, for reasons elaborated below I believe that the sustained fertility decline that began in the 1970s cannot be understood without taking the broadest possible measure of the profound changes wrought in Chinese society by the transition to socialism in the 1950s. In other words, an approach of the third, or institutional, sort is necessary. Briefly, I will argue that the explicit fertility policies of the 1970s and 1980s — the later-longer-fewer (*wan xi shao*) followed by the one-child policy — were necessary but not sufficient conditions for the fertility decline that occurred. The sufficient conditions include a range of implicit fertility policies — economic and political policies that restructured family and community institutions and changed state-society relations in ways that fundamentally altered both the economics of childbearing and the politics of fertility decision making.

A word on data and data sources. While the 1982 census and other large-scale demographic surveys conducted in the 1980s have provided a wealth of high-quality fertility data, because of the ban, lifted only recently, on field research by Western

1. John S. Aird, "Population Policy and Demographic Prospects in the People's Republic of China," in *People's Republic of China: An Economic Assessment, a Compendium of Papers Submitted to the Joint Economic Committee, U.S. Congress* (Washington, DC: Government Printing Office, 1972), pp. 327-31.

2. The role of the birth-planning program is stressed in John S. Aird, "Coercion in Family Planning: Causes, Methods, and Consequences," in U.S. Congress, Joint Economic Committee, *China's Economy Looks toward the Year 2000*, vol. 1, *The Four Modernizations* (Washington, DC: Government Printing Office, 1986). The joint-effects view is set forth in Nancy Birdsall and Dean T. Jamison, "Income and Other Factors Influencing Fertility in China," *Population and Development Review*, 9(4):651-75 (Dec. 1983). The institutional position is elaborated in Geoffrey McNicoll, "Institutional Determinants of Fertility Change," *Population and Development Review*, 6(3):441-62 (Sept. 1980).

TABLE 1

POPULATION SIZE; BIRTH, DEATH, AND
NATURAL INCREASE RATES; AND TOTAL FERTILITY RATES, 1970-88

Year	Year-End Population (10,000)	Crude Birth Rate	Crude Death Rate	Natural-Increase Rate	Total Fertility Rate		
					Country	Urban	Rural
1970	82,992	33.43	7.60	25.83	5.81	3.27	6.38
1971	85,229	30.65	7.32	23.33	5.44	2.88	6.01
1972	87,177	29.77	7.61	22.16	4.98	2.64	5.50
1973	89,211	27.93	7.04	20.89	4.54	2.39	5.01
1974	90,859	24.82	7.34	17.48	4.17	1.98	4.64
1975	92,420	23.01	7.32	15.69	3.57	1.78	3.95
1976	93,717	19.91	7.25	12.66	3.24	1.61	3.58
1977	94,974	18.93	6.87	12.06	2.84	1.57	3.12
1978	96,259	18.25	6.25	12.00	2.72	1.55	2.97
1979	97,542	17.82	6.21	11.61	2.75	1.37	3.05
1980	98,705	18.21	6.34	11.87	2.24	1.15	2.48
1981	100,072	20.91	6.36	14.55	2.63	1.39	2.91
1982	101,590	21.09	6.60	14.49	2.65[†]	1.73*	n.a.[‡]
1983	102,764	18.62	7.08	11.54	2.08[†]	1.61*	n.a.[‡]
1984	103,876	17.50	6.69	10.81	2.03[†]	1.46*	n.a.[‡]
1985	105,044	17.80	6.57	11.23	2.04[†]	1.23*	n.a.[‡]
1986	106,529	20.77	6.69	14.08	2.44[†]	1.43*	n.a.[‡]
1987	108,073	21.04	6.65	14.39	2.84[†]	1.38*	n.a.[‡]
1988	109,660	20.78	6.58	14.20	n.a.[‡]	n.a.[‡]	n.a.[‡]

SOURCES: Population size and birth, death, and increase rates for 1970-87 are from State Statistical Bureau, *1988 Statistical Yearbook of China* (Beijing: Zhongguo Tongji Chubanshe, 1988), pp. 97, 98; 1988 figures are from Cheng Hong, "Statistics Bureau Publishes Population Figures," *China Daily*, 13 Feb. 1989, p. 1. Total fertility rates for 1950-81 are from Ansley J. Coale, *Rapid Population Change in China, 1952-1982* (Washington DC: National Academy Press, 1984), pp. 47, 59. Country total fertility rates for 1982-87 are from Jiang Zhenghua et al., "Analysis of Fertility Change and Population Development in China" (Paper delivered at the Seminar on Population and Fertility Planning, Xi'an, China, May 1988). Urban total fertility rates for 1982-87 are from Griffith Feeney et al., "Recent Fertility Dynamics in China: Results from the 1987 One Percent Population Survey," *Population and Development Review*, 15(2):297-322 (June 1989).

*Rates are calculated by special estimation method from 1987 One Percent Survey and refer to years ending June 30. Other figures for 1983-88 are based on annual population survey conducted by the State Statistical Bureau. For discussion of accuracy see text. The estimation method is described in Feeney et al., "Recent Fertility Dynamics in China."

[†]1982-87 figures are based on annual survey and are adjusted for underreporting.

[‡]Not available.

scholars, in-depth data on the links between macroeconomic policies and microsocial change are scarce. For source materials on institutional change I draw on the results of a handful of field studies carried out in the last decade, my own field data gathered in a study of the demographic transition in Shaanxi Province, and earlier research based on interviews with refugees in Hong Kong. While the sociological data base remains slim, enough is known about these changes to warrant formulation of

FIGURE 1
TOTAL FERTILITY RATES FOR WOMEN OF CHILDBEARING AGE, 1950-87

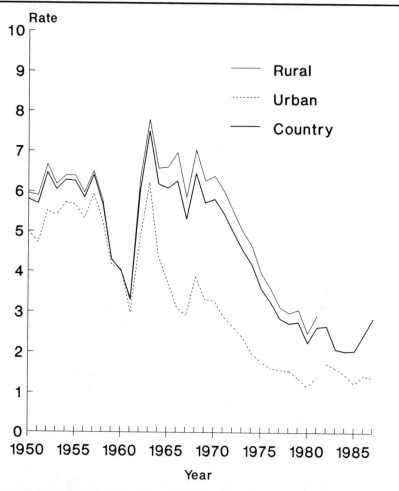

SOURCES: Reprinted from *Rapid Population Change in China*, 1984, with permission from the National Academy Press, Washington, DC. Total fertility rates for 1950-81 are from Ansley J. Coale, *Rapid Population Change in China, 1952-82* (Washington, DC: National Academy Press, 1984), pp. 47, 59. Country total fertility rates for 1982-87 are from Jiang Zhenghua et al., "Analysis of Fertility Change and Population Development in China" (Paper delivered at the Seminar on Population and Fertility Planning, Xi'an, China, May 1988). Urban total fertility rates for 1982-87 are from Griffith Feeney et al., "Recent Fertility Dynamics in China: Results from the 1987 One Percent Population Survey," *Population and Development Review*, 15(2):297-322 (June 1989).

tentative hypotheses linking the restructuring of China's economy and polity to the transformation of its society and thence to its fertility decline.

FERTILITY TRENDS, 1950-88

During the first twenty years after the founding of the People's Republic in 1949, total fertility hovered just above 6 children per woman (see Figure 1). It departed from this level only during the Great Leap Forward (1958-61), when it fell in response to famine, then rose in compensatory fashion. The year 1970 ushered in a decade of sustained fertility decline (see Table 1). During that extraordinary decade fertility fell virtually every year, bringing the total fertility rate (TFR) down to 2.2 by 1980, less than half its level of 5.8 ten years earlier. In the 1980s fertility fell further, to a low of 2.0 by mid-decade, then rebounded, reaching 2.8 in 1987, a level comparable to that of the late 1970s. These figures, based on annual surveys and adjusted for underreporting, should be taken as only a general indication of fertility trends in the 1980s. TFRs calculated from the One Percent Survey of 1987 by the own-children method[3] show a less pronounced fluctuation. According to those estimations, the TFR fell to a low of 2.3 in 1984, rising to 2.5 in 1987.

Beneath the national averages lie striking rural-urban differences in childbearing trends. While TFRs declined precipitously in both areas, urban fertility fell a decade earlier and reached a lower level, measuring 1.1-1.4 in the early 1980s, well below the level of 2.5-3.0 registered in the countryside at that time. In the mid-1980s TFRs in the urban areas remained low—in the range of 1.2-1.6—clear evidence that the rise in overall fertility is due to an upward swing in the countryside, which accommodates 70 to 80 percent of the population.

3. For the own-children estimates, see Griffith Feeney et al., "Recent Fertility Dynamics in China: Results from the 1987 One Percent Population Survey," *Population and Development Review,* 15(2):297-322 (June 1989). The estimation methodology is detailed in Lee-Jay Cho, Robert D. Retherford, and Minja Kim Choe, *The Own-Children Method of Fertility Estimation* (Honolulu, HI: East-West Center, 1986).

THE PLANNED-BIRTH PROGRAM

Small-scale campaigns to encourage birth planning were launched in 1956-58 and 1962-66. These efforts, however, were interrupted by the Great Leap Forward and the Cultural Revolution. Concerted, nationwide birth-control campaigns—the later-longer-fewer campaign, followed by the one-child campaign—emerged only in the 1970s, when the political climate favored the devotion of sustained attention to the problem of rapid population growth.

Reproductive rules and implementation methods

The later-longer-fewer policy, introduced in 1971, encouraged later marriage, longer spacing between first and subsequent births, and fewer children.[4] The last stipulation was initially interpreted as two children for urbanites and three for rural dwellers, but in 1977 a limit of two children was established for couples in all areas.

Although fertility fell rapidly in the 1970s, by the end of the decade a new post-Maoist regime had taken over that staked its legitimacy on lifting living standards out of the stagnant levels of the previous two decades. Higher per capita incomes were to be achieved by manipulating numerator and denominator simultaneously: a package of rural reforms, unveiled in December 1978, was to stimulate economic growth, while a one-child policy, announced a month later, was to depress population growth. So drastic a measure was deemed necessary to stanch the so-called echo baby boom that was expected to occur in the 1980s and 1990s, as the

4. For details of the policy, see Pi-chao Chen and Adrienne Kols, "Population and Birth Planning in the People's Republic of China," *Population Reports,* 1982, series J, no. 25, pp. J577-618.

generation born in the 1960s came of reproductive age.

The one-child policy encouraged all couples of the Han ethnic majority to limit themselves to one child in order to ensure achievement of the national population-size target of 1.2 billion in the year 2000. While the reduction in the number of children received the most emphasis, the policy's goals also included late marriage, late childbearing, and eugenic births.

Enforcing such drastic changes in the marriage and childbearing habits of a billion people was no easy matter. Implementation was to rely on education in the benefits of small families, coupled with economic and administrative incentives for compliance with the reproductive rules and, after 1979, penalties for having higher-order births. What China's leaders have understood with hindsight is that success in implementation hinged on the existence of certain institutional prerequisites involving the tight control of society by the state. Such conditions pertained in the cities throughout the 1970s and 1980s but vanished from the countryside in the latter decade.

The loss of control over rural society, triggered by economic reforms, made it virtually impossible to enforce the one-child rule among the peasantry. Accordingly, beginning in the mid-1980s the policy's goals, on both macro and micro levels, were relaxed. In 1985 the leadership changed the national target for the year 2000 from 1.2 billion to about 1.2 billion, officially interpreted as 1.25 billion. In late 1988 the minister in charge of the State Family Planning Commission announced that the population was likely to top 1.27 billion by century's end,[5] possibly paving

5. Xinhua, "Minister Admits Population Target May Not Be Met," broadcast on 2 Nov. 1988, reprinted in Joint Publications Research Service, *China Report,* JPRS-CAR-88-080, 19 Dec. 1988, pp. 48-49.

the way, politically, for another increase in the official target. At the individual level the number of conditions under which rural couples were allowed to have two children was increased in 1984 and 1988, so that by decade's end the majority of rural couples could have a second child.[6]

Changes in
*   contraception and fertility*

Scattered evidence suggests that on the eve of the later-longer-fewer campaign, birth control was widely practiced in the cities but little known in the rural areas.[7] Unfortunately, the fragmentary nature of the data on contraception do not allow us to trace with precision the rapid spread of family planning in the 1970s.

The quantitative record is much clearer for the decade 1978-87. The Chinese statistic on birth control, the birth-limitation rate, is somewhat higher than the standard measure of contraceptive prevalence employed in international comparisons.[8] In 1978 the birth-limitation rate countrywide was about 70 percent of married couples under age 50, the equivalent of approximately 60 percent contraceptive prevalence.[9] By 1982 the birth-limitation rate had risen to 70, and by 1987 it had climbed

6. Susan Greenhalgh, "Shifts in China's Population Policy, 1984-86: Views from the Central, Provincial, and Local Levels," *Population and Development Review,* 12(3):491-515 (Sept. 1986); Zeng Yi, "Is the Chinese Family Planning Program 'Tightening Up'?" *Population and Development Review,* 15(2): 333-37 (June 1989).

7. Aird, "Population Policy and Demographic Prospects."

8. The birth-limitation rate includes those practicing contraception any time during the year within the annual total of contraceptors. Chen and Kols, "Population and Birth Planning," p. J590.

9. Chen and Kols, "Population and Birth Planning," p. J598.

TABLE 2

DISTRIBUTION OF BIRTHS BY PARITY, 1973-87 (Percentage of total)

Year	First Order	Second Order	Third and Higher Order
1973	20.6	20.9	58.5
1974	21.9	22.3	55.9
1975	23.8	22.6	53.6
1976	26.3	23.1	50.6
1977	28.8	24.7	46.5
1978	32.4	25.1	42.5
1979	33.9	26.3	39.8
1980	37.8	27.2	35.0
1981	43.6	26.7	29.7
1982	50.1	25.3	24.7
1983	56.4	24.6	19.0
1984	55.5	25.0	19.5
1985	50.2	30.1	19.7
1986	51.2	31.5	17.3
1987	51.7	31.5	16.8

SOURCE: Wei Jinsheng, "An Evaluation of China's Population Planning Program During the Past Decade" (Manuscript, Dec. 1988).

to 77 percent, an extraordinary level in so poor a population.[10]

Chinese statistics on birth-control operations, including major and minor procedures, show a rapid rise from 1971, when the operations were first made available free of charge. Between 1971 and 1987 a phenomenal total of 470 million birth-control operations were performed in China, including 207 million insertions of intrauterine devices, 36 million IUD removals, 66 million female sterilizations, 28 million

male sterilizations, and 134 million induced abortions.[11]

Changes in the distribution of births by parity provide further evidence of the success of the planned-birth program (see Table 2). During the later-longer-fewer era the proportion of third- and higher-order births fell from 59 to 40 percent. In the one-child decade the proportion of third and higher births fell further, to 17 percent, while the share of first births rose from 34 to 56 percent in 1983, before falling back slightly to 52 percent in 1987.

Parity progression ratios showing the proportion of women with one child going on to have a second also show the dramatic effect of the one-child policy in the early

10. The 1982 figure is from Qiu Shuhua et al., "A Survey of Birth Control among Women of Childbearing Age in China," in *Analysis on China's National One-per-Thousand-Population Fertility Sampling Survey* (Beijing: China Population Information Centre, 1984), pp. 139-44. The 1987 figure is from State Family Planning Commission, "Statistics on Population and Family Planning of China" (Data sheet, State Family Planning Commission, Beijing, n.d.).

11. Ministry of Public Health, *1987 Chinese Health Statistical Digest* (Beijing: Ministry of Public Health, 1988), p. 79.

1980s, followed by a weakening of control in mid-decade. Before 1979, 95 percent of couples with one child went on to have a second. This proportion fell to 63 percent in 1984, then rose again, climbing to 77 percent in 1987.[12] Clearly, the policy that on paper advocated one child in practice allowed two.

The temporal correspondence between implementation of the later-longer-fewer policy and the dramatic decline in fertility leaves little doubt that a causal connection exists between the two. Closer inspection of Figure 1, however, suggests that the linkage between policy and practice is far from tight. First, urban fertility declined during the second birth-planning campaign (1962-66), but failed to fall during the first campaign (1956-58), which, press reports from the time suggest, was guided by clearer goals and administered with greater vigor.[13] Second, although the one-child policy, even in its more liberal phase, set stricter reproductive rules than the later-longer-fewer policy, at the end of the first decade of the one-child policy period, fertility was no lower than it was at the close of the later-longer-fewer era. In the following sections I argue that these anomalies can be explained by examining the socioeconomic and sociopolitical context in which the fertility policies were carried out.

INSTITUTIONAL CHANGE IN THE CITIES

The transition to socialism in the 1950s fundamentally altered the relations be-

tween state and society, incorporating family and community into the bottom rung of new, state-dominated institutions capable of influencing even the most private of decisions. These and other implicit fertility policies also altered family and community institutions, modifying the economics of childbearing in ways that encouraged lower fertility. While the changes occurring in China's cities and villages exhibited global similarities, urban-rural differences in the pattern and pace of change were pronounced enough to warrant my speaking of two institutional environments, urban and rural, and treating them separately here.

State-society relations and the politics of fertility decision making

The socialization of the means of urban production in the early 1950s led to the creation of the state sector — of state-run enterprises and government organizations — and collective sector — comprising smaller firms collectively owned by the workers — as the two major divisions of the economy in the cities. The simultaneous construction of a socialist society brought two new institutions of social life, the work unit and the residential unit.

The encapsulation of families into work and residential units gave the state and its cadres tremendous power over family life. Cadre power was rooted in the control over a wide range of essential resources and in the lack of alternative means of obtaining these resources. Work units controlled access to jobs, wages, housing, medical care, social security, and crisis insurance, to name only the most fundamental necessi-

12. Griffith Feeney and Dingding Wang, "Fertility and Population Growth in China: Recent Past and Prospects" (Manuscript, East-West Population Institute, Sept. 1989).

13. On urban fertility trends, see Ansley J. Coale and Ronald Freedman, "Fertility Change in the People's Republic of China and Selected Other East Asian

Populations: Similarities and Differences" (Manuscript, n.d.). Press accounts of the first two campaigns are analyzed in Aird, "Population Policy and Demographic Prospects."

ties of urban life. The cadres' access to an unusually broad range of administrative punishments deepened worker dependency, further ensuring compliance with state directives.[14]

The existence of a forceful birth-planning program makes it impossible to obtain straightforward answers to questions probing fertility decision making by Chinese couples. Nevertheless, there can be no doubt that the work units' control of potent economic and political sanctions worked to ensure adherence to the reproductive rules embodied in the later-longer-fewer and one-child policies. Solid evidence of the power of urban birth-planning cadres comes from the 1985 In-Depth Fertility Survey, which showed that the gap between fertility preferences and outcomes was much greater in the cities than in the countryside. Whereas the vast majority of both urban and rural couples wanted two children, 80-90 percent of urban couples pledged not to have a second child, while fewer than 20 percent of rural couples signed the one-child pledge.[15]

Urban institutions and the economics of childbearing

Because urban fertility began to fall well before the advent of the later-longer-fewer campaign, it is clear that state control over fertility decisions was not the only factor inducing fertility to decline. Also important were changes in social, economic, and cultural institutions that altered what is often called the cost-benefit ratio of children, reducing their attractiveness to prospective parents. Changes that impinged on the value of children to parents were evident in a great many institutions of Chinese life; given limitations of space here and later in the section on rural fertility, I can touch on only a few of the most salient changes.[16]

Before the 1949 Revolution, children, especially sons, brought abundant benefits to residents of China's cities. Setting aside the difficult-to-measure emotional or psychological value of children, the most important of these benefits, from the Chinese point of view, were perpetuation of the family line, or what might be called lineage security; economic contributions in the short run; and old-age economic support.

In the institutional climate of urban China after 1949, all of these benefits were sharply reduced. While urbanites may have continued, covertly, to believe in the notion of a partilineal descent line, antisuperstition campaigns made ancestor worship illegal and politically dangerous, so that few dared to perform the rites.[17]

Changes in the political economy of urban life also made financial contributions from working-age children less certain.[18] During the Maoist era (1949-76) radical shifts in development strategy led to lurches between periods of ultra-leftist and moderate political economy. The rules for getting ahead changed unpredictably, making parental returns on investments in children's training highly uncertain. Further-

14. Andrew G. Walder, "Organized Dependency and Cultures of Authority in Chinese Industry," *Journal of Asian Studies,* 43(1):51-76 (Nov. 1983).

15. Wang Feng, "China's One-Child Policy: Who Complies and Why?" (Paper delivered at the Annual Meeting of the Association for Asian Studies, Washington, DC, 17-19 Mar. 1989).

16. For a more extensive examination of these changes, see Susan Greenhalgh, "Fertility as Mobility: Sinic Transitions," *Population and Development Review,* 14(4):629-74 (Dec. 1988).

17. Margery Wolf, *Revolution Postponed: Women in Contemporary China* (Stanford, CA: Stanford University Press, 1985), p. 247.

18. For elaboration of the following arguments, see Martin K. Whyte and William L. Parish, *Urban Life in Contemporary China* (Chicago: University of Chicago Press, 1984).

more, state emphasis on capital-intensive, heavy industry in a labor-surplus economy produced an unemployment crisis so severe as to convince leaders to launch a massive rustification program in which 10 percent of the urban population, primarily young school graduates, were sent to the countryside. Far from supporting their parents, young people had to be supported by them during their stint in the countryside and the few years spent waiting for a job assignment after their return to the city. Once they were allocated a job, the general freeze on wages and bonuses, especially unbending during the years 1967-76, kept their wages at levels barely adequate to support their own nuclear families, certainly too low to provide remittances for aged parents.

The importance of the third benefit, old-age support, was greatly reduced by the assumption of this function by the state. Beginning in the early 1950s, the state provided pensions amounting to 70-80 percent of preretirement wages for state-sector workers, the great bulk of the work force. In later years pension support was extended to collective-sector workers, although at a lower level.[19]

While the benefits of children declined, the direct and indirect costs of raising a child rose. Direct costs included expenditures on schooling — an estimated 5 percent of a worker's salary per child[20] — as well as the burden of support through young adulthood. Nonmonetary costs included the heavy load of chores that fell largely on young mothers. With the vast majority of

reproductive-age women working outside the home, and few enjoying the help of older-generation live-ins, additional children exacerbated women's double burden, convincing many young mothers that one child was enough.

With the costs of raising children high and the benefits of many offspring low or uncertain, it is not surprising that preferred family sizes were small. In addition, the traditionally strong preference for sons, which put upward pressure on fertility, weakened with improvements in educational and occupational opportunities for women. In the 1960s many intellectual and cadre couples, feeling the pinch of tight housing and heavy work demands, voluntarily opted to have only one child.[21] In the 1970s, little pressure was reportedly required to enforce the two-child limit prescribed by the later-longer-fewer policy.[22] In the one-child-policy era of the 1980s, surveys indicate a mean preference for 1.5-1.8 children in urban areas of the country.[23]

In urban China, then, changes in the institutions of social life altered both the economics and the politics of childbearing. Beginning in the 1950s, the loss of family functions to the state made children less attractive in an economic sense, lowering family-size preferences years before the introduction of a strong planned-birth program. The creation of socialist work units altered the balance of power between state and society such that, after 1970, when the birth-control program gained muscle,

19. Deborah Davis-Friedmann, *Long Lives: Chinese Elderly and the Communist Revolution* (Cambridge, MA: Harvard University Press, 1983), pp. 22-31.

20. Jonathan Unger, *Education under Mao: Class and Competition in Canton Schools, 1960-80* (New York: Columbia University Press, 1982), pp. 21-22.

21. Elisabeth Croll, *Chinese Women since Mao* (Armonk, NY: M. E. Sharpe, 1984), p. 94.

22. William L. Parish and Martin K. Whyte, *Village and Family in Contemporary China* (Chicago: University of Chicago Press, 1978), p. 162.

23. Martin K. Whyte and S. Z. Gu, "Popular Response to China's Fertility Transition," *Population and Development Review*, 13(3):471-93 (Sept. 1987), p. 475.

birth-planning cadres had strong carrots and sticks with which to pressure urban couples to make the politically correct reproductive decisions.

INSTITUTIONAL CHANGE IN THE COUNTRYSIDE

During the first three decades of Communist rule, the economics of collective life gradually lowered peasant fertility aspirations, while the political structure of the commune facilitated the enforcement of birth planning after it was endorsed by the top leadership. In the late 1970s, however, rural socialist institutions were dismantled, enhancing fertility desires and undermining cadre power, so that, despite the existence of a more stringent birth policy, in the 1980s fertility shifted up and down but registered little overall change from the level of the late 1970s.

State-society relations and the politics of fertility decision making

The construction of socialism in the countryside followed a three-step process of collectivization, which culminated in the formation of huge People's Communes during the Great Leap Forward. Excessive centralization proved organizationally unworkable and economically disastrous. In the wake of the Great Leap in 1962, rural society was reorganized into a three-tier hierarchy of collectives—commune, production brigade, production team—which remained the organizational infrastructure of rural life until the introduction of liberalizing reforms in the late 1970s.

Whereas, traditionally, state power had reached only down to the county level, after 1949 peasants found themselves encapsulated in collective units run by a political elite occupying the lower rungs of a hierarchy that extended all the way up to Beijing.

Throughout the collective era local cadres maintained extensive control over peasant economic, cultural, and political life. In the economic sphere, cadres organized the production and distribution of crops and sideline enterprises, leaving less than 10 percent of the land for peasants to till as private plots. In the cultural arena, religious activities were largely proscribed; temples were turned into warehouses or pigsties. Participation in politics was now mandatory and, at times, all-consuming, entailing endless rounds of mass meetings and study sessions. In the social sphere, matters of marriage and reproduction were largely left to families themselves—that is, until the beginning of the later-longer-fewer campaign in the early 1970s.

Like their urban counterparts, rural cadres had many means with which to enforce the new norms of later marriage, longer spacing, and fewer children. As positive inducements, they could offer such benefits as less onerous jobs, more work points for work performed as part of the production team, or larger private plots. Local cadres also controlled a vast arsenal of sanctions with which to make life miserable for overly fertile couples. They could humiliate uncooperative couples in mass meetings, assign them to despicable jobs, take away private plots, even cut off rations of essential supplies. The temptation to use these and other, even more forceful measures was particularly strong during special birth-planning campaigns, when pressure on cadres to fulfill targets was intense. Unable to move away—cadres also controlled the household registers, which had to be moved, too, if migrants were to obtain rations of goods necessary for survival—ordinary peasants had little choice but to comply.

If collective social organization facilitated policy implementation in the 1970s, decollectivization undermined policy enforcement in the 1980s. The rural reforms introduced in the late 1970s and early 1980s dismantled the collectives, reestablishing the family as the basic unit of rural life. In most areas of the country the most crucial reform—the "contracting of everything to the household" (bao gan dao hu)—was not completed until 1983. Cadres lost much of their control over economic life, as peasants were given freedom to sell privately all produce in excess of a state quota, develop sidelines, find jobs outside the village, and even migrate to cities for short periods of time. Political levers were also lost, as the commune reform of 1984 separated politics from economics—at least in theory—and accelerated the decline in the status of the Party.

Deprived of a wide range of sanctions, rural cadres were hard-pressed to enforce the one-child policy. Their task was made more difficult by changes in marriage and fertility policies. The 1980 marriage law raised the legal age of marriage but lowered the effective age limits established by the later-longer-fewer policy, producing a marriage and subsequent baby boom that cadres had no authority to suppress. Changes in the one-child policy in 1984 included an injunction against the use of physical coercion, depriving cadres of a powerful if repugnant enforcement tool. Facing these and other obstacles, after 1984 rural birth-planning cadres generally muddled through, enforcing de facto two- or even three-child policies while

doctoring the statistics that went up the administrative hierarchy.[24]

Rural institutions and the economics of childbearing

The collectivization of rural life changed the economics of childbearing in ways that, while unanticipated by China's leaders, certainly facilitated their policy objectives. Under a collective economic regime many traditional family functions were taken over by the team, eroding the advantages children had historically conferred on rural parents. Through their work in the production team sons had been able to enhance the number of work points, and thus the size of rations and income, that the family enjoyed. With the collectivization of land, however, sons could no longer facilitate family wealth accumulation. Nor could they boost family fortunes by diversifying into nonagricultural jobs, one of the major advantages, traditionally, of having several sons.

If the short-run economic benefits of sons declined, the importance of having at least one son as a lineage and old-age security asset did not. Home ancestor worship was attacked as superstition in the 1960s, but many if not most peasants continued, surreptitiously, to perform the rites.[25] Surveys in the 1980s reveal that "carrying on the family line" was a major reason rural couples wanted sons.[26] An

24. Susan Greenhalgh, "States and Societies: Political Aspects of Population Policy and Family Planning in Developing Countries, with Special Reference to China" (Paper delivered at the IUSSP Seminar on the Role of Family Planning Programmes as a Fertility Determinant, Tunis, 26-30 June 1989).

25. Parish and Whyte, *Village and Family.*

26. Croll, *Chinese Women.*

even more important reason for desiring a son was to ensure economic support in old age. Although the collective offered the "five guarantees" to the childless elderly, the meager level of collective support brought home the fact that any rural resident wishing a decent level of living in old age had no choice but to have a son.

On the other side of the ledger, the costs of raising children remained low during the collective era. From the late 1960s until the early 1980s the costs of medical care to parents were modest, as they, like many other expenses, were largely borne by the collective. The major direct cost, schooling, could not have been overly onerous, as the shortage of rural schools meant the majority of boys would receive at most a junior high school education, while the majority of girls would graduate from primary school.

With sons bringing only moderate benefits and daughters remaining net economic burdens, as the latter continued to join their husbands' families at marriage, it is not surprising that preferred family sizes were not large. The evidence available suggests that in the early 1970s, when the later-longer-fewer campaign was launched, most rural couples wanted only two or three sons and one daughter.[27]

Decollectivization a decade later vastly increased the labor benefits of children, a fact made all too clear by the declining school enrollments at the primary and secondary levels. While the short-term impact on fertility preferences appears to have been positive, however, concurrent increases in the food, clothing, medical, and other costs of raising children depressed fertility desires in the more developed rural areas. By

27. Parish and Whyte, *Village and Family*, pp. 146-47.

the late 1980s low family-size preferences were commonly reported among agricultural couples in peri-urban areas.

Summarizing the rural experience, beginning in the mid-1950s a host of changes in family and community life lowered the value of children to parents while vastly enhancing the control of state cadres over ordinary peasants. This institutional context was crucial to the success of the later-longer-fewer policy in raising contraceptive use and lowering fertility in the 1970s. In the 1980s the reversion to more traditional forms of family and community life bolstered the values of children while partially freeing society from state control. These institutional reversals help explain why fertility in the 1980s returned to the level of the late 1970s, despite the existence of a more stringent fertility policy.

THE 1990s AND BEYOND

The rapid fertility decline of the 1970s stalled in the 1980s. What will happen in the 1990s? Experience has taught students of China the folly of predicting the future course of events in that country. At most one can hazard some speculations based on what is known about the present and the past.

If my hypotheses regarding the forces underlying fertility change are sound, the answer will hinge on developments in two policy areas, birth planning and the rural economy. Indications are that urban development policies, which affect only a small proportion of the population in any case, are unlikely to be significantly modified in the foreseeable future.

With regard to birth-planning policy, both official statements and discussions with Chinese scholars suggest that the policy is unlikely to be substantially revised in the 1990s.[28] One can expect that at the beginning of the decade, perhaps after the results of the 1990 census are clear, the target population for the year 2000 will be adjusted upward to 1.27-1.30 billion; if fertility continues to climb, the target may be raised again before decade's end. There is unlikely to be much change in the reproductive rules or the means by which they are enforced, however. While the current system — characterized by extensive manipulation and partial implementation by couples and cadres alike — is far from perfect, it works to a certain extent, and it is probably the best the state can hope for given the relaxation of political control in the countryside, which was necessary for economic growth.

As for rural economic policy, few observers expect that the regime will want to — or be able to — reverse the tide of liberalization that washed over the countryside in the 1980s. Certainly, few believe the state will try to reconstruct the collectives that dominated rural life in the 1960s and 1970s. Given that these units were the vehicle for the successful enforcement of the birth-planning policy, their absence from

28. Author's interview file 89/9/22nd.

the rural institutional scene will doubtless mean continued weak implementation of the policy in the 1990s.

If the basic institutional configuration, and thus the balance of power between state and society, is to remain unchanged, then the major contextual determinants of the fertility policy's success will be the set of economic policies affecting the nature, pace, and distribution of rural economic development. Among the most important policies will be those affecting peasant incomes and the costs and benefits of children — for example, policies on commodity prices, investment in urban construction, and the sectoral allocation of investment in manufacturing. Also important will be policies affecting the spatial distribution of economic opportunities, as between urban and rural areas and between macroregions of the country. As elsewhere, in China higher incomes are associated with lower fertility; thus, the more highly concentrated the pockets of economic growth, the more vast the area of high population growth. While it is impossible to say anything meaningful about the likely direction of change in so many key policy areas, it is clear that it is changes in economic, rather than population, policy that will shape the fertility trends of the 1990s.

ANNALS, *AAPSS,* **510,** July 1990

Population Change in a
Rural Area of Bangladesh, 1967-87

By JANE MENKEN and JAMES F. PHILLIPS

ABSTRACT: The Matlab subdistrict of Bangladesh is unique in the developing world in the extent of demographic data available over a long time period, during which a serious famine occurred and a family planning program that employed village women as home visitors was introduced within the context of maternal and child health services. These data demonstrate that fertility in this population is well below the maximum biologically feasible, primarily due to the long and intense breast-feeding practiced, that seasonality of births is pronounced, and that fertility drops in response to drastic food shortage. Sex differences in mortality favor males, but during famine the disparity was reduced. Despite arguments that family planning programs are ineffective and use resources that could be applied in areas more relevant to development, the Matlab family planning program has led to both reduced fertility and reduced mortality and may be changing the status and roles of women.

Jane Menken is the UPS Foundation Term Professor in the Social Sciences and director of the Population Studies Center, University of Pennsylvania. She is a member of the National Academy of Sciences and a consultant to the International Centre for Diarrhoeal Disease Research, Bangladesh.

James F. Phillips is senior associate in the Research Division of the Population Council. From 1980 to 1985, he directed family planning and maternal and child health projects at the International Centre for Diarrhoeal Disease Research, Bangladesh.

BANGLADESH, a rural densely populated nation of some 110 million people, achieved independence in 1971. Its
population lives in a lush riverain environment that is periodically beset by some of
the world's worst natural disasters due to
flooding, caused at least in part by conditions in its neighboring countries, and other
weather-related calamities. Indices of economic development and modernization are
low: at $160 in 1986, Bangladesh is fifth
lowest in the World Bank's ranking of
countries by 1986 per capita gross national
product; the large majority of the population — 82 percent in 1985 — lives in rural
areas; a high percentage — 75 percent in
1980 — of the labor force is in agriculture;
per capita food production in 1984-86 had
fallen slightly below its level at the start of
the decade, a level that itself barely exceeded that of 1974-76, a period of widespread crop failure and famine; daily calo-
rie supply had fallen from 1964 per capita
in 1965 to 1800; and literacy is low.[1] Yet,
despite poverty and adversity, mortality
declined during this century, probably
most rapidly in the period 1950-65.[2] Since
then the country has sustained a growth
rate of over 2 percent per annum; in this
century, its population has more than tri-

pled.[3] Bangladesh is considered a notable
example of increase that has led to diminishing returns to labor in agriculture. It is
believed that real agricultural wages have
fallen below their 1830s' level and that the
change was accompanied by a decline in
per capita caloric intake and, possibly, an
increase in landlessness.[4]

These conditions are considered highly
unfavorable for fertility decline and for
improving survival. It is, therefore, of unusual interest to track recent population
change in Bangladesh and to consider
some of the factors that influence its levels
and variation. Detailed and accurate information is not available for the entire nation.[5] There is, however, a remarkable body
of published data for an isolated rural region some forty miles southeast of Dhaka,
in Matlab Subdistrict. These data will be
used first to consider the basic trends since
the late 1960s in birth, death, migration,
and growth rates and then, selectively, to
examine some of the factors that influence
fertility and mortality.

1. World Bank, *World Development Report
1985* (New York: Oxford University Press, 1985),
p. 184, tab. 6; idem, *World Development Report 1988*
(New York: Oxford University Press, 1988), pp. 222
(tab. 1), 234 (tab. 7), 278 (tab. 28), 282 (tab 31), 284
(tab. 32).

2. M. A. Mabud, "Level and Trends in Fertility
in Bangladesh: Evidences from Sample Vital Regis-
tration System," in *Recent Trend in Fertility and
Mortality in Bangladesh: Proceedings of a National
Seminar,* ed. M. A. Mabud (Dhaka: Population Devel-
opment and Evaluation Unit, Planning Commission,
1987), p. 3; S. D'Souza, "Mortality Structure in
Matlab (Bangladesh) and the Effect of Selected
Health Interventions," in *Determinants of Mortality
Change and Differentials in Developing Countries,*
U.N. Population Studies no. 94 (New York: United
Nations, 1986), p. 119.

3. A. U. Ahmed, *Analysis of Mortality Trends
and Patterns in Bangladesh,* Asian Population Series
no. 72 (New York: United Nations, 1986), p. 1.

4. National Research Council, Working Group
on Population Growth and Economic Development,
*Population Growth and Economic Development: Pol-
icy Questions* (Washington, DC: National Academy
Press, 1986), pp. 21-22.

5. Andrew Kantner and Elizabeth Frankenberg,
"Levels and Trends in Fertility and Mortality in
Bangladesh," in *Bangladesh Contraceptive Prevalence Survey, 1985: Secondary Analysis,* ed. A. Kantner et al. (Dhaka: Mitra, 1988), pp. 4, 11, 13; National
Research Council, Committee on Population and Demography, Panel on Bangladesh, *Estimation of Recent Trends in Fertility and Mortality in Bangladesh*
(Washington, DC: National Academy Press, 1981),
pp. 1-3. Both sources conclude that the differential
coverage in the censuses and surveys taken between
1961 and 1985 in the region that is now Bangladesh
preclude definitive measures of change over time,
although there appears to be some evidence of fertility
decline in recent years — since 1983 — and of mortality decline over the period 1979-85.

MATLAB

Matlab lies in a flat deltaic plain criss-crossed by rivers and canals. There are few roads, so the primary means of communication is via small countryboats. The region is among the most densely populated agrarian areas in the world, with over 2000 people per square mile. Villages of about 1000 people consist of *baris,* or groupings of several houses around a central courtyard, that function as economic and social units. A *bari* usually contains two or more patrilineally related families, each of which has its own one-room or two-room house made of mud floor, jute-stick walls, and roof of thatched grass or — if they can afford it — galvanized tin. The area is 85-90 percent Muslim, and many women rarely venture outside their *baris.*

The most common occupations are agriculture — rice or jute — and fishing. The largest of the three annual harvests is the *aman* — over half the rice crop — in November. Smaller crops are harvested at the end of the *boro* (February) and *aus* (June) seasons.

THE DEMOGRAPHIC SURVEILLANCE SYSTEM

In the early 1960s, the Cholera Research Laboratory established a field station in Matlab from which research, including trials of cholera vaccines, could be undertaken.[6] The collection of population data was originally a by-product of cholera research. In order to carry out a vaccine trial, it was necessary to know how many people were at risk of contracting cholera at any given time. Therefore, in 1966, the Demographic Surveillance System (DSS) was established. The first census was taken of some 132 villages, containing well over 100,000 people, and registration of all births, deaths, and migrations in and out of those villages was begun. Each household was visited at least every three days to collect this kind of information, thereby minimizing the chance of missing events or misdating them. The interval between visits was later extended to one week. An important feature of the DSS is that the village workers are all female and can, therefore, enter each household.

In 1968, 101 more villages were surveyed and added to the DSS. The recording of marriages and divorces was initiated in 1975. Additional censuses were taken in 1974, 1978, and 1982.

By 1978, the population covered by the DSS had reached almost 279,000. To lessen the burden of data collection, in cost as well as magnitude, the area was reduced to 149 villages. The 1983 population included in the DSS was 191,000.[7]

The existence of the DSS and the presence of a cadre of well-trained workers has facilitated relatively small special studies that take advantage of the existence of high-quality data on vital events and collect additional information that permits examination of socioeconomic and biological determinants of both fertility and mortality. Also, since data are collected on a household basis, data sets that follow individuals and families over time can be constructed, although this feature is only beginning to be exploited because of the difficulties of linking records.

6. The Cholera Research Laboratory, founded in 1961 under the auspices of the Southeast Asia Treaty Organization, was succeeded in 1978 by the International Centre for Diarrhoeal Disease Research, Bangladesh (ICDDR,B).

7. M. R. Chowdhury et al., "Vital Events and Migration — 1978," *Demographic Surveillance System — Matlab,* Scientific Report no. 47 (Dacca: ICDDR,B, 1981), 7:2, 6; S. Zimicki et al., "Cause of Death Reporting in Matlab," *Demographic Surveillance System — Matlab,* Scientific Report no. 63 (Dacca: ICDDR,B, 1985), 13:2-3.

THE MATERNAL AND CHILD HEALTH AND FAMILY PLANNING PROGRAM

A second project that involved major longitudinal data collection began in October 1977, when a program providing maternal and child health and family planning (MCH-FP) services was introduced in 70 of the DSS villages — the treatment area — with the remainder serving as a comparison area so that the impact of the program could be assessed. The major difference between the MCH-FP program and the government health service is the intensive effort to reach mothers and children through regular home visits that are backed up by clinical services at local centers staffed by paramedical workers or the hospital. The time between visits was extended to 15 days in the treatment area, so that the village workers could spend sufficient time with each family to provide these new interventions. The program was implemented in stages, to avoid overloading workers with new responsibilities and to ensure that all intended services were operating well before adding others.[8]

The first services included family planning information and provision and nutrition counseling. Shortly thereafter, the local treatment centers were established. Starting in mid-1978, tetanus inoculation was offered to pregnant women, since neonatal tetanus was believed to be a major cause of infant death. Early in 1979, home-based oral rehydration therapy for treatment of certain types of diarrhea was introduced. The second wave of introduction of new services came in 1982, when, successively, the tetanus program was extended to all married women, measles vaccination

8. J. F. Phillips et al., "The Effect of a Maternal and Child Health-Family Planning Project on Infant and Child Mortality in Matlab, Bangladesh" (Manuscript, 1989), p. 7.

of children was begun, and efforts to improve the safety of childbirth were implemented, including training of traditional birth attendants, identification of women who were at high risk of difficult delivery or bearing frail infants, and provision of rudimentary childbirth equipment.[9]

A microcomputer-based record-keeping system was developed that permitted rapid feedback to the village workers, faster analysis of data, and flexibility in adding or deleting items of information to be collected. This initiative became one of the very few family planning programs that is properly designed to permit evaluation of its effectiveness.

FERTILITY IN MATLAB, 1967-87

The trend in fertility over the past 20 years is illustrated by the birth rates — births per 1000 population — shown in Figure 1 for the entire period for Matlab as a whole and for the treatment and comparison areas separately from 1978 to 1987.[10] A vivid feature of this graph is the drop in fertility that resulted from famine that followed flooding in 1974-75, which will be discussed further later in this article.

Following inception of the family planning program, the birth rate in the comparison area lies markedly above the treatment-area measure and is consistent with the pre-1978 pattern in Matlab. These rates taken alone do not, however, constitute incontrovertible evidence that fertility was the same in the two areas prior to the in-

9. Ibid., pp. 8-9.
10. All vital statistics are taken from the publications of the Demographic Surveillance System for the various years and from the annual reports of the ICDDR,B. Rates for Matlab are available in published form only until 1983; those given for 1984-87 are averages of the treatment-area and comparison-area rates.

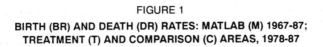

FIGURE 1

BIRTH (BR) AND DEATH (DR) RATES: MATLAB (M) 1967-87;
TREATMENT (T) AND COMPARISON (C) AREAS, 1978-87

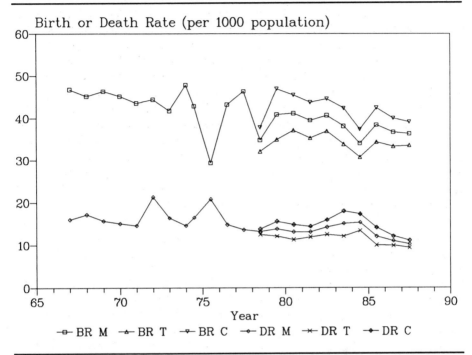

SOURCES: Publications of the Demographic Surveillance System for the various years; annual reports of the International Centre for Diarrhoeal Disease Research, Bangladesh.

ception of the MCH-FP program. Phillips et al. do provide that evidence by demonstrating that, on a month-by-month basis, the total fertility rate, a sensitive measure of reproduction, was virtually identical in the two areas in the period 1974-77 and consistently lower in the treatment area thereafter.[11] Annual age-specific birth rates — births per 1000 women in a five-year age group — were alike in the preprogram years. Thereafter the treatment area exhibited the typical pattern expected when a population begins to control its

fertility: change in birth rates is greatest among older women, while the youngest women — here under 20 — may not reduce their births at all.[12] To illustrate this type of change, the age-specific rates for 1974 and 1984 are shown in Figure 2.[13]

Two additional features of reproduction in Matlab are of note. First, fertility in the absence of family limitation is relatively low for a region in which marriage of women is early and near universal. Second, there is marked seasonality in births. Births peak in November and are high for the last three months of the year. In a study that

11. J. F. Phillips et al., "Determinants of Reproductive Change in a Traditional Society: Evidence from Matlab, Bangladesh," *Studies in Family Planning,* 19(6):318 (Nov.-Dec. 1988).

12. Ibid., pp. 319-21.

13. The rates were provided by James Phillips from original data.

FIGURE 2a

**AGE-SPECIFIC BIRTH RATES, MATLAB
TREATMENT (Trt) AND COMPARISON (Cmp) AREAS, 1974**

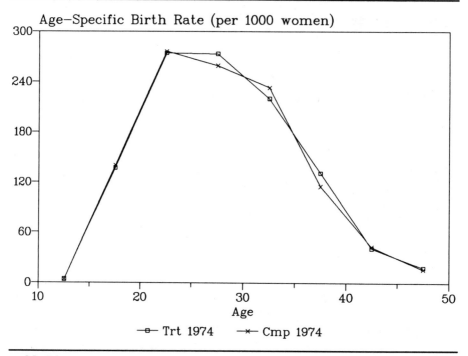

SOURCE: James Phillips, original data.

recorded all reproductive events in a four-year period for 2368 women, 37 percent of all live births took place in the last quarter of the year (Figure 3).[14] Pioneering studies in Matlab that will be discussed in this article illuminate the role of biological and social factors, including nutrition and breast-feeding, as determinants of fertility.

MORTALITY IN MATLAB, 1967-85

Figure 1 shows the trends in the death rate — deaths per 1000 population — during this period. Mortality peaks followed the

start of civil war in 1971 and the mid-decade famine; subsequent to 1978, death rates in the treatment and comparison areas diverged for reasons that will be considered further herein.

Males in Bangladesh can expect to live longer than females (Figure 4). The measure presented is the expectation of life at birth, the number of years an individual would live, on average, if he or she experienced the age-specific mortality conditions of a particular calendar year. In most countries of the world, women live longer than men; Bangladesh is one of the exceptions.

14. S. Becker, A. Chowdhury, and H. Leridon, "Seasonal Patterns of Reproduction in Matlab,

Bangladesh," *Population Studies,* 40(3):463 (Nov. 1986).

FIGURE 2b
**AGE-SPECIFIC BIRTH RATES, MATLAB
TREATMENT (Trt) AND COMPARISON (Cmp) AREAS, 1984**

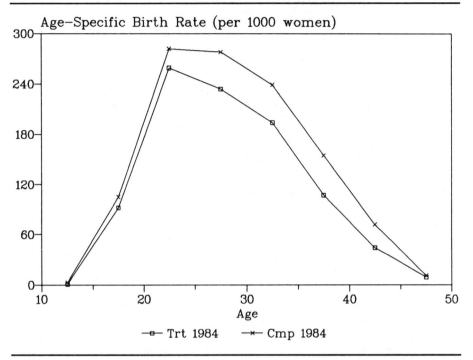

Age–Specific Birth Rate (per 1000 women)

—□— Trt 1984   —×— Cmp 1984

SOURCE: Phillips, original data.

MIGRATION

The Matlab data set is unique in the accuracy of measurement of migration in and out of the DSS area. Short stays, either within or outside the area, are ignored by the data system. An individual is recorded as migrating out if absent for at least six months, and as migrating in if remaining for at least that length of time.

Figure 5 shows that Matlab is a net sending area: in every year except 1971, out-migration has exceeded in-migration. The peak in 1975, which reflects the movement of people to find relief from the famine, appears not to have been followed by massive return of those who departed. Each year, the migration rate is higher

for women than for men. The peak age group for women is 15-19, when they are marrying and joining their new household. For men, the peak comes in the late 20s, when they are leaving to work outside the region.[15]

GROWTH RATES

The difference between the birth and death rates in a given year is a measure of natural increase — the population change that would occur if there were no migration. The actual growth rate takes into ac-

15. See, for examples, K. Shaikh et al., "Vital Events and Migration — Tables 1982," *Demographic Surveillance System — Matlab,* Scientific Report no. 62 (Dhaka: ICDDR,B, 1984), 12:46-48.

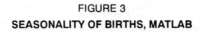

FIGURE 3
SEASONALITY OF BIRTHS, MATLAB

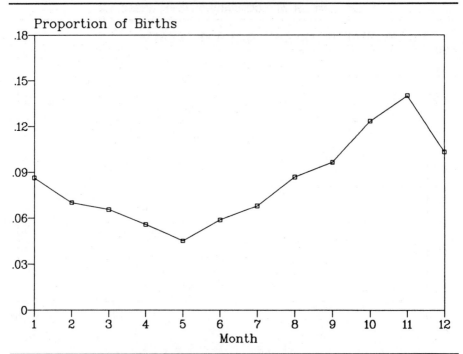

SOURCE: S. Becker, A. Chowdhury, and H. Leridon, "Seasonal Patterns of Reproduction in Matlab, Bangladesh," *Population Studies,* 40(3):463 (Nov. 1986).

count the difference between in-migration and out-migration as well. Both of these rates, which are customarily expressed as percentage change, are shown in Figure 6. In every year, the rate of natural increase was positive and usually over 2.5 percent. Even under the high-mortality and the low-fertility conditions of the famine, births still exceeded deaths so that the population would have grown by about 1 percent. Instead, however, the extent of out-migration led to population decrease for that single year. Migration, in every year except 1971, reduced growth below the potential offered by the fertility and mortality conditions that characterized the period. It therefore serves to reduce the population pressure on

land in this region. Some of the migration is temporary although long-term, involving men who work in distant cities or countries; in fact, many households receive and depend upon remittances from such kin.

SUMMARY

Striking features of population change emerge from even this cursory consideration of the accurate records from Matlab; the few that will be explored further in this article include these aspects of fertility:

— in the absence of family planning, fertility is well below the maximum biologically feasible;
— seasonality of births is pronounced; and

FIGURE 4
EXPECTATION OF LIFE BY SEX, 1967-83

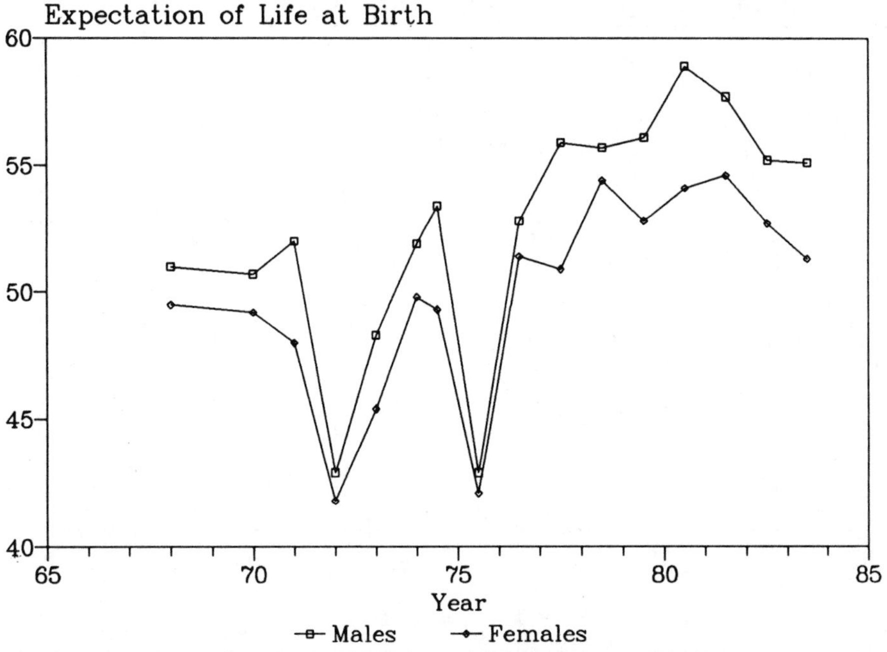

Expectation of Life at Birth

-⊟- Males   -•- Females

SOURCES: Publications of the Demographic Surveillance System for the various years; annual reports of the International Centre for Diarrhoeal Disease Research, Bangladesh.

— the MCH-FP program has led to marked reductions in fertility.

They will also include these aspects of mortality:

— sex differences favor males;
— famine mortality seems to affect males and females differentially; and
— mortality fell subsequent to the introduction of the MCH-FP program.

DETERMINANTS OF FERTILITY
AND FERTILITY CHANGE

Fertility in Bangladesh and in Matlab is low primarily because intervals between births are long, even in the absence of deliberate family limitation. Pioneering studies in Matlab have provided much of the data used to elucidate the roles that breast-feeding practices and nutritional status play in determining fertility.

In 1974, Lincoln Chen and his colleagues reported on a study in which some 200 women were followed for more than two years, with visits from the village workers occurring every two weeks. Conceptions were identified soon after they happened by means of pregnancy tests carried out after each visit. The women were asked whether they had resumed menstruating after their last birth, whether they were still breast-feeding their youngest child, and whether they were feeding the

FIGURE 5
MIGRATION RATES, MATLAB, 1967-83

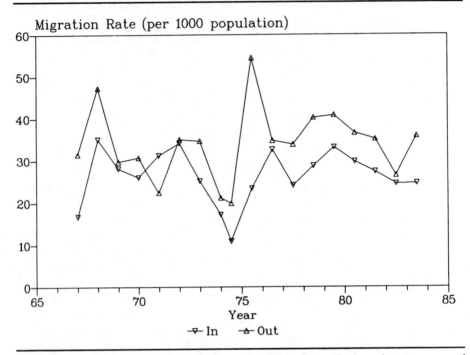

SOURCES: Publications of the Demographic Surveillance System for the various years; annual reports of the International Centre for Diarrhoeal Disease Research, Bangladesh.

infant anything other than breast milk. The results, confirmed by later larger-scale investigations, demonstrated that women in this population do not resume ovulation until long after a live birth.[16] The average duration of amenorrhea in well-nourished women who do not breast-feed their children is 1.5 to 2.0 months;[17] in Matlab, where children are breast-fed until the next pregnancy or the next birth, amenorrhea

lasts over 18.0 months.[18] These studies have led to intense research on the complex relationship between frequency and duration of suckling and amenorrhea that has documented the physiological and hormonal links.[19]

16. L. C. Chen et al., "A Prospective Study of Birth Intervals in Rural Bangladesh," *Population Studies,* 28(2):277-97 (July 1974).

17. E. Salber, M. Feinlieb, and B. MacMahon, "The Duration of Postpartum Amenorrhea," *American Journal of Epidemiology,* 82:347-58 (July 1966).

18. Chen et al., "Prospective Study"; S. Huffman, "Nutrition and Postpartum Amenorrhea in Rural Bangladesh," *Population Studies,* 32:251-60 (July 1978); S. Huffman, A. Chowdhury, and W. H. Mosley, "Postpartum Amenorrhea: How Is It Affected by Nutritional Status?" *Science,* 200:1155-57 (1978).

19. See, for example, J. Dobbing, ed., *Maternal Nutrition and Lactational Infertility,* Nestle Nutrition Workshop Series vol. 9 (New York: Raven Press, 1985).

FIGURE 6
GROWTH RATES, MATLAB, 1967-83

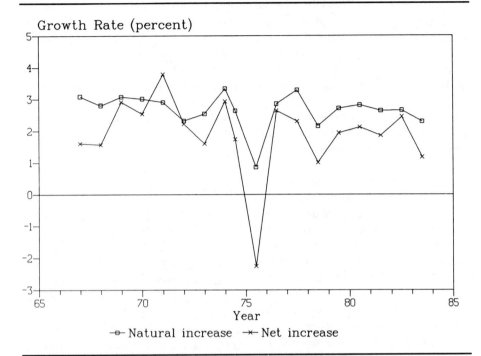

SOURCES: Publications of the Demographic Surveillance System for the various years; annual reports of the International Centre for Diarrhoeal Disease Research, Bangladesh.

One hypothesis proposed to explain why women in Bangladesh take so long to resume ovulating is malnutrition—that if they had been better fed, their bodies would have reacted by being able to resume ovulation sooner.[20] Undernourishment, however, does not seem to be an important explanation of low fertility except under famine conditions. When food supply exceeds famine levels, the better the nutritional status of a woman, the shorter, on average, the duration of amenorrhea, but the decrease is so small that the resulting differences in the length of the birth interval do not have a significant effect on

overall fertility.[21] Better-nourished girls reached menarche earlier than their more poorly fed peers, but again the effect on overall fertility is slight.[22]

Birth intervals are also long because the probability that a woman who has resumed ovulating conceives in any given month is relatively low and because the seasonal swing in conception rates is so marked.[23] Employment in agriculture and fishing

20. R. Frisch, "Population, Food Intake, and Fertility," *Science,* 199:22-30 (1978).

21. Huffman, "Nutrition"; Huffman, Chowdhury, and Mosley "Postpartum Amenorrhea."

22. A. Foster et al., "Female Reproductive Development: A Hazards Model Analysis," *Social Biology,* 33:183-98 (1986).

23. The maximum probability in any month found by Chen et al. was under 0.15. Chen et al., "Prospective Study." When seasonality was taken into account, the average monthly probability of concep-

keeps some men away from home a significant portion of the month, so low frequency of intercourse provides a partial explanation of the low conception rates. In the one study that investigated seasonal variation in the frequency of intercourse, the reported differences by month in the number of days since last intercourse and the proportion having had intercourse within the last 48 hours could account for only a small proportion of the wide seasonal variation in conception rates noted earlier.[24]

Another explanation, proposed by Jain, Hermalin, and Sun, suggested that women who had resumed menstruation but were still breast-feeding had lower conception rates than those who were not lactating.[25] Again, data could be collected in Matlab to examine this hypothesis. Among menstruating women, those who were fully breast-feeding were less likely to conceive than those whose child was receiving supplementary feeding or had been weaned. The longer a woman had been offering supplementary nourishment to her infant, the more likely was she to conceive.[26] Strong seasonality exists in resuming menstruation, probably because women are more likely to offer solid food to infants shortly after the large harvest in November. This seasonal pattern is therefore part of the expla-

nation for the seasonality in conceptions.[27]

When famine conditions prevail, conception rates and birth rates plummet. In Bangladesh, birth rates fell by about a third between 1974 and 1975, and the decline was nearly the same at every age.[28] The most likely causes are severe food deprivation that affects reproductive physiology, both male and female, and decreased coital frequency, whether induced biologically or resulting from increased stress or separation.

The family planning debate

By 1985, nearly 45 percent of all married women of reproductive age in the treatment area of the DSS were using some form of contraception or had been sterilized. The project has demonstrated that, even in the absence of obvious economic development, in an environment that is unfavorable to reproductive change, a well-planned, well-organized program that delivers integrated maternal and child health and family planning services in culturally appropriate ways—in this case, by women health workers who come to the homes—can reduce fertility. The work in Matlab is characterized by research on alternative ways of organizing programs and of delivering services to find avenues that permit relatively uneducated workers to provide effective care.[29] One outcome is a

tion was less than 0.08, according to J. Menken, "Estimating Fecundability" (Ph.D. diss., Princeton University, 1975), pp. 132, 135.

24. Becker, Chowdhury, and Leridon, "Seasonal Patterns," p. 470.

25. A. Jain, A. Hermalin, and T. Sun, "Lactation and Natural Fertility," in *Natural Fertility*, ed. Henri Leridon and Jane Menken (Liège: Ordina Editions, 1979), pp. 149-94.

26. A. M. John, J. A. Menken, and A.K.M.A. Chowdhury, "The Effects of Breastfeeding and Nutrition on Fecundability in Rural Bangladesh: A Hazards-Model Analysis," *Population Studies*, 41(3): 433-46 (Nov. 1987).

27. Becker, Chowdhury, and Leridon, "Seasonal Patterns," pp. 466-68.

28. L. T. Ruzicka and A.K.M. Alauddin Chowdhury, "Vital Events and Migration—1975," *Demographic Surveillance System—Matlab*, Scientific Report no. 12 (Dacca: Cholera Research Laboratory, 1978), vol. 4; A.K.M.A. Chowdhury and George T. Curlin, "Recent Trends in Fertility and Mortality in Rural Bangladesh, 1966-75" (Working Paper no. 3, Cholera Research Laboratory, 1978).

29. For an overview of the program, see J. Phillips, "Translating Pilot Project Success into National

project that is trying to introduce some of the elements of the MCH-FP program into the family planning program sponsored by the government in other regions of Bangladesh.

The research in Matlab has not neglected the role of social and cultural change in effecting fertility change. The problems of parental dependency on children for security, of a society that discriminates against women, and of low levels of education that produce resistance to new ideas have been examined through surveys and through group discussions.[30] Supplying the means of fertility control has led to greater change than expected by proponents of the "development is the only contraceptive" school; clearly, as well, the impact of even the best programs is ultimately limited by cultural patterns that must change in order to permit further development, including the shift to low mortality and low fertility.

MORTALITY DIFFERENTIALS AND DETERMINANTS

In Matlab, female mortality is higher than male mortality from the postneonatal period — 1-11 months — until near the end of the reproductive years.[31] There is little evidence that these differentials have changed over time. Their basis may lie in the preferential feeding of males that characterizes Bangladesh and may be exacer-bated under conditions of food shortage. Koenig and Wojtyniak note that there is little difference in mortality of young boys and girls in Teknaf, an area of Bangladesh with more abundant food supply than Matlab. Given limited resources, families may well choose to distribute them "according to culturally-determined criteria such as sex."[32]

During the Bangladesh famine of the mid-1970s, crude death rates rose by nearly 60 percent, but there were substantial differences by age and sex. The greatest rises occurred among children aged 1-11 months followed by children 5-9 years old and persons over 45, in that order. Children 1-9 years old experienced even higher mortality in the year after the famine than they suffered during the crisis. Because the neonatal death rate was virtually unchanged, infant mortality rose less than in the age groups already noted. The disadvantage of young females — under 10 — appears to have been exaggerated during the 1974-75 famine, but disaster diminished or even reversed the disadvantage of older women in most age groups by raising male death rates more than female death rates. In 1975, mortality was higher for men than for women from age 25 on.[33] Thus, although the youngest women suffered disproportionately, the advantage of older women compensated, leading to the near identical — but very low — expectations of life seen for men and women during the famine.

The MCH-FP program appears to be associated with declines in the treatment

Policy Development: Two Projects in Bangladesh," *Asia Pacific Population Journal,* 2(4):3-28 (Dec. 1987).

30. M. Rahman, *Tradition, Development, and the Individual,* Asian Population Change Series 1 (Canberra: Australian National University, 1986); M. Nag and M. B. Duza, "Secrets of Success in Bangladesh," *People,* 15(4):27-28 (Dec. 1988).

31. See, for example, M. K. Chowdhury et al., "Vital Events and Migration — Tables 1981" (Scientific Report no. 59, ICDDR,B, 1983), pp. 11, 30.

32. M. A. Koenig and B. Wojtyniak, "Excess Female Mortality during Infancy and Early Childhood: Evidence from Rural Bangladesh" (Working Paper Series no. 22, ICDDR,B, 1987), p. 39; Ahmed, *Analysis of Mortality Trends,* pp. 52-55.

33. Ruzicka and Chowdhury, "Vital Events — 1975."

area in mortality of children aged 1-4 years, although the components of the program responsible for the improvement have yet to be identified. It is likely, however, that measles vaccination is reducing mortality, especially among the children of the very poor.[34] Oddly enough, the program has had little effect on diarrheal deaths. The International Centre for Diarrhoeal Disease Research, Bangladesh, was one of the pioneers in the development of oral rehydration therapy. Yet it is impossible to show any direct effect of this therapy on mortality in either the treatment or the comparison area because the Centre, at its inception, established an effective center for treating diarrhea. They have, however, been able to demonstrate that distribution of oral rehydration packets, or instruction in producing the appropriate combination of sugar and salts from generally available staple foods, has led to fewer visits to the treatment center and no discernible increase in diarrheal mortality. On this basis, some analysts have concluded that oral rehydration therapy can avert some diarrheal-disease-related mortality in settings where clinical treatment is not available.[35]

The program has led to a reduction in maternal mortality, which is responsible for more than a third of the deaths among reproductive-age women. Women who become pregnant have no lower mortality risks than before the program, but many fewer are conceiving. The lack of change in the mortality ratio — deaths per 1000 live births — results from offsetting effects: fewer women whose pregnancies would be risky — older, high-parity women — become pregnant, which should cause the ratio to decline; however, the women who do become pregnant are more likely to be young childless women, for whom pregnancy is also riskier.[36]

The Matlab data have also documented the familiar relationships between socioeconomic status and mortality: mortality at all ages decreases as education of the father or head of household increases; it decreases with increased ownership of goods and with size of the dwelling unit.[37] Unfortunately, the social and economic measures are taken at long intervals — in the censuses — and are quite simple and limited. Therefore they have not proven especially useful in understanding the determinants of population change in Matlab and have offered little advantage over the kinds of information typically collected in surveys.

DISCUSSION

The Matlab DSS and MCH-FP projects continue to provide the best ongoing, detailed monitoring of population change in a developing country. They also offer lessons for development policy.

Family planning programs are frequently attacked, on the one hand, as being ineffective and, on the other, for using resources that could be applied in areas more relevant to development. What Matlab demonstrates is that family planning programs can be effective when organized well, which, in this case, occurs within the context of a maternal and child health pro-

34. J. D. Clemens et al., "Measles Vaccination and Childhood Mortality in Rural Bangladesh," *American Journal of Epidemiology,* 128(6):1330-39 (Dec. 1988); Michael Koenig, personal communication, 1989.

35. M. H. Merson et al., "Village-based Distribution of Oral Rehydration Packets in Bangladesh," *American Journal of Tropical Medicine and Hygiene,* 29(2):285-90 (Mar. 1980).

36. M. A. Koenig et al., "Maternal Mortality in Matlab, Bangladesh: 1976-1985," *Studies in Family Planning,* 19(2):69-80 (Mar.-Apr. 1988).

37. D'Souza, "Mortality Structure."

gram. A good program may serve as a model for establishing institutional approaches to other problems of development. A single-goal program cannot, however, be the only approach to improving conditions in Bangladesh or any other less developed country.

In terms of policy relevant to fertility change, there are limits to what family planning programs can be expected to yield. Cultural factors, especially within the family and the immediate community, affect reproductive decisions and influence both fertility and mortality. They establish the bounds within which individuals have some scope for autonomous action. According to M. Rahman, bari heads have latent understanding of population problems; they are men of experience who know the effects of land fragmentation when too many sons survive to lay claim to family property. But other social and cultural values that we fail to recognize adequately may outweigh their interest in preventing the slivering of land.[38] Despite decades of biomedical investigation, we understand little about the role of family structure and community ties in this arena.

In Matlab, the position of women stands out as a deterrent to change. Women are far less likely to receive education than men; their movements are restricted; their earning capacity is limited. The argument that the most effective route to improved conditions for men, women, and children in many parts of the world may be through improving conditions for women is not new; it seems particularly relevant, however, in the Bangladesh context.

Family planning and other programs directed at women may themselves become vehicles for influencing change. Some female village workers in Matlab report encountering opposition from bari members and other relatives to their work, especially to their independent movement around the village. In response, a few were forced to give up their positions; for others, employment was eventually legitimated by their contributions to family income. These women now act as role models for other women and, especially, for young girls. The attitudes of men, especially influential men, may be changing as a result of the growing status and prestige associated with the role of female village worker.[39]

In considering the short-term prospects for population change in Bangladesh, fertility decline seems more readily achievable than much improvement in mortality. Matlab has experienced significant innovation in reproductive behavior under conditions that do not seem radically different from those of other parts of the country. One model for the needed machinery appears to be working. But mortality decline has not kept pace. The experience of recent years does not encourage the expectation that new magic bullets or barefoot-doctor programs will suddenly appear to reduce mortality risks. The strategy for Bangladesh may be to continue to invest in improving its family planning programs while exploring new ways of reducing mortality, through providing care that will be effective in increasing survival and through increased attention to the role of food supply and nutrition in establishing and maintaining health.

38. Rahman, Tradition, Development, pp. 173-74.

39. R. Simmons, R. Mita, and M. A. Koenig, "The Effect of the Matlab Project on Women's Status" (Paper delivered at the Rockefeller Foundation Workshop on Women's Status and Fertility, Belagio, Italy, June 1988).

Changing Intergenerational Family Relations in East Asia

By LINDA G. MARTIN

ABSTRACT: Intergenerational family relations in China, Japan, and South Korea are changing. Multigenerational coresidence and dominance of patrilineal relations are declining. In some ways, the diffusion of so-called Western values and practices that are in conflict with Confucian ideals parallels the earlier process of the Confucianization of Japan and Korea. The demographic changes that are influencing families are new, however, and East Asians of the future will have fewer but longer-lasting kinship relations. At the same time, population aging and the expected declining role of the family in elder care are causing growing concern among policymakers.

Linda Martin is director of the Committee on Population, National Academy of Sciences, and a senior research scholar at Georgetown University. She is currently on leave from her positions as research associate at the East-West Population Institute and professor of economics at the University of Hawaii, where she was employed from 1979 to 1989. She received her undergraduate degree from Harvard University and a master's in public affairs and Ph.D. in economics from Princeton University. In recent years, her research has focused on aging and family issues in Asia.

NOTE: The author is very grateful to Glenda Roberts, Diane Wolf, and especially Minja Kim Choe for providing useful information and comments and to the East-West Population Institute for its support. The views expressed here are those of the author alone and not those of the National Academy of Sciences.

THE countries of East Asia are known for their Confucian heritage, which emphasizes the importance of the family and filial piety. In the face of rapid socioeconomic change, the completion of the demographic transition, and population aging, however, there are conflicts between the ideal of living in a multigenerational household and the economic and demographic realities.

Japan is the most advanced economically of the East Asian countries and completed its transition to low mortality and fertility in the 1960s. South Korea is considered a newly industrialized country, and in recent years its fertility level has also fallen to the replacement level of 2.1 children per woman, in part due to the success of its family planning program. China has also experienced substantial economic growth in the 1980s, and it has implemented the strongest population-control policy in human history. As a result, fertility is approaching the replacement level in China, although the goal of the one-child-per-family policy has not yet been met throughout the country.

Such success in reducing fertility and population growth is leading to dramatic population aging, since relatively fewer births mean that, on average, a population will grow older. As indicated in Table 1, all three countries are projected to experience considerable aging of their populations. By 2025, over one-fifth of Japan's population will be ages 65 and older, as will be about one-eighth of the populations in the other two countries. Also important for future provision of public services to the elderly is the fact that between 1985 and 2025, the absolute numbers of the elderly will more than double in Japan, triple in China, and quadruple in Korea.

Although initially mortality decline results in a younger population — since infant and child mortality are especially high in high-mortality populations — in demographically more advanced countries, such as Japan, mortality decline is beginning to contribute to population aging, as gains in survival are increasingly concentrated at older ages. Japan has the longest-lived population on earth, and substantial progress in increasing survival has also been made in China and Korea, as shown by the expectations of life at birth in Table 1. Besides contributing to population aging, such mortality decline allows individual aging. Overall, then, East Asians of tomorrow can expect to have fewer family members, as a result of fertility decline, but these kinship relations will last much longer, as a result of mortality decline.

Concomitant with the effects of demographic change, economic and social changes are also influencing family relations. As industrialization occurs, the family is decreasingly the focus of production, and on a daily basis, individuals are likely to spend a greater proportion of their time interacting with non-kin and with institutions other than the family. Moreover, migration may result in the generations of a family living in different places.

The issue of family change is of special concern to policymakers for a variety of reasons, but in East Asia one of the foremost concerns is that as populations age, governments will be increasingly expected to provide support to the elderly that was, at least in theory, traditionally provided by families. Accordingly, policy pronouncements often pay lip service to the role of the family in the care of the elderly, and governments are searching for ways to increase the benefits and reduce the costs of family support. Efforts have ranged from attempts to legislate filial piety in China to tax incentives for living with an elderly parent in Japan.

TABLE 1

FERTILITY, MORTALITY, AND AGING INDICATORS, 1985-2025

	China	Japan	Korea
Total fertility rate (children per woman)			
1985-90	2.4	1.8	2.1
2025-30	2.1	2.1	2.1
Expectation of life at birth (years)			
Males: 1985-90	68.3	74.7	65.7
2025-30	73.0	76.6	71.1
Females: 1985-90	70.6	79.7	72.4
2025-30	78.1	82.5	78.0
Proportion of total population ages 65 and over (percentage)			
1985	5.2	9.9	4.3
2025	12.1	20.6	12.5
Number of persons ages 65 and over (millions)			
1985	53.9	11.9	1.8
2025	185.7	26.9	7.4

SOURCE: K. C. Zachariah and My T. Vu, *World Population Projections 1987-88 Edition: Short- and Long-Term Estimates* (Baltimore, MD: Johns Hopkins University Press, 1988).

A critical constraint, however, in family support of the elderly, especially caregiving to the frail, is the allocation of women's time, since women are the usual caregivers of the old as well as the young. Besides facing demands on their time from family members, the women of East Asia are increasingly being relied on to contribute to economic growth through employment outside the home.

Furthermore, there is evidence that individual attitudes and expectations about family relations are changing or, at least, that with greater economic resources, individuals may have more options in choosing the form of those relations. With increased income, East Asians may opt for greater privacy, especially in living arrangements, as has been the case in the West.

In this article, the family ideals and traditions—especially with regard to intergenerational relations—are reviewed and actual changes in family relations in recent decades are documented for China, Japan, and Korea. The conclusion speculates about possible future family change in East Asia.

IDEALS, TRADITIONS, AND LAWS

To talk about change the past must first be examined. This is especially important, since it is often tempting to think of behavior in the past as homogeneous and static or to assume that traditional behavior was equivalent to cultural ideals, legal prescriptions, or the practices of elites.

Ideals and traditional behavior

Popular Western conceptions of family traditions in China, Japan, and Korea presume that East Asian families have been uniformly and long influenced by Confucian thought, when just the opposite is the case. Even in China, the home of Confucius, the Confucian patriarchal ideals of supremacy of the eldest male in the family, the reckoning of descent and inheritance in the male line, and residence in large households with husband's parents and brothers after marriage have in the past not been achieved by all Chinese.[1] Although data for earlier centuries are limited, most certainly high mortality constrained multigenerational living, and there is evidence from the early twentieth century of variation by regions and socioeconomic groups in the extent to which the other patriarchal ideals — such as virilocal residence, or living with husband's family — were realized.

More surprising, perhaps, is the fact that widespread Confucian influence on family relations began to be felt only as recently as the seventeenth century in Korea and the eighteenth century in Japan.[2] Prior to the Confucianization of Korea in the middle of the Yi dynasty (1392-1910), the principle that men were superior to women did not apply, female lines were as important as male lines, and inheritance was equally divided among children of both sexes. It is thought that in the preceding Koryo period (918-1392), uxorilocal marriage — residence with wife's family — was the custom.[3] Similarly in Japan, pre-Confucianization family relations were both patrilineal and matrilineal, and postnuptial residence was not strictly virilocal. It was not until approximately the turn of the twentieth century that virilocal residence became common throughout Japan.

In both Korea and Japan, the adoption of Confucian ideals and practices was gradual and from the elite down. Neo-Confucian ideas were first introduced in thirteenth-century Korea by the upper-class *yangban* and in seventeenth-century Japan by the *samurai*. In both cases, there was resistance to the adoption of Confucian practices, even though they were, at least in part, codified in the law of the land during the Yi dynasty in Korea and in the Meiji era (1868-1911) in Japan. In fact, in neither country were the ideals ever completely adopted or the practices completely accepted.

For example, if we use pre-World War II East Asia as the benchmark for recent family change, then there were substantial differences between the three countries. The ideal household type in China remained a so-called joint-stem family in which all sons brought their wives — who had been selected by their parents — to their natal home to live. In Korea and Japan, the expectation was that only the oldest son would do so, that is, the ideal was a stem family.[4] The reality at any given time, however, was that most households did not match the ideal type. In Japan in 1920, 60 percent of the households were nuclear and 30 percent stem, and demographic analysis indicates that only three-quarters of the possible number of three-generation households were realized.[5] Data from Taiwan from 1906 to 1946 indicate that households

1. Maurice Freedman, ed., *Family and Kinship in Chinese Society* (Stanford, CA: Stanford University Press, 1970).

2. Mark Peterson, "Women without Sons: A Measure of Social Change in Yi Dynasty Korea," in *Korean Women: View from the Inner Room*, ed. Laurel Kendall and Mark Peterson (New Haven, CT: East Rock Press, 1983), p. 33; Takao Sofue, "Family and Interpersonal Relationships in Early Japan," in *Religion and the Family in East Asia*, ed. George A. De Vos and Takao Sofue (Osaka: National Museum of Ethnology, 1984), p. 219.

3. Martina Deuchler, "The Tradition: Women during the Yi Dynasty," in *Virtues in Conflict: Tradition and the Korean Woman Today*, ed. Sandra Mattielli (Seoul: Samhwa, 1977), p. 8.

4. Kwang Kyu Lee, "Family and Religion in Traditional and Contemporary Korea," in *Religion and the Family in East Asia*, ed. De Vos and Sofue, p. 187.

5. Minako Kurokawa Maykovich, "The Japanese Family," in *The Family in Asia*, ed. Man Singh Das and Panos D. Bardis (London: George Allen & Unwin, 1979), p. 385; Makoto Atoh, "Changes in Family Patterns in Japan" (Paper delivered at the Seminar on Theories of Family Change, sponsored by the International Union for Scientific Study of Population, Tokyo, 29 Nov.-2 Dec. 1988), fn. 7.

were about equally divided among nuclear, stem, and joint-stem types.[6]

Ideal patterns of inheritance and adoption practices also varied across countries. In principle, in China all sons received equal shares, in Korea all sons received shares but the eldest got more, and in Japan the eldest son took it all.[7] In all three countries, young men, especially daughters' husbands, were sometimes adopted into families to serve as heirs, but such cases were rare in Korea and occurred only when there was no son or other appropriate male member of the paternal kinship group. In China also, adoption from the broad paternal group was preferred, but it was not practiced so strictly as in Korea. In Japan, adoption from outside the kin group was done freely.[8] The goal in Japan was to preserve the ie — sometimes described as the family corporation — rather than to preserve the blood line.[9]

Thus, in discussing family change in East Asia, it is essential not to assume Confucian or Chinese ideals as a starting point for all three populations, and it is important to distinguish historically between family ideals and the actual practices in each country. Furthermore, just as in the past, there has been tension between actual practices, ideals, and the codes of family law in the postwar period.

6. Arthur P. Wolf, "Chinese Family Size: A Myth Revitalized," in *The Chinese Family and Its Ritual Behavior*, ed. Jih-Chang Hsieh and Ying-Chang Chuang (Taipei: Institute of Ethnology, Academia Sinica, 1985), p. 35.

7. Jai-Seuk Choi, "Comparative Study on the Traditional Families in Korea, Japan and China," in *Families in East and West*, ed. Reuben Hill and Rene Konig (Paris: Mouton, 1970), p. 207.

8. Ibid., p. 203.

9. Harumi Befu, "Corporate Emphasis and Patterns of Descent in the Japanese Family," in *Japanese Culture: Its Development and Characteristics*, ed. Robert J. Smith and Richard K. Beardsley (Chicago: Aldine, 1962), p. 34.

Laws

The 1950 Marriage Law of China prohibited child betrothal, interference in choosing one's spouse, and interference in the remarriage of widows, who in the past were ideally to have remained devoted to their deceased husbands.[10] It also gave women equal rights in the possession and inheritance of property. The law sought to end the subordination of individuals, especially women and young people, to family authority, and it sought to establish the conjugal or nuclear family as the basic unit of the socialist society. Nevertheless, the effects of these reforms were limited and uneven across the country, and provisions were not always enforced. There were periodic campaigns, such as the 1973-74 anti-Confucius campaign, to wipe out "feudalistic-patriarchal" ideology, but they were often viewed by the people as just one more propaganda barrage that would soon dissipate.[11]

The 1980 Marriage Law of China reaffirmed many of the provisions of the earlier law but added the imperative that birth control be used and modified other provisions in an attempt to provide incentives for becoming a one-child — in particular, a daughter-only — family.[12] The legal age of marriage was raised to 20 for females and 22 for males, but the law noted that the limits were to be viewed as minimums, and separate administrative directives specified that women should not marry until their mid-twenties and males until their late twenties. Both the 1950 and 1980 laws

10. Michael Palmer, "The People's Republic of China: Some General Observations on Family Law," *Journal of Family Law*, 25(1):48-54 (1987).

11. Kay Ann Johnson, *Women, the Family and Peasant Revolution in China* (Chicago: University of Chicago Press, 1983), pp. 200-201.

12. Palmer, "People's Republic of China," pp. 55-68.

stressed the duty of parents and children to support each other, but the 1980 law emphasized the responsibility of daughters — not just sons, as in the past, when married daughters were often not considered members of their natal families — and added a stipulation that grandchildren had a duty to care for their grandparents, both maternal and paternal. Other 1980 provisions to encourage small families and increase the value of daughters included articles stating that either virilocal or uxorilocal marriages were acceptable and that children might be given either their father's or their mother's family name.

The postwar constitutions of Japan and Korea also embodied efforts to transform family relations. Although there was a small movement before the war in Japan to change the law, it was basically the influence of the American occupation forces that led to the 1947 constitution and associated civil code, which disestablished the *ie*, or Japanese family system of the Meiji civil code.[13] The constitution assured freedom of choice of spouse and equal rights of women to own property and to inherit. Inheritance solely by the eldest son was no longer required, as it had been in the past, and widows were given rights to half their husbands' estates and the children had rights to equal shares of the other half. Furthermore, lineal ascendants — that is, parents — were no longer given priority over children and spouses in an individual's obligations to support various family members.[14]

The 1948 constitution of the Republic of Korea also guaranteed individual freedom and sexual equality, but these ideals were not fully implemented in the civil codes.[15] For example, the civil code of 1960 stipulated that the family head could decide the place of residence of the family and that men under 27 and women under 23 years of age needed their parents' permission to marry. Wives were allowed to succeed to the family headship, but only if there were no children. The code also granted inheritance rights to wives and daughters, but wives and unmarried daughters had a right to only one-half the amount given sons, and married daughters, only one-fourth. In the late 1970s, the code was revised to allow freedom of marriage for persons over age 20. It also gave widows inheritance shares equal to those of the new family heads. Daughters who were not in the household received one-sixth shares, and all sons — no matter where they lived — and daughters in the household were allotted two-thirds shares. Thus equal rights within the family for women have not yet been achieved in Korean law. Moreover, actual practices fail to match the model behavior prescribed by law — a phenomenon common to all three countries.

CHANGING BEHAVIOR, ATTITUDES, AND EXPECTATIONS

The so-called nuclearization of East Asian households in the postwar period is often cited as evidence of the growth of the pernicious influence of Western values and as cause for alarm in planning for elder care. As it has already been noted, however, nuclear households were common in some East Asian populations early in the twentieth century. Furthermore, for several reasons, changes from one time to another

13. Robert J. Smith, "Gender Inequality in Contemporary Japan," *Journal of Japanese Studies*, 13(1):12-13 (1987).

14. Toshi Kii, "Status Changes of the Elderly in Japan's Legal, Family, and Economic Institutions," in *The Situation of the Asian/Pacific Elderly*, ed. Charlotte Nusberg and Masako M. Osako (Washington, DC: International Federation on Ageing, 1981), p. 70.

15. Deuchler, "The Tradition," pp. 43-44.

in the proportion of households in a population that are nuclear in form may not be a good measure of changes in underlying intergenerational family behavior.

First, household definitions imposed in data collection efforts, such as censuses, may draw inappropriate boundaries that divide family members. For example, in Japan there is the phenomenon of older parents' living under a separate roof but in the same compound, and in Taiwan some family members eat but do not live together or vice versa.[16] Nevertheless, 1988 Japanese survey data indicate that only about 3 percent of adults reported living next door to their parents, and Taiwanese survey data show that the percentage in the either-or category declined from 10 to 3 percent between 1973 and 1985.

Second, cross-sectional data may obscure the true life-cycle nature of coresidence. Members of a stem or joint-stem family may pass through stages in their lives in which they live in nuclear households simply because the requisite relatives to form the ideal type of household are not alive.

But the most important reason for not relying on distributions of household types for the population as a whole is that the demographic availability of relatives changes over time. For example, given no change in the extent to which people form stem households when there are appropriate family members available, one might expect with fertility and mortality decline to see an increase in the incidence of stem

households and a decline in the incidence of nuclear households, as Zeng has demonstrated for China.[17] More parents would be available to each adult offspring for forming a stem household. On the other hand, fertility decline would also reduce the number of brothers available, so it might become more difficult to form a joint-stem household. Of course, fertility effects on the availability of kin would operate with a lag in comparison to mortality effects, so initially the latter would outweigh the former and the availability of all types of kin might increase.

It is for these reasons that understanding the degree of nuclearization over time is fraught with difficulty, especially when underlying behavior or propensities to live together, as well as demographic availability of kin, are changing. Accordingly, in the discussion of family change that follows the focus will be on more specific family behavior of an intergenerational nature — arrangement of marriage and postnuptial coresidence, living arrangements of the elderly, and contact across household boundaries.

Arrangement of marriage and postnuptial coresidence

In all three countries, there is evidence that the incidence of arranged marriages has declined in the postwar period.[18] Almost 90 percent of Korean women who married between 1950 and 1959 had their

16. Linda G. Martin and Noriko O. Tsuya, "Interactions of Middle-Aged Japanese with Their Parents" (Paper delivered at the Annual Meeting of the Population Association of America, Baltimore, MD, 1989), p. 45; Maxine Weinstein et al., "Household Composition, Extended Kinship, and Reproduction in Taiwan: 1965-1985" (Paper delivered at the Annual Meeting of the Population Association of America, Baltimore, MD, 1989), p. 8, tab. 5.

17. Yi Zeng, "Changes in Family Structure in China: A Simulation Study," *Population and Development Review*, 12(4):675-703.

18. Sae Kwon Kong et al., *Change of Korean Family Structure* (Seoul: Korean Institute of Population and Health, 1987), p. 84; Margery Wolf, "Marriage, Family, and the State in Contemporary China," *Pacific Affairs*, 57(2):228 (1984); Mainichi Newspapers and Nihon University, 1988 Japanese National Family Survey, unpublished data.

marriages arranged by their parents, while only 81 percent of the 1960-69 marriage cohort, 55 percent of the 1970-79 cohort, and 45 percent of the 1980-86 marriage cohort did. For the most recent cohort, 26 percent had been introduced by friends or family, but not for the express purpose of considering marriage, and 16 percent had met at work — virtually unheard of among the earliest cohort.

Data collected in 1980-81 from four rural communes in China indicate that parents selected women's husbands for 90 percent of the group ages 60 years and over, 95 percent of the 50-to-59-year-old group, 68 percent of the 40-49 group, 65 percent of the 30-39 group, and 55 percent of the 20-29 group.

The sharp drop for the 40-49 group, who would have been ages 10 to 19 around 1950 and entering the years of eligibility for marriage, is remarkable, although there is some chance that answers were influenced by their social acceptability.

The change is smoother in Japan. Data from a 1988 national survey indicate that the percentage of women whose marriages were arranged in each of the same age groups was 68, 57, 48, 36, and 11, respectively. Of course, in Japan, as in the other two countries, the average age at first marriage has increased, so those women in the 20-29 group are relatively early marriers. It is not known if young brides would be more or less likely to have their marriages arranged, but it is probably safe to conclude that the parental role in spouse selection has declined over time.

There has also been change in the characteristics considered in spouse selection in Japan. About 50 percent of the two youngest groups reported that an important consideration was whether or not they would be expected to live with their husbands' parents. Only about one-third of the older groups said that this factor had been very or somewhat important. A saying that has been popular at least since the early 1970s in Japan is that an ideal husband comes with a house, with a car, and without a mother-in-law.[19]

These changing tastes about living with husbands' parents are also reflected in changes in postnuptial coresidence, that is, residence right after marriage. Among Japanese eldest sons married between 1960 and 1964, 58 percent lived with their parents immediately after marriage, whereas only 41 percent of eldest sons married between 1980 and 1982 did so.[20] In recent years, there has been a slight increase in the proportion of noneldest sons living with their parents after marriage to about 15 percent, but the proportion of daughters residing postnuptially with their parents has remained at only about 4 percent. Altogether, since the late 1940s, the proportion of all newlyweds living with their parents decreased from 59 to 31 percent in the early 1970s and since then has not changed substantially. The lack of change in recent years may be due to the fact that as fertility has fallen, a greater proportion of newlyweds each year comprises eldest sons, who remain relatively more likely to live with their parents.

The pattern of change over time in postnuptial residence in China is mixed and is thought to have been influenced in recent years by housing shortages. Neolocal residence — residing separately from both sets of parents — increased to over 50 percent in

19. David Plath, " 'Ecstasy Years' — Old Age in Japan," *Pacific Affairs,* 46(3):428 (1973).

20. Atoh, "Changes in Family Patterns in Japan," p. 35.

urban areas in the 1950s, but gradually declined in the 1960s and 1970s.[21] Both virilocal and uxorilocal residence increased, although the former remained greater than the latter and was the case for about one-half of urban newlyweds for the 1977-82 period. Besides housing shortages, another possible reason for this change is the increased availability of parents with whom to coreside.

Living arrangements of the elderly

From the perspective of the other end of the age distribution — the elderly — there is evidence in all three countries of declining coresidence. In Japan, the percentage of the noninstitutional population ages 65 and over living with children fell from 77 percent in 1970 to 65 percent in 1985.[22] Although coresidence remains greater in rural than in urban areas, it has declined in both.[23] An increasing proportion of the elderly is living with spouse only or alone. Less than 2 percent of the elderly are in nursing homes at any one time, but hospital stays of the elderly are extremely long in Japan, indicating a phenomenon known as social hospitalization.

Some Japanese scholars have argued that the decline in coresidence measured cross-sectionally does not mean that there will be a reduction in the proportion of the elderly that ever live with their adult children. Rather, they argue that coresidence is simply being delayed and taking on a more strategic and less of an obligatory charac-

ter. This view is supported by attitudes of the middle-aged about whether or not adult children should live with their parents. A 1987 national survey showed that 51 percent of the respondents ages 30-49 said that children should live with parents in general, whereas over 80 percent said that they should do so if one of the parents were in poor health or widowed.[24] Nevertheless, cohort trends in living alone and in institutions and hospitals indicate that an increasing proportion of the Japanese elderly will be living apart from family members in the future.

Japanese parents are certainly lowering their expectations of future coresidence and support. The results of the *Mainichi Newspaper*'s biennial national survey of wives of childbearing age show that the proportion planning to depend on their children in old age declined from 55 percent in 1950 to 18 percent in 1988.[25] There has also been a shift in whom among family members Japanese would want to rely on if they needed help. As of 1986, 65 percent of men over age 60 said that they would look to their wives for care. Among elderly women, 29 percent named their daughters-in-law — this response consistent with the ideal stem family — but almost as many, 23 percent, named their daughters.

The departure from the ideal is also reflected in attitudes toward inheritance. The proportion of women of childbearing age who said they would leave their property to the child who took care of them increased from 18 percent in 1963 to 32 percent in 1977. Among middle-aged males, it

21. H. Yuan Tien and Che-fu Lee, "New Demographics and Old Designs: The Chinese Family amid Induced Population Transition," *Social Science Quarterly*, 69(3):615 (Sept. 1988).

22. Linda G. Martin, "The Graying of Japan," *Population Bulletin*, 44(2):14 (June 1989).

23. Atoh, "Changes in Family Patterns in Japan," p. 36.

24. Daisaku Maeda, "The Role of Families in the Care of the Elderly" (Paper delivered at the United Nations Conference on Population Aging in the Context of Urbanization, Sendai, Japan, Sept. 1988), tab. 2.

25. Martin, "Graying of Japan," p. 15.

is those in lower-status occupations who are more likely to live with their parents, reflecting perhaps their families' lesser capability of purchasing privacy and their greater need for the inheritance that coresidence may facilitate.[26]

In Korea, the proportion of persons over age 60 living with their married adult children or other married relatives declined from 71 percent in 1970 to 64 percent in 1980.[27] In 1970, more educated, married elderly persons living in urban areas were least likely to be living with children. Although changes in the composition of the population, such as increased educational attainment, greater urban residence, and less widowhood, contributed to the decline in coresidence over the decade, more important were changes in the underlying propensities for all groups to coreside. By 1980, the rural elderly were less likely to reside with their married children than the urban elderly. This change perhaps reflects the migration of the younger generation to the cities, leaving the rural elderly behind, and increased urban housing shortages.

Age differences in expectations of support in old age in Korea indicate that perhaps in the future the elderly will be more self-supporting and rely less on family members, especially on eldest sons. In 1988, 48 percent of persons ages 60 and over said that they relied on their eldest son, 20 percent on all sons, and 20 percent on sons and daughters together, while 8 percent were self-supporting. Persons 20-29 years of age had quite different expectations: 17 percent indicated that they expected reliance on eldest son; 16 percent, all sons; 44 percent, sons and daughters together; and 17 percent, self.[28]

In mainland China, estimates of the proportion of the elderly living with their adult children are available only from small surveys in the 1980s and generally are in the 60 to 80 percent range, with rural coresidence greater than urban. At the low end are estimates from a 1985 study of persons 60 and over in Shanghai, which has the highest concentration of older people in China. The study found that 33 percent were living with a married son, 14 percent with a married daughter, 7 percent with more than one married child, 23 percent in nuclear families, and 19 percent alone.[29] The proportion living with daughters was especially high in light of the Confucian ideal and the experience of the respondents' parents, only 6 percent of whom had lived with a married daughter, while 51 percent had lived with a married son.

Evidence of decline over time in coresidence in a Chinese population is also available from Taiwan. Survey data from married women ages 20-39 indicate that the proportion of their husbands' parents living or eating with a married son declined from 81 percent in 1973 to 69 percent in 1985.[30] These changes in behavior were preceded by considerable changes in expectations about coresidence in old age. The proportion of women 20-39 expecting to live with their sons in old age declined from 94 percent in 1965 to 54 percent in

26. Martin and Tsuya, "Interactions of Middle-Aged Japanese," p. 21.

27. Susan DeVos and Yean-Ju Lee, "Change in Extended Family Living among the Elderly in South Korea, 1970-1980" (CDE Working Paper no. 88-43, Center for Demography and Ecology, University of Wisconsin, Madison, 1988).

28. National Bureau of Statistics, *Social Indicators in Korea 1988* (Seoul: Economic Planning Board, 1989), p. 276.

29. Tamara K. Hareven, "Reflections on Family Research in the People's Republic of China," *Social Research*, 54(4):676 (Winter 1987).

30. Weinstein et al., "Household Composition," tab. 5.

1973.[31] Declining expectations were found for all educational groups and for both urban and rural residents, indicating that it was not simply compositional shifts in the population that led to the decline but rather change that permeated all sectors of the population.

Of course, living together is only one measure of family relations, and, just as in most societies, there are stresses of coresidence. Living in a multigenerational household is no guarantee of emotional or financial well-being of the elderly, and some elderly may be better off living separately.[32] Furthermore, in the case of the frail elderly, considerable stress on the younger generation may result. Daisaku Maeda, a leading Japanese gerontologist, notes, "The term 'family care' has a beautiful and noble connotation, but, in many cases, it is accompanied by the painful sacrifice of the caretakers, and the quality of care is frequently poor."[33]

Tales of disagreements between mothers-in-law and daughters-in-law are common in East Asia, although there is evidence that the balance of power is shifting from the older to the younger generation, which is better educated and more likely to be employed outside the home. In Japan, the child-care assistance given by mothers-in-law is thought to have facilitated the labor force participation of younger married women and to have helped perpetuate multigenerational coresidence.[34] Accord-

ingly, it should not be assumed that coresidence represents only a one-way flow of support from the younger to the older generation.

Contact across household boundaries

Intergenerational support across household boundaries is also an important part of family relations, as is strongly demonstrated in the West. Only for Japan is there limited information about such interaction, and most of it focuses on social contact and distinctions between urban and rural households. Survey data from 1964-65 indicate that urban dwellers were generally less likely to rely on family members for various forms of assistance than were rural dwellers.[35] Friends and coworkers were depended on relatively more in the urban area. Visits between noncoresident family members were also less frequent in the city. Surprisingly, perhaps, in the urban area, contact with wife's family was more frequent than contact with husband's family. Contact on ritual occasions, such as marriages and funerals, was relatively greater with husband's family, but more informal association was greater with wife's.

Data from a 1988 national family survey in Japan indicate that even though men ages 30-59 were more likely to live with their parents than were women the same age—35 versus 9 percent—and lived closer to their noncoresident parents than did women, women saw their noncoresident parents almost as frequently as men saw theirs, and they phoned them more often.[36] The importance of relations with wife's kin is also exhibited in the extent to which ancestor

31. Lolagene C. Coombs and Te-Hsiung Sun, "Familial Values in a Developing Society: A Decade of Change in Taiwan," *Social Forces,* 59(4):1241 (June 1981).

32. Linda G. Martin, "The Aging of Asia," *Journal of Gerontology: Social Science,* 43(4):S110 (July 1988).

33. Maeda, "Role of Families," p. 17.

34. S. Philip Morgan and Kiyosi Hirosima, "The Persistence of Extended Family Residence in Japan: Anachronism or Alternative Strategy?" *American Sociological Review,* 48:270 (Apr. 1983).

35. Takashi Koyama, "Rural-Urban Comparison of Kinship Relations in Japan," in *Families in East and West,* ed. Hill and Konig, pp. 318-37.

36. Martin and Tsuya, "Interaction of Middle-Aged Japanese," p. 31.

worship in Japan has become less exclusively patrilineal and more bilateral.[37]

Increasing contact with wife's natal family is also thought to be occurring in Korea and China, although ritual forms may remain the same.[38] It is argued that because of later ages at marriage, there is a longer period in which daughters form relations with their families. Furthermore, as female education and labor force participation increase, daughters — especially those who live in cities — are seen as increasingly valuable resources for the entire kin group.[39]

CONCLUSION

The cynic might ask, "If the ideal of filial piety were truly practiced, why has there been a need for penalties against unfilial children in the criminal codes of China from the time of the Tang dynasty (618-907) to the present?" The reality is that through the centuries in East Asia, there has been tension between family ideals, laws, and practices.

The postwar period has been a time of great political, economic, and social change, and intergenerational relations, though not totally transformed, have also changed. Even so, it is not the first time that new ideals and practices have come into conflict with the old. In fact, in some instances, today's changes represent returns to pre-Confucianization practices.

Although the three societies start from different points and have been influenced by different policies and historical events, in recent decades similar forces have operated in all. Demographic change has led to population aging and, for individuals, fewer but longer kin relationships. Migration has separated the generations, and there is some indication that even where coresidence is possible, individuals with greater economic resources are opting for greater privacy. To the extent that today's cross-sectional predictors of coresidence and changing attitudes and expectations can foretell the future, the trend toward family generations' living separately is likely to continue in East Asia.

Also affecting intergenerational relations is the changing role of women. Although in none of the societies is the constitutional model of equal rights matched in practice and although patriarchal ideology remains strong, the increased economic role of women outside the home, as well as the demographic reality that there simply will not be as many adult sons per family in the future, means that bilateral ties will continue to grow in importance.

To the extent that the older generation needs help from the younger generation, however, families — women in particular — will be less available to provide time-intensive services. Public and private-market providers will increasingly be called upon. But it should be noted that just as families are changing, so are the elderly. Tomorrow's elderly will most likely be healthier, better educated, and richer than today's, and they may have prepared for old age with very different expectations. Accordingly, tomorrow's elderly are likely to be more independent and to increasingly prefer the intimacy at a distance in their

37. Kiyomi Morioka, "Ancestor Worship in Contemporary Japan: Continuity and Change," in *Religion and the Family in East Asia,* ed. De Vos and Sofue, p. 206.

38. Chae-Sok Choe, "Family and Kinship Organization," in *Introduction to Korean Studies* (Seoul: National Academy of Sciences, 1987), p. 690; Deborah Davis-Friedmann, *Long Lives: Chinese Elderly and the Communist Revolution* (Cambridge, MA: Harvard University Press, 1983), p. 59.

39. Susan Greenhalgh, "Networks and Their Nodes: Urban Society on Taiwan," *China Quarterly,* 99:551 (1984).

relations with family members that is the norm in the West today.

Even so, it is unlikely that East Asian families will soon resemble Western families or that families of the three societies examined in this article will converge in form and practices. Change is not necessarily unidirectional. Besides different starting points, different policies may affect family life in each country. The new responsibility system in China, for example, is thought to be reversing the decline in the economic role of the family, though that was not its express purpose. What remains to be seen is whether governments can successfully influence changes in other family relations in such a way that support for the elderly does not increasingly become a government function.

ANNALS, *AAPSS*, **510**, July 1990

Transformations in Sub-Saharan African Marriage and Fertility

By CAROLINE BLEDSOE

ABSTRACT: Among populations that value high fertility, marital practices often play important roles in regulating fertility. This article interprets ethnographic and demographic data to examine changes in contemporary African marriage. It shows that female education exacerbates inequities between de facto polygynous women who previously would have lived together, shared household resources, and acknowledged each other as cowives. These new forms of polygyny, however, hold an important key to explaining why polygyny and high fertility still proliferate. Men sustain the costs of polygyny and of high fertility in large part by marginalizing low-status women, usually those with the least education, as outside wives and their children as outside children.

Caroline Bledsoe is associate professor of anthropology at Northwestern University. She received her Ph.D. in anthropology from Stanford University. She has written on marriage, fertility, child fosterage, child mortality, literacy, and politics in Liberia and Sierra Leone.

AS late as 25 years ago, many experts predicted that areas such as Southeast Asia and Latin America would sustain high birth rates until population cataclysms forced reductions. Yet fertility rates throughout the world have declined dramatically. The major exception is sub-Saharan Africa where, according to 1989 Population Reference Bureau figures, the total fertility rate — the number of children a woman can be expected to bear — is 6.3, the highest in the world. Most demographers believe that overall African fertility will decline, and recent information from demographic and health surveys suggests that fertility levels are declining slightly in a few areas. But how or when major transitions in reproduction may occur is unclear.

To address this question, this article examines marriage, an important determinant of fertility among populations wherein people make few attempts to regulate births. Incorporating ethnographic data with overall trends in the marriage market, I examine the social dynamics behind apparently clear-cut demographic figures, focusing on people's efforts to construe marital status and parenthood to their advantage. The analysis applies to much of sub-Saharan Africa but draws most examples from Sierra Leone, where I have conducted ethnographic fieldwork.

DETERMINANTS OF FERTILITY IN NATURAL-FERTILITY POPULATIONS

Like families elsewhere, those in Africa face mounting difficulties in raising children. Urbanization and economic recession have eroded the utility of children as subsistence laborers and have increased the costs of their maintenance and education. Yet on the whole, families still value

high fertility.[1] Girls of five and over help with farm work, cooking, cleaning the house, bringing water, and looking after smaller children. Boys are put to work also, though they have more license to roam about town with friends. As adults, children who leave for urban employment are reminded at every opportunity that their remittances are vital to their rural kin. Those who remain at home take over the household and its financial matters, allowing their parents to assume the roles of elder statesmen who bestow advice and blessings on the young and to die peacefully, relying on their children to give them a decent burial and to keep alive their names and deeds. In Sierra Leone, even the changes wrought by Christianity and education have not dampened the attitude that unmarried mothers are far better off than childless women. Indeed, anxious kin may pressure an older educated daughter to begin having children, although no permanent husband may be in sight.

Men want children as much as women do. Although men have fewer immediate uses than women for children's labor, a child creates a firmer link for a man to a woman's potentially advantageous family. Children also enhance men's long-term hopes for improving the material well-being of their families and their ability to compete with rival families for positions of political leadership and material pos-

1. One reason why fertility remains valued in Africa is that many people take responsibility for, and can demand benefits from, children. For example, fostering children out temporarily to be raised or trained adjusts family size and composition socially and takes economic pressure off parents without limiting their biological fertility. See Caroline Bledsoe, "The Politics of Children: Fosterage and the Social Management of Fertility among the Mende of Sierra Leone," in *Births and Power: The Politics of Reproduction,* ed. W. Penn Handwerker (Boulder, CO: Westview Press, 1990), pp. 81-100.

sessions, including rights to preferred farmland. Not surprisingly, men are warned against marrying infertile women; some even require proof of fertility before marriage.

Most demographers agree that where the demand for children is high and few women employ birth-control measures, "natural fertility"[2] determines reproductive levels. That is, women do not alter their fertility behavior appreciably from the first to the last child. In such populations, one important determinant of fertility levels is the range of social practices that affect child spacing. In Africa, most child spacing occurs through long periods of breast-feeding, which prolongs amenorrhea, and of sexual abstinence while a baby nurses: up to two years or more. Such practices are sustained in part by widespread beliefs that male sexual fluids contaminate breast milk and harm nursing babies.

Another factor that determines fertility in natural-fertility populations is marital practices, especially the time that fertile women spend in conjugal union. Age at first marriage is particularly important because the total number of births women have through the reproductive period is largely a function of the age at first marriage, which usually initiates regular child-bearing. Changes in this variable and other demographic underpinnings of marriage — prevalence of polygyny; proportions of fertile women who are married; and rates of divorce, widowhood, and remarriage — offer key areas for researchers interested in potential fertility declines.

MARRIAGE IN AFRICA

What is marriage like in sub-Saharan Africa? Despite extraordinary diversity across the continent as well as within soci-eties, almost all women marry, and they remarry quickly after divorce or widow-hood. Women also marry comparatively young; mean ages range from 16 to 18 years. They marry men substantially older, on average, than themselves. The institution that maximizes the time women spend in union, despite wide age gaps between spouses and often high rates of divorce, is polygyny.

Contrary to predictions that polygynous societies will inevitably become monogamous, sub-Saharan Africa is the only major world region in which polygyny is still widely practiced, despite the welter of legal and religious codes that colonial as well as modern states have created to curb it. Although not every marriage is polygynous, men who manage to marry more than one wife gain power and prestige as well as the possibility of numerous children. Polygyny also offers a man links of political alliance and economic support with a wide range of families. On the other hand, women, as cowives, can gain help from each other with domestic chores and with child care. Given a choice, however, most young women prefer monogamous marriage to gain greater leverage with husbands and liberate themselves from the work demands of domineering senior wives. Not surprisingly, as they grow older and gain junior wives of their own, their opinions of polygyny often improve.

Transformations occurring in conjugal relations have been truly dramatic, at least on the surface. Twenty-five years ago, Evans-Pritchard described marriage in so-called simple African societies as a given: there was no such thing as an unmarried adult woman.[3] Moreover, companionship in marriage was described as weak, and

2. Louis Henry, "Some Data on Natural Fertility," *Eugenics Quarterly*, 8(2):81-91 (1961).

3. E. E. Evans-Pritchard, *The Position of Women in Primitive Societies and Other Essays in Social Anthropology* (New York: Free Press, 1965).

women were seen as having little choice in whether to marry. Although these generalizations were too broad, the last quarter century has seen sweeping changes. Especially among educated people, many marriages are celebrated under the auspices of the Christian church or national civil codes, marriage age appears to be rising, partner selection is becoming more a matter of personal choice than of family dictate, distant formality between spouses is being replaced by love and companionship, bridewealth — money or goods given to the woman's family by the man in exchange for her labor and reproductive services — is growing less common, and educated women or those with independent incomes can more easily divorce unsatisfactory husbands.[4]

These changes appear to have come about more through pragmatic adaptations to the exigencies of economic and social life, however, than through national civil or religious codes, which often remain remote from, if not irrelevant to, their intended beneficiaries. Today, bridewealth is being replaced by help from the man with his wife's school fees or her parents' taxes or medical expenses, most civil or religious marriages begin as customary marriages before being formalized by religious or

4. Christine Oppong, *Marriage among a Matrilineal Elite: A Family Study of Ghanaian Senior Civil Servants* (New York: Cambridge University Press, 1974); Barbara Harrell-Bond, *Modern Marriage in Sierra Leone* (The Hague: Mouton, 1975); Caroline H. Bledsoe, *Women and Marriage in Kpelle Society* (Stanford, CA: Stanford University Press, 1980); Christine Obbo, *African Women: Their Struggle for Economic Independence* (London: Zed Press, 1980); Kristin Mann, *Marrying Well: Marriage, Status and Social Change among the Educated Elite in Colonial Lagos* (New York: Cambridge University Press, 1985); the contributions to *Transformations of African Marriage*, ed. David Parkin and Davin Nyamwaya (Manchester: Manchester University Press, 1987).

civil ceremony, and married Christian men sometimes marry additional wives by customary law or by taking outside wives.

PROBLEMS IN DEFINING AND ANALYZING AFRICAN MARRIAGE

These changes occurring in marriage and their possible links to fertility change open fascinating areas for new research. Before addressing these questions, however, we must confront three issues concerning marriage that complicate attempts to analyze African material and weaken the reliability of causal inferences between marriage and fertility.

Defining marriage

The first problem is that of defining when marriage begins and ends. African marriage is often a long, ambiguous process rather than a unitary event.[5] It may extend over a period of months or even years, as partners and their families work cautiously toward more stable conjugal relationships. A girl, sometimes with her family's implicit permission, may test out potential relationships with several young men before establishing a more permanent one. For many a girl, youth consists of preparing for life with a man with whom her family began marital negotiations when she was a toddler or even before birth, while her conjugal life may be marked by periodic disputes about outstanding bridewealth debts.

Even as a process, marriage transactions do not constitute a clear linear sequence. At some point, ceremonies may be performed, cash or tokens exchanged, cohabitation and sexual relations begun, and

5. See especially John L. Comaroff and Simon Roberts, "Marriage and Extra-Marital Sexuality: The Dialectics of Legal Change among the Kgatla," *Journal of African Law*, 21:97-123 (1977).

children born. But these events do not follow predictably from each other, and people may move back and forth between forms of union with little fanfare. And if analysts are confused about the legal status of a union, conjugal partners themselves may disagree about this point or change their minds well after the relationship appears settled.

To accommodate the difficulty that these definitional problems pose, some demographers are trying to reformulate their definitions to encompass new forms of marriage or reemerging old ones. Others attempt to identify the culturally relevant stages in the conjugal process and the conditions under which the order may change.[6]

Despite such efforts, a more substantial definitional problem threatens to undermine all attempts to categorize unions: that is, conjugal relationships are becoming more fluid, particularly as conjugal forms diversify with rapid societal transformation. Examining the Yoruba of Nigeria, Guyer points out that as national economic crises deepen, and cash, petrol, and food grow more scarce, a woman maximizes her chances for economic security by creating links to several men.[7] Because a man is much more likely to respond to his child's need for support than the needs of a temporary girlfriend, a woman can press her economic demands on a particular man, whether or not they call their relationship a marriage, with far greater leverage if she has a child by him. Therefore, although a woman cannot marry polygamously, she can be managing ties with several men at once, through what Guyer calls "polyandrous motherhood," making marriage almost incidental to her reproductive career.[8] Thus, to bemoan the demise of stable African marriage and family structures, as some observers have, is to misunderstand their intrinsic dynamism, as Burnham stresses:

It seems analytically valuable to consider all forms of conjugal relations, from consensual unions to "ordinance" or "church" marriages, as representing a bundle of interactional possibilities with associated political, economic, legal and other implications. How these interactional possibilities are utilised by male and female actors is a central, if very complex, question for future research.[9]

Multiple-partnership unions

Another factor undermining our confidence in straightforward links between marriage and fertility is the ease with which women can be absorbed into polygynous unions. The overall effects of polygyny at the societal level are still unclear.[10]

6. See, for example, Etienne van de Walle and Dominique Meekers, "Marriage Drinks and Kola Nuts" (Paper delivered at the IUSSP Seminar on Nuptiality in Sub-Saharan Africa: Current Changes and Impact on Fertility, Paris, 1988).

7. Jane I. Guyer, "Changing Nuptiality in a Nigerian Community: Observations from the Field" (Paper delivered at the IUSSP Seminar on Nuptiality in Sub-Saharan Africa: Current Changes and Impact on Fertility, Paris, 1988).

8. Such strategies obviously become riskier in the era of acquired immune deficiency syndrome. Yet condoms, because they block fertility, face an uphill battle for acceptance in Africa because they undermine the core of stable heterosexual relations.

9. Philip Burnham, "Changing Themes in the Analysis of African Marriage," in *Transformations of African Marriage*, ed. Parkin and Nyamwaya, p. 50.

10. For recent discussion, see Monique Borgerhoff Mulder, "Marital Status and Reproductive Performance in Kipsigis Women: Re-Evaluating the Polygyny-Fertility Hypothesis," *Population Studies*, 43:285-304 (1989); Michel Garenne and Etienne van de Walle, "Polygyny and Fertility among the Sereer of Senegal," *Population Studies*, 43:267-83 (1989); Noreen Goldman and Anne Pebley, "The Demography of Polygyny in Sub-Saharan Africa," in *Reproduction and Social Organization in Sub-Saharan Africa*, ed. Ron Lesthaeghe (Berkeley: University of California Press, 1989), pp. 212-37.

Polygyny may (1) increase fertility by absorbing more women in marriage, (2) decrease fertility by reducing each woman's number of sexual encounters or increasing the spread of sexually transmitted diseases, or (3) have no effect on fertility, particularly if extramarital affairs are common. Previous assumptions that polygyny decreased fertility, for example, have been questioned on the grounds that infertile women are more likely than others to be divorced and thus to become attached to polygynous unions as secondary wives.

If the complications posed by polygyny make inferences about fertility difficult, then contemporary proliferations among types of informal union compound the problem. More freedom of partner choice, increased geographical mobility, higher female education levels, and access to more economic resources all mean that young women are less compelled to marry, or remain with, older, more traditional men and uneducated senior wives. But although formal polygyny does appear to be diminishing, it is being replaced, especially in urban areas, with de facto polygynous templates: serial monogamy, *deuxieme bureau* ("second office"), outside marriage, polyandrous motherhood, and sugar-daddy relationships. Because polygyny appears to be thriving through these alternative forms, it is difficult to draw reliable inferences about fertility's association with reported marital status.

Formal education for women

Many rural African girls see education as their primary hope of leaving low-status subsistence farming and becoming urban career women and monogamous wives, since most men with a secondary-school education have only one legal wife at a time. All 26 girls in a rural Sierra Leonean secondary school I surveyed, which had 112 boys, wanted to be lawyers, doctors, nurses, bank managers, teachers, or accountants. All wanted to attend college, and many wanted Ph.D.'s and M.D.'s.

Despite these ambitions, the numbers of rural female students dwindle rapidly as girls approach puberty. Families that contemplate the substantial expenses of secondary schooling usually choose a boy to send ahead, hoping that he, in turn, will help his siblings with their schooling. One reason families give girls lower priority is that they fear that an educated woman swelled with her own importance will become an arrogant wife who quarrels with her uneducated cowives, refuses farm work, and flaunts the authority of her husband, whose allegiance the family has cultivated. But the bottom line is often economic: investing in a girl's education risks a substantial waste of money, since people fear that her school career may be terminated abruptly by pregnancy. Still, many parents recognize the benefits to be gained from an educated daughter, particularly her ability to secure a white-collar job and to marry a man with one.

In other areas of the world, increases in the education of girls have dramatically lowered fertility levels by, among other things, delaying marriage. In Africa, fertility is indeed somewhat lower among educated women. But substantial fertility declines are offset by reduced periods of breast-feeding and postpartum abstinence, as educated mothers learn that concurrent breast-feeding and sex do not harm babies and as they begin to use commercial infant formulas. Education also erodes associations between fertility and marriage through rising premarital fertility among girls who want to continue schooling. This suggests that one of the principal tenets of demography, that educated women have lower fertility because of their educations, may prove problematic for Africa. In fact, because education is so valued, the reverse may apply: young women who manage to avoid pregnancy through birth control, abortion, or infertility get more education.

Education poses a more subtle difficulty for fertility inferences, however, one that brings us back to the problems of defining marriage and reckoning with informal unions. The analytical problem is that educated women who enter forms of union that precede or supplant formal marriage are much less likely than uneducated women to claim they are married. Using Brandon's 1984 survey, we found that educated women in Freetown reported the longest delays in marrying.[11] But we believe that many of these reported differences are artifacts of different definitions of marriage to which the two groups of women subscribe. Lacking an objective definition of marriage that is independent of education makes it impossible to test hypotheses linking the two variables.

Uneducated women appeared willing to declare themselves married after customary ceremonies, at earlier stages in the marital process, and to enter polygynous unions with already married men. By contrast, educated women may have acknowledged being married only if their partners had no other wives — and if they had undergone the church or civil ceremonies that betoken so-called modern women, events that usually come late in the conjugal process. Hence external influences, including injunctions from Christian churches to distinguish once and for all between married

11. Anastasia Brandon and Caroline Bledsoe, "The Effects of Education and Social Stratification on Marriage and the Transition to Parenthood in Greater Freetown, Sierra Leone" (Paper delivered at the IUSSP Seminar on Nuptiality in Sub-Saharan Africa: Current Changes and Impact on Fertility, Paris, 1988).

and unmarried people, appear less to constrain behavior or eliminate ambiguity than to create new idioms, such as church marriage or outside wife, for legitimizing choices.

Significantly, even though highly educated women in the survey married much later than uneducated women, education had remarkably little effect on age at first birth; both groups had their first births at about the same ages. It is striking, in fact, that educated — thus largely Christian — women preferred to define these births as premarital, rather than admit being married solely through customary rites.

EFFECTS OF EDUCATION ON THE MARRIAGE MARKET

As these problems suggest, analysts increasingly recognize the futility in trying to pigeonhole phenomena that are inherently ambiguous and fluid. To gain insight into the social dynamics that create demographic outcomes, therefore, we need to abandon the search for categorical precision and confront squarely the fact of ambiguous conjugal unions. After establishing more realistic notions of conjugal relations that reflect people's efforts to shape their family commitments through social means, we can return to ask how fertility may be changing in response to actors' needs and goals in the context of educational and economic changes.

Though education may have less effect on age at first union or first birth than on women's efforts to label their unions strategically, it has powerful effects on the formal marriage market: sheer numbers of marriageable individuals. Female education effectively constricts the formal marriage market for educated women by decreasing the number of men they find most acceptable — those who are both educated and unmarried — and by making them delay entry into formal union in hopes of better matches.[12] As a Sierra Leonean man affirmed to me:

I don't know of any woman who was in secondary school who is married polygamously. Any woman who has finished Class 8 [eighth grade] will probably be a sort of mistress [outside wife], rather than a polygamous wife. . . . Many of the women working in the offices now who are educated and unmarried are somebody's mistress. But especially now, people don't look down on this so much.

If, however, we incorporate the phenomenon of informal polygyny, we gain important insights into these demographic processes; we find that female education is exacerbating inequities between de facto polygynous wives and their respective children. Polygyny is often seen as an equalizer in Africa, spreading resources among a man's wives and children.[13] This is perhaps going too far; even in the past, polygynous wives were differentiated by family status and seniority in the household. But nowadays if a man already has an educated wife, then his newly acquired uneducated woman will likely remain a country or outside wife and live in a more rural area or a poorer neighborhood.

On the other hand, a newly acquired educated woman will almost certainly displace an uneducated wife, as a case from my fieldwork illustrates. A young rural man with a few years of primary education married an illiterate woman through customary procedures. Within a few years, his trading business grew, and a local family removed one of its daughters from primary school to become his second wife. Both women bore children. As his urban career began to spiral, he moved to Freetown, bought some large cargo trucks and a supermarket, and celebrated a church marriage to a highly educated Freetown woman. From that time, little was heard about the first two wives or their children; the man kept them in the background and downplayed the validity of their ties to him. Indeed, the new wife insisted that she was the only wife. Her children were educated in Freetown, while the others managed to attend school up-country by drawing on the meager resources of their maternal families. These children became increasingly marginalized, geographically as well as socially.

Although strong incentives for polygyny remain, therefore, a man facing economic and social pressures can initiate several potential conjugal links but minimize his costs by eventually selecting a principal wife and marginalizing the rest as outside wives.[14] In effect, education intensifies differences between women who previously would have lived together, shared household resources, and acknowledged each other as cowives.

12. See also Wambui Wa Karanja, " 'Outside Wives' and 'Inside Wives' in Nigeria: A Study of Changing Perceptions in Marriage," in *Transformations of African Marriage*, ed. Parkin and Nyamwaya, pp. 247-62. Very elite urban men, however, may disregard these proscriptions and openly acknowledge multiple wives. See, for example, Remi Clignet, *Many Wives, Many Powers: Authority and Power in Polygynous Families* (Evanston, IL: Northwestern University Press, 1970).

13. Jack Goody, *Production and Reproduction: A Comparative Study of the Domestic Domain* (New York: Cambridge University Press, 1976).

14. Data from a recent historical ethnography document findings for a Portuguese village that bear striking parallels to contemporary African trends. They show that illegitimacy has provided a key source of cheap labor for the wealthy and the landed without posing threats to local patrimonies. See Brian J. O'Neill, *Social Inequality in a Portuguese Hamlet: Land, Late Marriage, and Bastardy, 1870-1978* (New York: Cambridge University Press, 1987).

EFFECTS OF EDUCATION AND ECONOMIC RECESSION ON MARRIAGE AND FERTILITY

As long as children remain women's best claims to male resources, the ambiguity and flux in marriage that education produces mean that women will continue, on the whole, to want many children. This means, in turn, that age at first birth will be related tenuously at best to marital status. Yet just as we looked beyond formal marriage as the only significant union, insights into the dynamics of reproduction begin to emerge when we move beyond initial biological events to social aspects of fertility that occur after the birth of a child: in particular, to male efforts to sustain high fertility, yet minimize its escalating costs, by according different degrees of support and recognition to their children.

Strategies for shaping families by social means fall into two categories: additive and decremental. Concerning additive marital strategies, men and women can add partners either serially or concurrently, whether or not these unions are recognized formally as marriage. Conversely, divorce or separation shapes marital links by decrement.

For fertility, additive reproductive strategies include curing infertility, taking in foster children, and so on. But shaping fertility by processes of decrement raises the most unsettling questions. We can best address them by recognizing that because of the uncertainty of their own future welfare, young adults at the beginning of their reproductive careers would be foolish to outline a clear fertility-limitation strategy. Rather, they try to keep their options open, shaping their family size and composition as conjugal events unfold and new options and constraints emerge. In this view, pregnancies and births constitute an array of potentialities that adults can reassess and adjust as future circumstances arise.

A woman, of course, can employ selection strategies. A woman trying to build stable relations with a man would be foolish to contracept. Deteriorating conjugal relations can undermine the potential of a pregnancy for her, however, and induce her to abort.[15] Selection strategies also account for many cases of child fosterage, as when a woman contracts a relationship with a new man who is not her child's father,[16] and for associations between mother's conjugal status and child survival.[17]

Recognizing that families can be shaped and pruned brings us back to the issue of de facto polygyny, wherein men's perspectives become vital. In fact, because polygyny traditionally allowed most women to marry, these new forms are central to current transformations in African marriage and fertility.

Some scholars argue that because all children belong, in theory, to the mother's or father's family, there is no such thing as an illegitimate child in sub-Saharan Africa. But a man contemplating sending all his children to elite schools, perhaps abroad, or buying equally expensive books and

15. This is suggested by the findings in John Caldwell and Pat Caldwell, "Marital Status and Abortion in Sub-Saharan Africa" (Paper delivered at the IUSSP Seminar on Nuptiality in Sub-Saharan Africa: Current Changes and Impact on Fertility, Paris, 1988).

16. Hilary Page, "Child-Rearing versus Child-Bearing: Co-Residence of Mother and Children in Sub-Saharan Africa," in *Reproduction and Social Organization*, ed. Lesthaeghe, pp. 401-41; Caroline Bledsoe, "Differential Care of Children of Previous Unions within Mende Households in Sierra Leone" (Paper delivered at the Health Transition Workshop, "Cultural, Social and Behavioural Determinants of Health: What Is the Evidence?" Canberra, Australia, 1989).

17. Olukunle Adegbola "A Comparative Analysis of Children of Informal and Formal Unions" (Paper delivered at the IUSSP Seminar on Mortality and Society in Sub-Saharan Africa, Yaounde, Cameroon, 1987); Dominique Meekers, "Consequences of Marriage and Premarital Childbearing in Côte d'Ivoire" (Manuscript, University of Pennsylvania, 1989).

uniforms for them all — and in a badly inflated economy — would find his costs prohibitive. Hence economic pressures as well as social pressures to maintain the appearance of monogamy are now inducing many men to draw harder lines between their inside and outside children.

Since the potential value of children remains as great for men as for women, foreclosing options by limiting biological fertility makes poor sense to men. Just as a man can decrease the costs of polygyny by marginalizing outside wives, so he can try to control socially the costs of fertility by investing selectively in children. This makes maternal status — always a point of potential differentiation within polygynous families — a locus of increasing discrimination. A man may single out the children of high-status, educated women for substantial educational investment, while casting the children of low-status or ephemeral unions as outside children whose costs of rearing and educating can be minimized.

Escalating costs further deepen these disparities. While children of educated, high-status mothers become defined as inside children and move up the ranks of society through education or prestigious marriages, their success stories mask an equally potent tendency for other women and children to become defined as outside and to slide down the scale. Children who become defined as illegitimate or outside are more likely to become malnourished, live with caretakers who exploit their labor, and eventually produce outside children themselves.[18]

In sum, the thesis that men can prune their familial obligations by singling out inside wives and children and marginaliz-

18. See also Harrell-Bond, *Modern Marriage in Sierra Leone*, p. 134.

ing the rest suggests that men do not necessarily abandon polygyny or high fertility because they have ingested Western beliefs or norms, a common scholarly assumption. Nor do men necessarily decide at the outset of their marital careers to marry monogamously. Rather, they can become monogamous — and high fertility can become low fertility — through decremental social processes of withdrawing support and recognition from low-status wives and children.

CONCLUSION

Africa is clearly experiencing vast shifts in marriage and fertility patterns. The trajectories of these two domains are not immediately obvious, however. Nor is the relationship between marital and fertility change as straightforward as we might expect if we looked merely, for example, at reported ages of first marriage. One reason, as I have suggested, is that the combination of intrinsic ambiguity and radical change in marriage particularly among educated individuals is making men reduce their fertility costs less by decreasing their biological fertility or numbers of conjugal partners than by marginalizing children whose maternal families have the least access to wealth, power, or education.

Yet we must interpret this trend carefully. It would be misleading to create a dichotomy between societies with ambiguous, vacillating rules governing marriage and responsibility toward children and those with clear-cut, stable rules. Adults in all societies constantly reshape their family structures through social means: creating new ties, strengthening old ones, or redefining burdensome ones, in ways that cumbersome biological fertility cannot do. As such, any society can create maneuvering room, if needed, to regulate the costs of children, even within monogamous unions that everyone regards as legitimate. For example, I find striking parallels between the situations of outside wives in Africa and those of young in-married wives in extended households in prerevolutionary China. Greenhalgh and Qiaozhuan attribute high child mortality rates in China before the 1950s to the fact that senior members of patriarchal families accorded low status to young wives and allocated them few resources to expend on their children.[19]

Whereas a superficial analysis might conclude that deteriorating morals as well as the erosion of traditional norms in Africa are producing more outside marriages and children, I favor a different interpretation: in the crunch between their efforts to advance in the ranks of the educated elite and increasing economic difficulties, men respond by constricting the range of wives and children whom they are willing to recognize as legitimate.

Because individual children's chances for survival as well as social mobility are uncertain, adults would be foolish to outline at the outset of their reproductive careers a clear fertility-limitation strategy. It makes more sense to keep one's options open by continuing to initiate conjugal links and to bear children, treating each event as the beginning of a long, continuously assessed relationship that may eventually merit either greater investment or termination, depending on future circumstances.

Expanding the question of the costs and benefits of children to the postnatal stage thus demands that we ask how trends in marriage affect people's expenditures for children already born. Shifts in the statuses of different kinds of conjugal unions may have more impact in the immediate future on child health and welfare than on fertility.

19. Susan Greenhalgh and Liang Qiaozhuan, "The Family Revolution and Child Mortality in Rural Shaanxi, 1940s-1980s" (Paper delivered at the IUSSP Seminar on Mortality Transition in South and East Asia, Beijing, 1988). Other practices in various parts of the world that effectively reduce the costs of fertility include the neglect of girls, high-order siblings, fostered children, and deformed children. For a review of these issues, see Caroline Bledsoe and H. Kimball Hirschman, "Case Studies of Mortality: Anthropological Contributions" (Paper delivered at the Twenty-First General Conference of the IUSSP, New Delhi, 1989).

Fertility and Mortality Decline
in Latin America

By ALBERTO PALLONI

ABSTRACT: During the twentieth century the population of Latin America has undergone three momentous shifts. One of these affected mortality, and the other two involved marital and general fertility. Different countries, however, experienced these shifts at different times and with different intensities. As a consequence, the patterns of population growth are very diverse and difficult to classify. In this article an attempt is made to construct a typology of population trends in Latin America by identifying similarities and differences in the levels, patterns, and changes of fertility and mortality. The typology is used to review the most important macro and micro determinants of the observed population trends.

Alberto Palloni is a professor of sociology and demography at the Center for Demography and Ecology, University of Wisconsin. He received his B.A. in sociology from the Catholic University of Chile in 1971 and his Ph.D. in sociology from the University of Washington in 1977. He has done research on indirect methods of estimation, formal demography, mortality, and fertility. He is currently engaged in research on the modeling of the spread of acquired immune deficiency syndrome in Africa and Latin America. He is also completing two books on the history of the population in Latin America since 1850.

IN 1859 Juan Bautista Alberdi, an Argentinean intellectual, proclaimed that "to govern is to populate." This pro-growth posture was officially incorporated in the Argentinean Constitution and has until very recently permeated at least the rhetoric if not the actions of a significant number of Latin American governments. Strong nationalism, suspicion and rivalries between neighboring countries, and, at least in some countries prior to 1930, perceived needs for manpower and a skilled labor force fueled liberal immigration policies and pronatalism. The official pronatalist stance reinforced high-fertility norms inherited from the era of the Spanish Conquest. This ideology was strengthened by the staunch opposition of the Catholic Church to any form of birth control.

Although rapid population growth in the continent is not totally unrelated to official ideology, the deeds and omissions of governments, or popular adherence to the dogma of the Catholic Church, it would certainly be an oversimplification to search no further for explanations of Latin American growth patterns. Population trends in Latin America are the outcome of a complex set of factors, some of which are rooted in particular historical conditions of specific places while others are more pervasive, although experienced with different timing and intensity. The result is a variety of population regimes not unlike that of the so-called more advanced nations of Western Europe or North America.

Starting in 1900, population trends in Latin America underwent three important shifts with long-lasting consequences. The first and perhaps best known is the change in the levels and patterns of mortality. Beginning shortly before 1945 and extending through the mid-1980s, life expectancies began an irreversible increase from values of about 35 years to values above 60. The rapidly ascending trend in life expectancies proceeded undisturbed for at least two decades and resulted in a period of unprecedented expansion of the rates of natural growth. A second shift, much less known, more debatable, and less pervasive than the previous one, is a transient, short-lived, but perceptible increase in fertility within the period between 1950 and 1960. The third and final shift is of more recent origin and parallels very closely in speed and magnitude the past changes in mortality: a very sudden and accelerated decline of fertility that began in the late 1960s to middle 1970s and that swept across most countries in Latin America. Although it has yet to run its full course, this fertility decline has already left an important imprint that will set the tone of future trends.

The characterization of Latin American population trends by means of these three landmark shifts is far from optimal. First, one removes from examination international migration flows that were particularly important at several points during the periods between 1860 and 1920 and between 1945 and 1955 in countries of the Southern Cone — Argentina, Uruguay, and, to a much lesser extent, Chile — and in Brazil, Cuba, Mexico, and Venezuela. Since the demographic impact of these migratory currents is overshadowed by those of fertility and mortality changes, however, I have chosen to make only passing references to them. Second, while the identification of three shifts is useful for extracting the most relevant features characterizing very different fertility and mortality patterns, it inevitably masks diversity in the magnitudes and variability in the timing of the country-specific shifts and obscures important national idiosyncrasies.

In what follows I review the nature of mortality decline and the trends of fertility experienced in Latin America during the period stretching from 1900 to 1985. I analyze the main features of the three population shifts by identifying the recurrent, common characteristics and by reconstructing the contrast between the demographic transition in Latin America and the demographic transition in Western Europe. But the appearance of unity in the process hides diversity of patterns. In a modest effort to capture the richness of the various patterns, I construct a typology of demographic regimes. Its goal is not so much to reproduce actual historical cases as it is to establish significant boundaries between them. The typology will make it clear that there is no single Latin American pattern of population change. I hope to show that to invoke the image of a unique experience, even if only for descriptive purposes, is highly misleading.

For the purpose of this review, the label "Latin America" will be applied to the set of countries in Central America, excluding Belize; the subset of Spanish-speaking Caribbean countries, excluding Puerto Rico; tropical South America, excluding Suriname and Guyana; and temperate South America. Altogether there are 19 countries examined in this document.

THE INITIAL AND FINAL CONDITIONS: TRENDS FROM 1900 TO 1985

By 1900 the global weighted annual natural rate of growth in Latin America hovered around .017. This was the combined outcome of a global weighted crude birth rate of about .044 and a global weighted crude mortality rate of about .027. With these rates and the implied 41 years of doubling time, the population of Latin America was far removed from the stationary demographic regime that prevailed in Western Europe on the eve of the secular transformations that swept the old continent after 1750. These conditions persisted in Latin America until the 1930s, when most countries experienced the onset of a slow but steady mortality decline. Thus, in the mid-forties, the rate of natural increase had inched upward to about .025, the crude death rate had decreased to levels around .017, and the crude birth rate remained virtually constant at levels of about .042. It is during the post-World War II period that the demographic revolution began in earnest: by 1960 the rates of natural increase had peaked at a level of .028, the crude death rate had reached .013, and the crude birth rate leveled off at .041. In the following two decades, and after a fleeting but significant period of increase, the crude birth rates began a gradual decline and so did the rates of natural increase while mortality continued at a somewhat slower pace the downward course initiated almost forty years earlier.

At the turn of the century the population of Latin America numbered no more than 61 million. By 1930 it had increased to about 100 million and by 1950, right before the rapid and massive downturn in mortality, it had already surpassed 150 million. Estimates for 1985 indicate that the total population had reached a level of about 400 million. Thus, during this century, the population of Latin America has more than quadrupled, and about three-fourths of the total growth has occurred since 1950. If the post-1950 mortality decline had followed the same average pace of the pre-1950 decline and if we neglect the potential reciprocal influence between mortality and fertility, the population in 1985 would have reached a level not higher than 269 million. Thus the accelerated post-1950 pace of mortality decline added 65 percent to the growth that would have occurred if pre-1950 mortality trends had persisted. This excess growth is partly the result of accumulated built-in momentum in the population—a younger age distribution with higher growth potential—and partly the result of the higher rates of survival to childbearing ages.

A continent of contrasts:
Heterogeneity in population trends

Since the beginning of the century, Latin American countries have shown sharp variability in population trends. The diversity is pervasive and encompasses not only population size but also the internal distribution of populations, their ethnic composition, the degree of prevalence of foreign-born populations, and, of course, fertility and mortality. Over time, diversity has alternatively shrunk and expanded as countries have responded to similar exogenous conditions and as some of them, the forerunners, have ceased to undergo trends that others, the latecomers, have experienced with some considerable delays. Yet, as I will try to show later, the various demographic transitions fall into a few classes with easily identifiable features, all of which are potentially useful for tracing the determinants and conditions that account for them.

Elsewhere, I have shown that during the period between 1900 and 1930, the natural rate of increase in most Latin American countries was close to 1.7 per thousand per annum.[1] The rates grew sharply between 1930 and 1970 as a result of falls in mortality that were not offset by fertility reductions. Finally, the rates decreased again, during the period 1970-85, as a result of a downturn in fertility. Intercountry variabil-

1. Alberto Palloni, "A Brief History of Population Trends in Latin America: 1900-1985" (Working series paper 90-02, Center for Demography and Ecology, University of Wisconsin, 1990).

ity was at a maximum during the first period and attained a minimum during the second period, when most societies went through rapid mortality decline. Throughout these periods, however, there was an intriguing grouping of countries: Argentina, Uruguay, Cuba, Costa Rica, Chile, Colombia, Panama, and Venezuela had the highest rates of increase during the first period and the lowest during the last period. These are countries that started with lower than average fertility and lower than average mortality and whose mortality transition was both more gradual and closely followed by relatively early fertility declines. Among the other countries the main differences are found in the patterns of decline in the rate of increase. Six countries— Bolivia, Guatemala, Honduras, Nicaragua, Paraguay, and Peru—showed either increases or trifling reductions between the second and third period. Finally, Brazil's and Mexico's values closely approached the values characteristic of the countries in the first group. This is the result of significant decreases in fertility that took place during the 1970s.

The sharp rises in the rates of natural increase observed in the second period had a pervasive and persistent impact on the age structure of populations. Thus, in 1960, approximately 10-15 years after the onset of the mortality decline, more than 40 percent of the population in Latin America— the exceptions being Argentina, Chile, Uruguay, and Cuba—was below age 15. By 1980-85, the populations had become less youthful, as the bulge created by earlier mortality declines at the youngest ages passed age 15. But, with the same exceptions noted previously, the proportions below age 15 were still larger than 30 percent.

It is important to note that while this preliminary clustering of countries serves heuristic purposes, it has a severe shortcoming since it masks important inter-country variability. Thus, among the members of the first group, Argentina and Uruguay resemble each other more than they do the remaining members of the group. Similarly, Chile, Cuba, and Panama are closer to each other than to Colombia and Venezuela. As I will show later in this article, the boundaries between the various groups and the lines separating the countries within each group are strongly associated with the timing and intensity of mortality and fertility decline.

MORTALITY REGIMES

The inception of different mortality regimes is by no means recent. As early as 1900 there was a slow but gradual and sustained mortality decline in countries of the Southern Cone in South America—Argentina, Uruguay, and Chile—as well as in Brazil, Colombia, Cuba, Costa Rica, and Panama. The estimated life expectancies for the period 1880-1900 in these countries were within the range 27-35. By 1930 Argentina, Costa Rica, Cuba, and probably Uruguay had attained life expectancies of 40 years or more, and by 1945 virtually all of them had reached levels of life expectancies surpassing 45 years. Although mortality declines were observed in other countries as well, they were much slower and started from considerably higher levels. On the eve of World War II, the gap between the forerunners and laggards in the mortality transition had gradually widened, but the variance within the more advanced group had also increased: some countries were benefiting more than others even though the whole group was advancing at a faster pace than the remaining countries. Table 1 displays estimated values of life expectancies in five-year periods before and after World War II.

With a few exceptions, the pre-1940 improvements in survival revealed in Table 1 cannot possibly be attributed to the application of novel medical technology. A medical or public health argument is probably pertinent only for Cuba, Panama, and Venezuela, where efforts of malaria eradication may have contributed in more than trivial ways to mortality changes. But Argentina, Uruguay, and Chile never had a high prevalence of malaria, and, as a consequence, the vector-eradication or population-relocation campaigns that were so successful in Cuba, for example, cannot be held responsible for more than trivial contributions. The bulk of medical innovations—including antibiotics, sulfonamides, and vaccines against common infections—that are broadly applicable appeared only after 1935. Taking into consideration the long lags in the diffusion of these innovations to large sections of the population in Latin America, one must conclude that their real impact has to be sought after World War II, not before. Table 2 illustrates this claim by assessing the approximate timing of the introduction of chemotherapies and prophylaxis for 10 of the most common causes of deaths in Latin America during the period of interest.[2]

But if medical innovations were unimportant before 1945 or 1950, how can one account for the sizable gains in survival during the first thirty or forty years of the twentieth century?

The handful of countries that made important advances in the mortality transition prior to 1930 or 1940 were those whose populations experienced significant improvements in standards of well-being.

2. J. B. McKinlay and S. M. McKinlay, "The Questionable Contribution of Medical Measures to the Decline of Mortality in the United States in the Twentieth Century," *Milbank Memorial Fund Quarterly*, Summer 1977, pp. 405-29.

TABLE 1
ESTIMATED LIFE EXPECTANCIES IN LATIN AMERICA, 1900-1985

Country	1900-05	1930-35	1940-45	1950-55	1960-65	1970-75	1980-85
Argentina	40.3	55.2	59.2	61.8	66.5	65.7	71.0
Bolivia	26.0	27.0	28.0	35.8	41.0	48.7	53.1
Brazil	29.0	38.0	44.2	47.1	50.2	57.0	59.0
Chile	30.2	35.0	43.0	53.0	57.1	61.5	69.0
Colombia	33.0	38.5	42.3	47.0	53.4	59.2	67.0
Costa Rica	35.0	40.3	46.8	59.0	62.3	69.3	73.0
Cuba	33.0	43.0	45.0	60.0	64.0	70.0	73.5
Dominican Republic	—	31.0	36.5	48.0	54.3	58.9	64.7
Ecuador	—	—	36.7	46.0	54.2	59.7	63.5
El Salvador	—	29.4	34.5	44.0	54.5	57.4	60.3
Guatemala	24.0	28.0	35.5	43.0	49.0	54.5	58.3
Honduras	35.0	35.0	39.0	45.3	50.0	55.1	60.2
Mexico	25.0	35.0	43.0	50.6	58.6	62.0	65.5
Nicaragua	—	29.0	37.0	42.5	48.0	57.0	60.8
Panama	37.8	38.0	45.0	53.0	63.0	67.5	70.2
Paraguay	25.8	—	43.0	49.7	57.0	62.1	68.4
Peru	—	—	38.3	42.1	49.7	54.6	59.8
Uruguay	—	—	61.0	67.0	68.5	71.5	72.0
Venezuela	—	33.5	45.0	55.9	61.5	66.0	69.5

SOURCE: Adjusted vital statistics and census counts.
NOTE: All estimates are based on adjusted vital statistics or derived from the application of indirect techniques. Linear interpolation was used in cases where two estimates separated by no more than 10 years were available.

This occurred partly as a result of better diet and partly as the outcome of environmental changes brought about by massive works of infrastructure such as roads and communication networks and systems of excreta disposal and of potable water supply. By and large, the countries that experienced earlier improvements — Argentina, Chile, Cuba, Mexico, Uruguay — were also those favored by unusually advantageous conditions in international markets and by unprecedented state-directed efforts to diversify the national economies, to extend fundamental rights of participation to the citizenry, to broaden access to education, and to liberalize the delivery of social and health services. It is no coincidence that in these countries the period 1890-1935 is characterized by strongly nationalistic governments that deployed considerable resources to secure the political unification of dispersed territories, the formation of a centralized bureaucracy, and the establishment of a free-market economy that favored an incipient but weakened indigenous bourgeoisie. In some cases these efforts began before 1914, but without exception they were especially prominent in the aftermath of World War I and, later, as a response to the 1929 Great Depression. The Depression marks the onset of the industrialization phase characterized by import substitution that in spite of its final unequivocal failure, produced massive transformations in these societies. If none of the medical innovations that revolutionized the treatment of the most prevalent infectious diseases could have had significant effects before 1945 or 1950, we must invoke the structural transformations that occurred during the period to find an explanation for the more than trivial mortality decline that

TABLE 2

CHEMOTHERAPEUTIC AND PROPHYLACTIC
MEASURES FOR 10 COMMON DISEASES IN LATIN AMERICA

Disease	Medical Intervention and Year of Introduction
Tuberculosis	Isoniazid, streptomycin, 1950
Scarlet fever	Penicillin, 1946
Influenza	Vaccine (?), 1943
Pneumonia	Sulfonamide, 1935
Diphtheria	Toxoid, 1930
Whooping cough	Vaccine, 1930
Measles	Vaccine, 1963
Smallpox	Vaccine, 1800
Typhoid	Chloramphenicol, 1948
Poliomyelitis	Salk vaccine, 1955

SOURCE: John B. McKinlay and Sonja M. McKinlay, "The Questionable Contribution of Medical Measures to the Decline of Mortality in the United States in the Twentieth Century," *Milbank Memorial Fund Quarterly*, pp. 405-29 (Summer 1977).

NOTE: Since no information on morbidity or mortality by causes is available before 1950, I have used cause-of-death statistics for the period 1950-55 and selected the 10 most commonly found causes for the age groups zero to 55. Consequently, the diseases in the table are not necessarily the most prevalent either before or after 1945.

no fewer than six countries underwent before 1945.

The changes in mortality that took place between 1945 and 1965 have been the subject of abundant reviews and the facts are relatively clear. Much less attention has been given to the changes that followed, during the period 1965 to 1985, which, as I will show later in this article, represent a drastically different pattern. A comparison of the annual absolute gains in life expectancies in the periods between 1945 and 1965 and between 1965 and 1985 reveals several interesting features.[3] The first is that the pace of gains is quite heterogeneous in both periods: the average gains decrease from .68 to .48, but the dispersion around the mean remains high and at a constant level. The second feature is a clustering of countries around distinctive patterns of decline. Argentina and Uruguay, the most conspicuous of the forerunners, show the lowest gains in life expectancy

3. Palloni, "Brief History."

per year in both periods. Their levels of mortality decline gradually rather than in sudden jumps. At the other extreme is a group of countries that make unusually rapid progress. But this group is a startling blend of those with very low initial life expectancies and those that had progressed a great deal before 1945. The net result of this clustering is a very weak association between the initial levels of mortality and the subsequent pace of gains. This is prima facie evidence supporting the idea that exogenous changes produced gains in survival regardless of initial conditions. During the second period, from 1965 to 1985, there is a generalized plummeting of the rate of annual gain. Only a handful of countries experienced increases in the annual rate of gain of life expectancies. The remaining countries underwent substantial drops in the rate of gain irrespective of the levels they had attained by 1965.

The evidence presented so far raises two interrelated questions: (1) What were the factors behind the mortality decline during the period 1945-85? and (2) Has there been a slowdown in the progress toward higher levels of life expectancy that was unexpected given the history of mortality decline in the more advanced societies in Western Europe and North America?

Structural changes and
upward shifts of life expectancy

In a series of well-known studies, Preston has shown that about 20-30 percent of the changes in life expectancy between 1930 and 1965-70 are accounted for by increases in real income per capita.[4] The remaining changes are imputed to exogenous shifts, the result of the availability of low-cost, easily accessible medical technology. These findings were obtained from cross sections including developed and developing nations. This estimation exercise was carried out with some modifications for 23 countries in Latin America, with a sample that includes the 19 countries considered in this review plus Barbados, Jamaica, Haiti, and Trinidad and Tobago. The estimation procedure was first applied to the entire period 1945-85 and then separately for the periods 1945-65 and 1965-85.

The results of these analyses reveal several important features of the mortality decline in Latin America. First, the proportion of total gains in life expectancy attributable to changes in socioeconomic conditions — real income, education — is

4. Samuel H. Preston, "The Changing Relations between Mortality and Level of Economic Development," *Population Studies,* 29:231-48 (1975); idem, "Causes and Consequences of Mortality Decline in Developed and Developing Countries during the Twentieth Century," in R. A. Easterlin, ed., *Population and Economic Change in Developing Countries* (Chicago: University of Chicago Press, 1987), pp. 289-360.

about 45 percent during the first period and about 75 percent in the second period. Although the actual figures are somewhat different, these results confirm Preston's conjectures that, at least in a first phase, the increase in life expectancy is heavily dependent on exogenous factors. The dominance of socioeconomic conditions during the second period is to be expected if there is a gradual erosion of the effects of low-cost, easily transferable medical technology.

The second feature is that the relation between life expectancy and socioeconomic conditions becomes stronger, not weaker, as time passes. This is consistent with the results for the pooled sample of developing and developed countries and confirms once more the dangers of overplaying the potential benefits of medical technology that is not accompanied by significant socioeconomic transformations. The interrelation between medical technology and knowledge and socioeconomic transformations may exist because the accessibility of the technology depends directly on improved standards of living and/or because the effects of its application have a threshold that can only be removed by raising standards of living.

The third and final feature of the mortality decline is that the countries that experience the strongest gains associated with exogenous factors are those that, during the period 1950-55, had the highest prevalence of malaria. Curiously enough, this association found for the period 1945-65 persists into the latter period. The association found in the first period is in part a result of the synergism between malaria, malnutrition, and other infections: the elimination or drastic reduction of malaria, a feat that can be accomplished without heavy expenditures per capita, has spillover effects and leads to reduction in the fatality and incidence rates of other major diseases. It is less clear why the association between the magnitude of exogenous changes in 1965-85 and prevalence of malaria in 1950-55 remains still in force, nearly thirty years after the initiation of the eradication and relocation campaigns.

Latin America and Western Europe: Divergent patterns

Has mortality decline in Latin America experienced a slowdown? This is a question posed a few years ago that has not yet received a satisfactory answer. It is a slippery issue since it involves comparison with an undefined standard or baseline. If one compares properly standardized gains in survival in, say, England and Wales to those observed in Latin America, it would appear that the answer is affirmative: after a period of rapid gains, most countries succeed in attaining only a fraction of the gains experienced by England and Wales at comparable levels of initial life expectancy. If, however, the standard is changed, one obtains different results, some of which can contradict the hypothesis of a slowdown.

While the exercises invoking standards of comparison may raise justifiable skepticism, however, the mortality decline and the mortality patterns in Latin America have two inescapable characteristics: the former is sluggish, and the latter is conspicuous for its higher levels of infant mortality relative to the levels of total mortality. These features are two sides of the same coin and go a long way in explaining the peculiar profile of mortality decline in Latin America and its relations to endogenous and exogenous factors.

By 1985, roughly forty years after the introduction of medical technologies that revolutionized the treatment of diseases, only five countries had attained life expec-

tancies exceeding 70 years, six had reached levels between 65 and 70, and five had not yet even attained 60 years. The life expectancies of all the other countries remain between 60 and 65 years. That is, roughly one-fourth of the countries are exposed to levels of survival that were attained in Western Europe before the massive application of novel medical technology for the containment of infectious diseases. This is a paradoxical situation: on the one hand, gains in survival that were facilitated by vector-eradication campaigns, the distribution of vaccines, and the application of novel chemotherapy appear to be of unprecedented magnitude. On the other hand, a combination of conditions of a yet unknown nature has conspired to arrest the decline below levels that should have been achieved given the available technology. Observing the mortality decline through the narrow lens of the 1950s and 1960s yields the wrong impression, and as the lens is widened to cover a longer period of history, the gains are diluted and fall short of the mark. Elsewhere, I have shown that this apparent paradox is partly explained by the pattern of decline in infant mortality.[5]

REPRODUCTIVE REGIMES

The patterns of fertility in Latin America are at least as diverse as its mortality regimes. By and large, fertility remained virtually unchanged from about 1900 to 1965, when the beginning of a generalized decline set in. Just as in the case of mortality, however, we can distinguish forerunners and laggards. Within each of these groups we can introduce further distinctions according to the initial levels of fertility and the timing and pace of subsequent

5. Palloni, "Brief History."

declines. Table 3 displays the relevant information. For the period before 1950 I have estimated crude birth rates from a variety of sources, including indirect estimates derived from stable, quasi-stable, and generalized stable populations. As a consequence, comparisons across countries are somewhat treacherous and the inferences are necessarily tentative. In spite of these qualifications, however, a periodization of changes is possible.

Pre-1950 regimes

Up to 1950 there are three regimes: one with very high levels of fertility, another with low levels, and a third that falls in between these extremes. Argentina and Uruguay pertain to the low-fertility regime; Chile, Cuba, and Panama to the intermediate one; and the remaining countries are part of the high-fertility regime. The levels of the crude birth rates in Argentina and Uruguay before 1950 are very close to those experienced in England and Wales just before the secular decline of fertility begins around 1870. Although this comparison is misleading, since the crude birth rates are affected by the age structures, the conclusion is confirmed by examination of the age-standardized index, I_f. This index is the ratio of the observed births, adjusted for underregistration, to the births that would have occurred if all women of reproductive ages had been exposed to the age pattern of Hutterite fertility.

While the values of I_f observed in England and Wales and other Western European countries right before the secular fertility decline fall within the range .300-.540, the values in 1950 for Argentina and Uruguay are near or lower than the minimum of the range. Cuba's fertility levels in 1950 already resembled those of Western Europe on the eve of the secular decline, and it is very likely that Cuban fertility was already falling before this date. All other countries, including those that underwent a perceptible decline before 1950 — such as Chile and Panama — have I_f values that are at least 50 percent higher than the lowest observed in Western Europe before the onset of the decline. One factor explaining these differences is the differential in marriage patterns: while in Latin America marriage — including legal and consensual unions — has been early and nearly universal, the Western European marriage pattern was more restrictive, with proportions of never married women on the order of .15 and very late ages at first marriage. As I will show later in this article, however, this is not the only explanation that accounts for excess fertility in Latin America. In fact Latin American patterns of marital fertility are also much higher than the European ones prior to — and also after — the secular decline.

Post-1950 regimes

With values of I_f that fall by about 25 percent in just one decade, Cuba unambiguously joins the ranks of the forerunners. Although this decline is partly associated with the turmoil brought about by the Cuban Revolution, Cuba's levels before 1950 suggest a secular decline that was already under way and that would have continued even in the absence of the Revolution. While Argentina and, in all likelihood, Uruguay continue a slow descent, all other countries maintain their past levels of fertility, but several of them — Chile, Costa Rica, Ecuador, El Salvador, and Panama — experience more than trivial increases. The remaining countries are divided in two groups. For the first, the onset of fertility decline occurs in the late 1960s and early

TABLE 3
INDICES OF FERTILITY, 1900-1985

Country	1900 CBR	1930 CBR	1950 CBR	1950 TFR	1950 I_f	1960 CBR	1960 TFR	1960 I_f	1970 CBR	1970 TFR	1970 I_f	1980-85 CBR	1980-85 TFR	1980-85 I_f
Argentina	.042	.029	.025	3.1	.285	.024	3.0	.273	.024	2.9	.263	.025	3.3	.308
Bolivia	.045	.045	.042	6.7	.577	.046	6.6	.536	.045	5.3	.502	.043	5.1	.470
Brazil	.046	.046	.044	6.2	.529	.042	6.1	.532	.038	5.9	.490	.031	4.1	.365
Chile	.045	.040	.037	4.6	.402	.036	5.3	.462	.031	3.9	.352	.023	2.8	.259
Colombia	.043	.042	.044	6.8	.592	.044	6.6	.582	.040	5.3	.391	.030	3.5	.305
Costa Rica	.047	.045	.045	6.7	.581	.045	7.3	.629	.040	4.8	.412	.031	3.6	.361
Cuba	.045	.031	.030	4.6	.362	.035	4.2	.331	.028	3.9	.307	.017	1.6	.155
Dominican Republic	—	—	.046	7.8	.681	.048	7.6	.679	.042	6.5	.546	.034	4.4	.397
Ecuador	.048	.049	.047	6.7	.583	.046	6.9	.624	.042	6.6	.583	.038	5.4	.484
El Salvador	.044	.047	.048	6.3	.549	.047	6.9	.614	.044	6.3	.550	.042	4.3	.430
Guatemala	.046	.046	.031	6.9	.609	.048	6.6	.583	.046	6.0	.521	.043	6.4	.551
Honduras	.045	.042	.046	7.5	.597	.050	7.8	.682	.048	7.2	.638	.045	6.0	.530
Mexico	.047	.044	.045	6.7	.565	.045	6.9	.578	.041	6.5	.541	.032	3.9	.350
Nicaragua	—	—	.046	7.3	.678	.051	7.3	.665	.048	—	—	.042	6.0	.547
Panama	.040	.037	.039	5.8	.506	.040	6.0	.536	.036	5.4	.496	.028	3.2	.341
Paraguay	—	—	.043	6.6	.576	.043	6.3	.567	.040	5.8	.503	.038	5.0	.426
Peru	.047	.045	.046	6.9	.593	.046	6.9	.592	.043	.63	.441	.037	5.0	.438
Uruguay	.036	.028	.025	2.7	.308	.022	3.0	.460	.021	2.6	.269	.018	—	.256
Venezuela	.042	.040	.044	6.5	.584	.044	6.6	.593	.040	5.4	.484	.033	4.1	.346

SOURCE: Estimates based on adjusted vital statistics and census counts.

NOTE: All measures are centered around the indicated years. Linear interpolation was used for countries whose censuses did not fall in the years selected for this table; however, no interpolation was performed in intervals longer than 10 years. (CBR is the crude birth rate, TFR is the total fertility rate, and I_f is the index of overall fertility.

136

1970s and is rapid and swift. The second group is characterized by either stationary levels or very slow and late fertility declines.

Table 4 compares the pace of decline of I_f in Latin American countries with that in England and Wales. To construct the table I defined the date of the onset of the decline as the year after which there was a reduction in I_f of 10 percent or more. The first column of the table shows the I_f levels observed during that year, and the third displays the annual rate of decline — as a percentage — in the interval between the time of the onset of the decline and the middle of the period 1980-85. The fourth column displays comparable rates in England and Wales, which correspond in all cases, however, to lower absolute levels of I_f.[6] With the exception of Argentina, where the index increases slightly, all other countries experience a decrease in I_f. There are important differences, however. Bolivia, Ecuador, El Salvador, Honduras, Paraguay, Peru, and Uruguay show a pace roughly equal to or slower than the one observed in England and Wales. Instead, Brazil, Colombia, Costa Rica, Cuba, the Dominican Republic, Mexico, Panama, and Venezuela experience declines of magnitudes at least 50 percent larger than those of England and Wales.

Two disturbing features of the reproductive regimes just discussed are worth mentioning. First, the common conjecture that once fertility begins to drop it will drop very fast, faster than in developed coun-

6. The values in the fourth column of the table were calculated as the rate of decline in I_f experienced by England and Wales within a period equal in length to that used in column 3 of the table. The period starts at the time of onset of fertility decline in England and Wales and the definition of the date of the onset of fertility decline is the same as the one used for Latin American countries.

tries, is only partially confirmed. Admittedly, the largest and most populous countries seem to be following that pattern, but just about half of them have proceeded at lower than expected speed. Second, countries that experienced a fertility decline for well over twenty years have not yet reached the levels of fertility that would be commensurate with the contraceptive technology that is available today. One of them, Argentina, has experienced a complete stall in fertility changes. Only Chile and Cuba — and possibly Uruguay — have levels of total fertility below 3.0 children per mother. Will fertility in other countries fall below this threshold? Information on fertility preferences in the countries with total fertility close to 3.0 — Costa Rica, Colombia, Panama, and Mexico — confirms that the demand for children is still at relatively high levels, between three and four children, on average. This finding suggests that further falls in fertility of the magnitude observed in the 1970s are unlikely to occur any time soon. Since relatively high fertility preferences have also been detected in the remaining countries, it is unlikely that additional reductions among the latecomers — with levels of total fertility exceeding 4.0 children per mother — will be forthcoming, at least in the short run.

Marriage, marital fertility, and inhibiting effects

The previous discussion did not make the important distinction between marital and general fertility. I_f, the index of fertility, as well as total fertility, displayed in Table 3, is the combined outcome of fertility within marriage and the pattern of marriage. In what follows I discuss the observed trends in these two components of general fertility.

TABLE 4

INITIAL LEVELS OF GENERAL FERTILITY (I_f) AND PACE OF FERTILITY DECLINE
IN LATIN AMERICAN COUNTRIES: A COMPARISON WITH ENGLAND AND WALES

Country	Initial Level I_f	Date of Onset	Annual Percentage Decline from Date of Onset to 1980-85	Annual Percentage Change in an Equivalent Time Interval in England and Wales
Argentina	.285	1950	−.24	1.47
Bolivia	.502	1970	.55	1.43
Brazil	.490	1970	2.45	1.43
Chile	.462	1960	2.63	1.43
Colombia	.582	1960	2.94	1.39
Costa Rica	.629	1960	2.94	1.39
Cuba	.362	1950	2.66	1.47
Dominican Republic	.679	1960	2.44	1.39
Ecuador	.583	1970	1.55	1.43
El Salvador	.555	1970	1.67	1.43
Honduras	.613	1970	1.21	1.43
Mexico	.541	1970	.47	1.43
Nicaragua	—	1970	—	—
Panama	.496	1970	3.42	1.43
Paraguay	.565	1960	1.28	1.39
Peru	.530	1970	1.40	1.43
Uruguay	.308	1950	.58	1.47
Venezuela	.593	1960	2.18	1.39

SOURCES: Estimates for Latin American countries are based on adjusted vital statistics and census counts. Estimates for England and Wales are based on Michael Teitelbaum, *The British Fertility Decline: Demographic Transition in the Crucible of the Industrial Revolution* (Princeton, NJ: Princeton University Press, 1984), p. 81.
NOTE: Changes with sign reversed.

Nuptiality in Latin America. The study of marriage patterns in Latin America is hampered by the prevalence of consensual unions. These are difficult to treat for two reasons. First, since they do not ordinarily involve the same amount of exposure to sexual intercourse, it is not entirely correct to treat them as if they were conventional, or legal, marriages. If we do, we will be biasing downward the rates of marital fertility. Second, and more important, consensual unions are difficult to trace either in surveys or in censuses since the definitions and classifications are not consistent over time or across countries. In fact, results from the World Fertility Survey have shown that, unless interviewees are probed carefully, the proportion of women who are identified as being single is usually overestimated since many who are in consensual unions are simply not classified as married or in unions. Since each country has different classification practices and differential stigmas attached to nonlegalized unions, intercountry comparisons must be carried out with a great deal of caution. In this article, I treat reported consensual unions as if they were regular unions.

Examination of the singulate mean age at marriage (SMAM) during the period 1950-85 shows that although the timing of marriage has experienced a uniform upward trend, it has remained quite early.[7] With the exception of Cuba and the Do-

7. Palloni, "Brief History."

minican Republic, where the index shows decreases of about one to two and one-half years between 1950 and 1980, in most countries the trend has been upward, that is, toward a later marriage pattern. In some cases these increases are substantial, on the order of two to three years over a period of twenty to thirty years. Similar though more muted increasing trends were detected in cohort comparisons of median ages at marriage from data collected from individual interviews in the World Fertility Survey.

How do the nuptiality patterns in Latin America compare with those of other countries? As of 1980, the SMAM in Latin America was two to three years higher than those in Africa, just about the same or slightly higher than those observed in Asia — but two to three years higher than in Bangladesh and Nepal — and two to three years lower than in Western Europe and North America. Right before the irreversible fertility decline, the SMAM for England and Wales was between 25 and 26 years, values that have never been reached by any Latin American country.

Thus the regime of reproduction in Latin America has always had a built-in potential toward higher fertility since the constraints on marriage are few. There are only faint signals that this is changing in any drastic way.

Marital fertility. Like the study of nuptiality patterns, the study of marital fertility is affected by idiosyncrasies in the classification of females according to marital status. Consequently, the same cautions issued before are applicable here.[8]

To study marital fertility we use I_g, the marital fertility index whose theoretical maximum is unity when the observed level of marital fertility equals that of the Hutterites. With the exception of Argentina,

8. Ibid.

Cuba, and Uruguay, the Latin American levels of I_g in 1950 exceeded .70. Only a few countries in western and southern Europe experienced such high levels right before the onset of the secular decline, and for most of them the transition to lower levels started from levels of I_g within the range .60-.70.

With the exception of Cuba, the most recent estimates of I_g for Latin America are well above .400, a barrier broken in Western Europe right before World War I or World War II. In spite of this rather ominous sign of high marital fertility, it should be noted that a significant number of Latin American countries showed sharp fertility falls in I_g between 1960 and 1980-85. Among forerunners such as Argentina and Uruguay, I_g has changed only slightly but remains at relatively low levels — .40 to .50. Among the laggards — Bolivia, Ecuador, Guatemala, Honduras, Nicaragua, Peru, and Paraguay — the values of I_g remain at levels exceeding .70 and show only minor indications of impending changes. In the remaining countries, particularly Chile, Costa Rica, and Cuba, decline has been sudden and appears to be well under way although the most recent levels of I_g are, by Western European standards at least, somewhat high. Analyses of an indicator of parity-dependent birth control suggest that in only five countries, the forerunners of fertility decline and those that followed suit early during the 1960s, are there significant indications of more than trivial volitional birth control. In the remaining countries the indications of declining marital fertility are few and far between.

The review of marital fertility and nuptiality indices indicates that there are three types of fertility decline: early, with a date of onset prior to 1950; intermediate, with a date of onset between 1960 and 1965;

and late, with a date of onset after 1970. I showed that the decline among those that experience early onset is not uniform. On the one hand, Argentina and Uruguay move slowly and gradually and even show a tendency to slow down or to experience minor fertility increases. On the other hand, Cuba proceeds swiftly to reach the lowest levels of fertility in the continent. After undergoing a period of fertility increases between 1950 and 1960, countries with an intermediate date of onset experience a rapid decline but reach levels of total fertility exceeding replacement. The fall in fertility among those with intermediate and late dates of onset is unprecedented when compared with the fertility decline in Western Europe. It is too early, however, to say whether the decline will continue unabated toward replacement levels, and, if and when the decline proceeds, it is certainly premature to anticipate the speed of the decline. Finally, examination of indicators of nuptiality and of marital fertility suggests that the process of decline is almost entirely due to changes in marital fertility and that delayed marriage makes a detectable but unimportant contribution to the process.

The inhibiting effects of nuptiality, breast-feeding, and contraception. Most populations never achieve the maximum biologically possible reproduction levels since a variety of mechanisms exert inhibiting effects. Among these the most important are nuptiality, breast-feeding, and contraception. In some societies, involuntary and voluntary abortion can also play an important role. Societal rules preventing early marriage or regulating remarriage or conditions affecting marital disruption in general will affect the time of exposure to intercourse and, ceteris paribus, the actual levels of fertility. Breast-feeding affects

the length of the anovulatory period and therefore the chances that, under exposure to intercourse, a conception will take place. Thus universal and prolonged breast-feeding increases the period of postpartum infecundity. Contraception reduces marital fertility in obvious ways although the efficacy of various means varies substantially. Finally, abortion, as well as involuntary intrauterine mortality, reduces fertility even further. While nuptiality operates on general fertility, the other mechanisms are, by and large, inhibitors of marital fertility. Only two of these, however — contraception and abortion — are considered volitional and strongly attached to fertility preferences.

Table 5 displays the values of indices reflecting the inhibiting effects of nuptiality, breast-feeding, and contraception for Latin American countries; all indices are evaluated at the latest period of time for which data were available. The index is designed to show the proportionate impact of a particular behavior on the total fertility rate. The closer the values of the indices are to unity, the less powerful is the corresponding inhibiting effect on fertility.

Although the data are incomplete, the table shows some interesting features. First, note that Argentina and Uruguay are the countries with the strongest inhibiting effects attributable to nuptiality: their total fertility would increase between 10 and 20 percent if their pattern of nuptiality were more like the ones experienced by the rest of Latin America. The second feature, which is, unfortunately, only partially shown in the table, is that the countries that experience the sharpest and fastest fertility decline with intermediate and late dates of onset are also those that have the highest inhibiting effects due to contraception.

Two issues are relevant in this connection. The first is that in Brazil and more

TABLE 5
MAJOR PROXIMATE DETERMINANTS OF FERTILITY IN
COUNTRIES WITH AVAILABLE INFORMATION AT MOST RECENT DATE

	Index of Marriage	Index of Contraception	Index of Postpartum Fecundity
Argentina	.403	—	—
Bolivia	.690	—	.708
Brazil	.640	.550	.930
Chile	.380	—	—
Colombia	.602	.633	.846
Costa Rica	.567	.432	.908
Cuba	.693	.519	.897
Dominican Republic	.689	.697	.852
Ecuador	.656	.709	.782
El Salvador	.619	.598*	.725
Guatemala	.681	—	—
Honduras	.702	.750*	.821
Mexico	.684	.730	.842
Nicaragua	.594	—	—
Panama	.618	.508	.850
Paraguay	.626	.711	.811
Peru	.629	.755	.769
Uruguay	.435	—	—
Venezuela	.635	.580	.865

SOURCES: United Nations, Department of International Economic and Social Affairs, *Fertility Behavior in the Context of Development* (New York: United Nations, 1987), p. 168; National Academy of Sciences, Committee on Population and Demography, *Fertility Determinants in Cuba,* 1983, p. 121; National Academy of Sciences, *The Determinants of Brazil's Recent Rapid Decline in Fertility* (Washington, DC: National Academy Press, 1983), p. 56.

*These indices were estimated using information on the relation between the index of marriage and the proportion of women in union using an effective method of contraception.

recently in El Salvador and the Dominican Republic, there has been a sharp increase in sterilization, the most efficient method of contraception. It is likely that the inhibiting effects of contraception in these countries owe a great deal to sterilization rather than to the use of the pill, the intrauterine device, or other less efficient methods. The second issue regards the role of abortion. It is well known that abortion has become quite widespread in Cuba and has been important, although less widespread, in Chile. Preliminary calculations show, for example, that the inhibiting effects of abortion in Cuba contribute to reduced marital fertility by about 70 percent. It is possible that the various reproductive regimes identified before can be further disaggregated according to the prevalence of different strategies to reduce marital fertility.

Table 5 shows that the inhibiting effects of breast-feeding are, at least relative to Africa and some countries in Asia, quite minor. It is only in Bolivia, Ecuador, El Salvador, and Peru that the index dips below .80. Although it is possible that breast-feeding has been moving toward a less universal and shorter norm, there is little evidence to suggest that the pattern of breast-feeding in Latin American countries has experienced drastic transformations. If this inference is correct, then the high levels of marital fertility detected prior to the irreversible declines were in part the result of a norm of breast-feeding that shortened the periods of infertility after the birth of a child.

By and large, countries that have been lagging behind in the process of fertility decline have the strongest inhibiting effects of breast-feeding. If under the onslaught of modernization they were to experience an overhaul of the breast-feeding norm faster than they can adopt a new, controlled reproductive regime, fertility could increase. But another consequence of reduced breast-feeding is, ceteris paribus, an increase in infant mortality. Thus the final impact on the rate of natural increase is ambiguous because it will depend on the relative size of the fertility and infant-mortality effects of breast-feeding.

THE DETERMINANTS OF FERTILITY DECLINE

Our review of nuptiality and other intermediate determinants of fertility indicates that actual fertility levels as well as the bulk of historical changes are dominated by levels and changes in marital fertility. With the exception of Cuba and possibly Chile, the most important factor explaining levels of marital fertility is the use of conventional contraception or sterilization.

The determinants of fertility decline among the forerunners must be traced to conditions that kept the demand for children at lower levels long before modern contraception became available. A tempting but weak explanation is a diffusion process initiated by the influential, low-fertility immigrants from Western Europe.

A more compelling explanation is the existence of social conditions that produced a more permeable society, one where habits and customs, as well as aspirations and goals, could be passed on more easily across strata. One factor responsible for added permeability is the liberalized access to education. The forerunners of fertility decline are the same societies that experienced the sweeping post-Depression social and economic transformations that we invoked to explain mortality declines before the 1950s. A second factor is the strength of the state centralized bureaucracy and its willingness and capability to launch concerted campaigns to satisfy the demand for birth control. But these centralized efforts could have been successful only where the social and economic conditions constrained individual choices and lowered the demand for children. Why do Colombia, Brazil, and Mexico undergo sharp declines, whereas Peru, Bolivia, and Ecuador experience minor changes? What can explain the differences in speed and levels between Chile and Costa Rica on the one hand and Brazil, Colombia, and Mexico on the other?

A simple analysis of total fertility in the periods 1940-65 and 1965-75 and in 1975 and 1985 indicates that over time, levels and socioeconomic conditions — measured by real income per capita and education — explain an increased proportion of the variance, with the most important determinant being education. Confirming results obtained by Lapham and Mauldin for a larger sample of countries,[9] a measure of family planning efforts also appears to contribute

9. Robert J. Lapham and W. Parker Mauldin, "Family Planning Program Effort and Birth Rate Decline in Developing Countries," *International Family Planning Perspectives*, 10(4):109-18 (1984).

to the explanation of intercountry variability in fertility. Its importance pales, however, relative to that of education. A shift analysis shows that over time the proportion of changes attributable to exogenous factors increases, just the opposite of what happens with mortality. It is unclear what these exogenous factors are, although they surely reflect conditions affecting demand for children or fertility preferences.

A determinant that we have not explored in depth is the level of infant and child mortality. One mechanism linking infant mortality and fertility operates by shifting fertility preferences. But there is a second, equally powerful mechanism that is purely biological and that involves lengthening the period of postpartum amenorrhea by providing opportunities to breast-feed longer. The appeal of this explanation of fertility decline is undermined by the fact that most Latin American countries have had relatively short breast-feeding patterns. But a cursory examination of the types of reproductive and mortality regimes distinguished before reveals that there is indeed a correspondence between infant mortality and fertility. Elsewhere I have shown within repeated cross sections that the relation is very strong but that its strength is diluted when a longer period of time is considered in a pooled cross-section time-series.[10]

Like the determinants of mortality, those affecting fertility remain elusive and must wait for more detailed analyses that integrate socioeconomic conditions, political factors, and biological mechanisms.

10. Alberto Palloni, "Health Levels and Care in Latin America: The Case of Infant and Child Mortality, 1900-1985" (Working Series Paper 89-17, Center for Demography and Ecology, University of Wisconsin, 1989).

SUMMARY AND CONCLUSION

Most Latin American countries are currently undergoing what could be considered the third revolution in their demographic patterns. The first was the decline in mortality; the second was a somewhat mysterious though transient increase in fertility that some countries experienced between 1950 and 1960. The third is the downward shift in fertility. I have highlighted the first and the last of these revolutions and have attempted to show that the countries in Latin America did not experience them uniformly. Despite the diversity, there are many salient regularities that suggest that the population shifts affected groups of societies at the same time and in similar ways. Neither mortality nor fertility reductions have made Latin America less diverse than it was at the beginning of the century or after World War II. The heterogeneity in current mortality levels is formidable and by itself is sufficient to falsify the thesis that mortality changes have been mostly a consequence of the diffusion of medical technology. The heterogeneity in general and of marital fertility levels in particular is even more salient and calls into question the idea that well-established family planning programs are sufficient to produce irreversible shifts: the forerunners of fertility decline underwent fertility changes in the absence of any such programs; some of the official policies of the latecomers, such as Brazil, have been less than sympathetic to family planning programs; and, finally, some societies that experienced rapid declines and have strong family planning programs in place, such as Costa Rica and Colombia, show signs of transient slowdowns in actual fertility and a stalemate in the levels of fertility preferences.

Although this review has paid less attention to the determinants of either mortality or fertility, I have constructed types of demographic regimes that should be useful for identifying the societal mechanisms common to the members of the various types and those that are responsible for intertype differences. The typology supports the idea that exogenous changes fall short as explanatory factors of both mortality and fertility. Further examination of the types should yield insights into the endogenous factors that exert important influences on the trends.

The review has been virtually silent on a fascinating but difficult problem that has puzzled historical demographers for some time: Is the decline of mortality responsible for the decline in fertility that follows? And does the relation differ in the various types of regimes that were distinguished in this review?[11] The identification of endogenous determinants together with the exploration of the interrelation between fertility and mortality in the various demographic regimes is a task that demands more than, but should rest on, the modest descriptive accounting provided here.

11. See Palloni, "Brief History."

ANNALS, *AAPSS*, **510**, July 1990

Recent Changes in American Fertility, Marriage, and Divorce

By ANDREW CHERLIN

ABSTRACT: This article discusses recent trends in fertility, marriage, and divorce in the period since 1965 in the United States. It describes briefly the sharp changes in patterns of births, marriage, informal unions, divorce, and remarriage. Very recent developments of note include the increasingly important place of cohabitation in the life course, the continuing postponement of marriage, and the rise in birth rates to women in their thirties. Explanations are examined that emphasize both the increased economic opportunities for women and the cultural shift toward a greater emphasis on individualism and self-fulfillment. In the concluding section, it is argued that concerns about fertility and the family in the years ahead will focus less on the number of children than on whether their upbringing and education will be adequate to meet the needs of a society with a relatively small labor force and a large dependent population.

Andrew Cherlin is professor of sociology at Johns Hopkins University. He received his Ph.D. from the University of California, Los Angeles, in 1976. He is the editor of The Changing American Family and Public Policy *and currently is revising his 1981 book,* Marriage, Divorce, Remarriage. *He is chair of the Family Section of the American Sociological Association and is a member of the Committee on Child Development Research and Public Policy of the National Academy of Sciences.*

THE fundamental transformation of the American family since the mid-1960s has been the increasing separation of sexual intercourse, marriage, and child-bearing. These three aspects of reproductive behavior were highly linked in the 1950s — perhaps more so than in any period previously. But over the past 25 years, they have drifted apart, with important consequences for the amount and timing of fertility and for family formation and dissolution. In this article, I will begin by describing this transformation briefly. Then I will discuss its causes — notably, the changing labor market opportunities for women and changing societal norms about family and personal life. Finally, I will discuss the implications for American family life and fertility as we approach the year 2000.

1945-1965: THE FIRST POSTWAR GENERATION

The years since World War II can be divided into two periods: 1945 to 1965, and 1965 to the present. Although this article is about the latter period, it is helpful to keep the family patterns of the earlier era in mind. Throughout the West, the period from 1945 to 1965 was characterized by the high birth rates of the postwar baby boom, early marriage, and relatively modest increases in divorce.[1] Although Americans often look back on this period as if it were typical of the past, in fact the 1945-65 period was the most unusual and distinctive era in twentieth-century American demography.[2] It was the only period since the

early 1800s during which fertility increased. Women who reached their peak childbearing years in the 1950s gave birth to about three children on average. Moreover, young adults married at earlier ages than at any time before or since in this century. Nearly half of all women who reached adulthood in the 1950s married while they were teenagers. Finally, the increase in the rate of divorce was unusually low by historical standards.[3]

Although reliable information is limited, it appears that for a majority of women, and for many men, their first experience of sexual intercourse occurred with their future spouses — and often only after their marriages began.[4] If a pregnancy resulted while still single, it was likely to lead to a hasty marriage. The now antiquarian phrase "shotgun wedding" conveys the moral tone of the 1950s, when over 70 percent of premaritally conceived first births to white women were legitimated by a wedding before the child was born.[5] Only 4-5 percent of babies were born out of wedlock in the 1950s.[6]

The low proportion of children born out of wedlock was one reason why a high proportion of children lived with both parents. In addition, the loss of a parent due to death had become less common, and the divorce rate was relatively modest by today's standards. As a result, 88 percent of all children in 1960 were living with both

1. On the pervasiveness of this pattern in Western Europe, see Louis Roussel and Irène Théry, "France: Demographic Change and Family Policy since World War II," *Journal of Family Issues,* 9:336 (Sept. 1988).

2. See Andrew J. Cherlin, *Marriage, Divorce, Remarriage* (Cambridge, MA: Harvard University Press, 1981).

3. Ibid.

4. For information on a sample of white, middle-class men and women, see Elaine Tyler May, *Homeward Bound: American Families in the Cold War Era* (New York: Basic Books, 1988), pp. 120-21.

5. Martin O'Connell and Maurice J. Moore, "The Legitimacy Status of First Births to U.S. Women Aged 15-24, 1939-1978," *Family Planning Perspectives,* 12:22 (Jan.-Feb. 1980).

6. Arland Thornton and Deborah Freedman, "The Changing American Family," *Population Bulletin,* 38(4):21 (Oct. 1983).

parents.[7] To a large and perhaps unprecedented extent, then, children were being reared by both parents during the first postwar period.

But family patterns have changed dramatically since 1965. Sexual activity is more commonly initiated prior to marriage, marriage itself has been postponed, cohabitation has emerged as a common stage of life prior to or after marriage, divorce has increased greatly, the birth rate has fallen sharply, and a greater proportion of births occur out of wedlock.

Union formation

Since the 1950s, young adults have increasingly postponed marriage. For example, in 1960 just 28 percent of women aged 20 to 24 had never married; by 1970 the comparable figure was 36 percent; by 1980 it was 50 percent; and in 1988 it was 61 percent. The median age at marriage increased by over three years between the 1950s and the 1980s.[8] Yet it is too simple to interpret this trend as a movement away from forming unions. Since 1970, a great rise has occurred in the number of unmarried couples who are living together, and the increase in cohabitation has compensated, in part, for the postponement of marriage.

Prior to the mid-1960s, cohabitation largely was restricted to persons with little education and low incomes; it often constituted a de facto marriage of the type found among the poor in many parts of the world. Starting about 1970, cohabitation began to increase among the better educated as well. The common perception at the time was that cohabitation rose first and fastest among a young, urban, college-educated vanguard and then spread to the middle and working classes. But retrospective histories obtained by the 1987-88 National Survey of Families and Households (NSFH) show that cohabitation was increasing simultaneously for all educational groups after 1970. Furthermore, at all times, less well educated persons were more likely to cohabit than were the better educated.[9]

As a result, the propensity of young adults to enter a union—either cohabiting or marital—has changed far less than one might suppose. Comparing cohorts in the NSFH who reached age 25 around 1970 with those who reached 25 around 1985, one finds that the proportion who had married declined substantially from 72 percent to 55 percent. But the proportion who had entered either kind of union declined only from 75 to 69 percent. The increase in cohabitation had compensated for about two-thirds of the decline in marriage.[10]

Overall, nearly half of the recent cohorts of young adults in the NSFH report cohabiting before marriage. Most of these cohabiting relationships are relatively brief; about half end within one and one-half years. When they do end, about 60 percent result in a marriage and 40 percent result in the end of the relationship.[11] At least in the

7. U.S. Department of Commerce, Bureau of the Census, "Marital Status and Living Arrangements: March 1988," *Current Population Reports,* Series P-20, no. 433 (Washington, DC: Government Printing Office, 1989), p. 61.

8. Ibid., pp. 59-60

9. Larry L. Bumpass, James A. Sweet, and Andrew Cherlin, "The Role of Cohabitation in Declining Rates of Marriage" (NSFH Working Paper no. 5, Center for Demography and Ecology, University of Wisconsin, Aug. 1989).

10. Ibid., tab. 1.

11. Larry L. Bumpass and James A. Sweet, "Preliminary Evidence on Cohabitation" (NSFH Working Paper no. 2, Center for Demography and Ecology, University of Wisconsin, 1988).

United States, cohabitation is still a stage in a process that leads rather quickly to a marriage or a breakup; it is not, for most young adults, a long-term alternative to marriage. To be sure, the nature of cohabiting unions may differ from formal marriages, a point that will be discussed later.

Union dissolution

Between the early 1960s and the mid-1970s, the divorce rate doubled; since that time it has been relatively stable. At current rates, about half of all marriages end in divorce.[12] In fact, one recent estimate suggests that the proportion ending in divorce or separation may be above 60 percent.[13] Thus marriage has become much less stable. The new cohabiting unions are even less stable; their short half-life already has been noted. Most people who divorce eventually remarry, but here again behavior has changed. Remarriage rates declined in the 1970s and 1980s.[14] Cohabitation appears to be even more prevalent among the formerly married than among the never married. More than two-thirds of the previously married young adults in the NSFH report having ever cohabited, a greater proportion than among the never married.[15] Thus it seems likely that an increase in cohabitation after marital dissolution has compensated, at least in part, for the decline in remarriage.

Overall, the trends in union formation and dissolution suggest that many adults will move into and out of several different

unions during their life course. It will not be unusual for someone reaching adulthood in the 1990s to form a cohabiting union, end it, form another one, marry their cohabiting partner, subsequently divorce that partner, enter another cohabiting relationship, and then remarry. This great flux is in sharp contrast to the relative stability — and uniformity — of the life course in the 1945-65 period.

Sexual relations

The great increase in cohabitation certainly indicates that sexual relations now begin well before marriage for young adults and continue after marriage for the growing number of adults who experience marital dissolution. In other words, the connection between marriage and sexual relations is much weaker than prior to 1965. The indication is confirmed by survey data. During the 1970s, for example, the proportion of never married young women in metropolitan areas who reported ever having sexual intercourse increased from 28 percent to 46 percent.[16]

Fertility

It is well known by now that the birth rate has plunged from the peak of the 1950s to the lowest level on record. Had women continued to give birth at the age-specific rates in existence in 1957, they would have had an average of 3.8 children.[17] But the rates dropped slowly until the mid-1960s and rapidly thereafter. By 1970, the total

12. Cherlin, Marriage, Divorce, Remarriage.

13. Teresa Castro Martin and Larry L. Bumpass, "Recent Trends in Marital Disruption," Demography, 26:37 (Feb. 1989).

14. U.S. Department of Health and Human Services, National Center for Health Statistics, "Advance Report of Final Marriage Statistics, 1986," Monthly Vital Statistics Report, 1989, 38(3), supp. 2, p. 5.

15. Bumpass and Sweet, "Preliminary Evidence."

16. Melvin Zelnik and John F. Kantner, "Sexual Activity, Contraceptive Usage, and Pregnancy among Metropolitan Area Teenagers: 1971-1979," Family Planning Perspectives, 12:230 (Sept.-Oct. 1980).

17. U.S. Department of Commerce, Bureau of the Census, Historical Statistics of the United States, Colonial Times to 1970, Part 1 (Washington, DC: Government Printing Office, 1975), p. 50.

fertility rate (TFR), the average number of births a woman could expect if the age-specific rates remained constant, stood at 2.48, which was similar to the lifetime childbearing of women who came of age during the Great Depression.[18] The TFR then fell to a low of 1.80 in 1983, well below the replacement level of 2.10. In recent years, the TFR has increased modestly. It stood at 1.87 in 1987, and the still provisional estimate for 1988 is 1.93.[19] If this estimate were to stand, it would mark the first time that the TFR was above 1.90 since 1972.

But the changes in fertility go beyond the falling birth rates. As the children of the baby-boom generation postponed marriage, they also postponed having children. This delay in timing further depressed the TFR, which reflects both the number of children women are having and the timing of their births. As they aged, however, these baby boomers began to reach the ages at which they could no longer postpone childbearing. Enough of them decided to have children so that the birth rates for women in their thirties rose by 15 to 30 percent in the 1980s, whereas the rates for women in their teens and twenties remained flat. The timing of births is now considerably later than was the case a generation ago, and the share of all births born to older mothers is greater. In 1976, women aged 30 and older accounted for 20 percent of all births to women aged 18 to 44; but in 1988, women aged 30 and older accounted for 35 percent.

Moreover, the proportion of births that occur out of wedlock has risen steadily since the mid-1960s, indicating the weakening link between marriage and childbearing. In 1987, one out of four births occurred to unmarried women.[20] The trend has developed despite the increasing recourse to abortion by unmarried women. For example, between 1971 and 1979, the percentage of pregnant unmarried teenagers who terminated their pregnancies by abortion rose from 23 to 37 percent.[21] A major reason for the increased ratio of out-of-wedlock births is that unmarried pregnant women are much less likely to marry before their child is born. Among unmarried teenagers who carried their pregnancies to term in the 1970s, the proportion who married before their delivery date dropped from 33 to 16 percent.[22] More generally, census statistics show that among all women under 25 who had an out-of-wedlock pregnancy that resulted in a birth in the period 1970 to 1974, 46 percent married before the birth of the child, whereas the comparable figure for 1985 to 1988 was 26 percent.[23] In sum, although unmarried women are less likely to carry their pregnancies to term, those who do so are less likely to marry in order to legitimate the birth.

It was not the case that birth rates for unmarried women — except for teenagers — were rising between 1960 and 1980; rather, they were falling — but not as fast as

18. The source of the recent rates cited in this paragraph is U.S. Department of Health and Human Services, National Center for Health Statistics, "Advance Report of Final Natality Statistics," *Monthly Vital Statistics Report,* 1989, 38(3), supp., p.18. On the Depression cohort, see Cherlin, *Marriage, Divorce, Remarriage,* p. 21.

19. This provisional estimate by the U.S. National Center for Health Statistics is as yet unofficial and subject to revision when final figures are compiled. The 1987 provisional estimate was 1.88 and the final estimate was 1.87.

20. National Center for Health Statistics, "Natality Statistics," tab. 18, p. 32.

21. Zelnik and Kantner, "Sexual Activity."

22. Ibid.

23. U.S. Department of Commerce, Bureau of the Census, "Fertility of American Women: June 1988," *Current Population Reports,* series P-20, no. 436 (Washington, DC: Government Printing Office, 1989), p. 9.

the rates for married women were falling. Since 1980, however, birth rates for unmarried women aged 20 and older have increased substantially, thus directly fueling the growth in the proportion of children born out of wedlock.[24] Some of these births are to cohabiting couples; by one estimate, one out of four out-of-wedlock births occurs to a woman who is cohabiting.[25] Others are postmarital births conceived before a marriage disrupted. But a substantial share undoubtedly are to single, noncohabiting women, whose propensity to give birth has increased in recent years.

OPPORTUNITIES AND CONSTRAINTS

This transformation in family and fertility has occurred because of changes in both the economic and the cultural spheres. The economic role of women has changed, providing the opportunity for alternatives to the patterns of the 1950s. Societal values about the family and personal life have changed also, weakening constraints against alternatives. Let us examine these changing opportunities and constraints.

Economic change

The classic economic argument for the fall in fertility relates to the well-known increases in the labor force participation of married women. The increase has occurred in stages. In the 1950s, larger numbers of married women began to join the labor force after their children were in school; in the 1960s and 1970s, the largest increases were among women with preschool-aged children; and more recently the largest rate of increase has occurred among mothers of infants. In fact, 51 percent of all mothers of infants—children under age 1—are now in the labor force. During the postwar period, then, the trend for women has been toward a nearly continuous attachment to the labor force throughout adulthood.[26]

Economists argue that the driving force behind this trend is the rising wages the women can earn. Sociologists might broaden the focus to include more attractive work opportunities—the possibility of doing more challenging, more fulfilling work. In either case, the argument is that as wages or attractive work opportunities increase, women have more to lose by staying home to raise children. Therefore, they increasingly join the labor force and they have fewer children. To the extent that early marriage is inconsistent with a career for women, the argument can be extended to the postponement of marriage: young women have more to lose economically by marrying early and more to gain by developing a career. It can also help explain the rise in marital dissolution, in that women's economic alternatives to marriage have increased. The basic principle is that as men and women become more economically independent of each other, it is less necessary for them to pool their labor and their housework. New opportunities are presented, and old constraints are eased.

Richard Easterlin is the best-known proponent of an alternative economic theory that stresses the impact of the size of

24. National Center for Health Statistics, "Natality Statistics," tab. 19, p. 33.

25. Larry L. Bumpass and James A. Sweet, "Children's Experience in Single-Parent Families: Implications of Cohabitation and Marital Transitions" (NSFH Working Paper no. 3, Center for Demography and Ecology, University of Wisconsin, 1989).

26. On the postwar trend, see Cherlin, *Marriage, Divorce, Remarriage,* pp. 51-54. On the current labor force participation rate for mothers of infants, see Bureau of the Census, "Fertility of American Women," p. 5.

one's birth cohort on one's life chances.[27] Persons who belong to small cohorts find themselves in greater demand by employers, who must fill jobs from a smaller pool of potential workers. According to this theory, the young adults of the 1950s, who were part of the small Depression cohort, could afford to marry earlier and have more children because men had good employment opportunities. But when their children, the large baby-boom cohort, reached adulthood, labor market prospects were poorer. Consequently, young adults delayed marriage, more women entered the labor force, and couples had fewer children. Easterlin's cyclical model suggests that as the children of the baby boomers enter adulthood in the late 1980s and the 1990s, the situation will reverse again and marriage and birth rates will once again increase.

Although it is too soon to judge, the patterns of fertility in the 1980s do not support the Easterlin model so far. If the cohort model were operating, one would expect that young adults would show the first signs of increasing birth rates. Yet as noted earlier, the increases in age-specific rates in the 1980s have occurred solely among women in their thirties and forties — the older baby boomers themselves, not their children. This pattern is consistent with baby boomers' trying to make up for lost time, rather than with their children's experiencing improved labor market conditions.

Cultural change

There is no question that profound cultural changes have occurred concurrently with economic changes, and a number of observers argue that cultural change has exerted an important, independent role in modifying family patterns. The fundamental shift in public opinion has been toward an increasing tolerance of alternatives to conventional marriage and childbearing.

For example, in 1957, men in a national survey were asked, "Suppose that all you knew about a man was that he did not want to get married. What would you guess he was like?" Women in the survey were asked the same question about a hypothetical woman. Half the sample responded that the person probably was deficient in some way: sick, immoral, selfish, or neurotic. But when the same question was asked in a 1976 national survey, only one-third of the sample gave such negative opinions.

The two surveys also included the question, "Thinking about a man's (woman's) life, how is a man's (woman's) life changed by being married?" In 1957, 40 percent of the sample responded positively, describing marriage as opening new opportunities and enlarging life. Just 20 percent expressed negative views emphasizing burdens and restrictions. In contrast, almost as many people in the 1976 sample expressed negative views as expressed positive views. The authors of a massive book about these surveys wrote, "Perhaps nowhere in the book will we see such a dramatic change from 1957 to 1976 as we have in men's and women's increased tolerance of people who reject marriage as a way of life."[28]

The two surveys are part of a series of studies conducted over the past three decades by social scientists at the Institute for Social Research at the University of Mich-

27. Richard A. Easterlin, *Birth and Fortune: The Impact of Numbers on Personal Welfare* (New York, Basic Books, 1980).

28. Joseph Veroff, Elizabeth Douvan, and Richard A. Kulka, *The Inner American: A Self-Portrait from 1957 to 1976* (New York: Basic Books, 1981), p. 191.

igan. These studies map changes in the beliefs of Americans about how people should live their family lives. In a recent article that reviews the studies, Arland Thornton reported striking changes in attitudes during the 1960s and 1970s.[29] Americans' increasing tolerance of people who reject marriage was matched by greater tolerance of divorce, childlessness, and more egalitarian family roles for men and women.

For example, in a 1962 study, only 51 percent of young adult women agreed with the statement that "divorce is usually the best solution when a couple can't seem to work out their marriage problems." When the same women were reinterviewed in 1977, 80 percent agreed with the statement. As for childlessness, 85 percent of the women, all of whom had recently given birth to children, answered positively in 1962 to the question, "Do you feel almost all married couples who can *ought* to have children?" But just 43 percent answered positively to the same question when reinterviewed in 1980.

What occurred was, in Thornton's words, an "erosion of norms" about family life, a weakening of the cultural rules that guide behavior. Americans became more tolerant of alternatives to conventional patterns of marriage and childbearing. The erosion appeared to be part of a broader cultural shift toward an emphasis on autonomy and personal growth. Family life and fertility became matters of personal choice in which individuals made decisions based on a calculus of self-interest and self-fulfillment.[30] Marrying and having children still were desirable, but one no longer had to be married or to have children to be a proper member of adult society.

Ron Lesthaeghe has been the most forceful advocate of the position that changes in the family and fertility throughout the West have been a response primarily to broad cultural changes.[31] He argues that concerns about self-fulfillment and personal growth have played an increasingly important role in the individual's decisions about family and fertility. Lesthaeghe locates the early roots of this long-term change in the individualistic philosophies that emerged in the West after the Reformation and the Enlightenment. These were the cultural roots of a greater emphasis on the nuclear family and on the well-being of children, he argues, as opposed to an emphasis on extended kin groups and community obligations.

The more recent continuation of the trend—in which concern for self-fulfillment increasingly displaces concern for one's children's fulfillment—derives from a general shift to a "post-materialist" culture, according to Lesthaeghe. The metaphor of post-materialism, developed by political scientist Ronald Inglehart, refers to the effects on people's values of a rising level of affluence that removes worries about satisfying basic material needs such as food and shelter.[32] With an increase in affluence, the emphasis shifts from survival to satisfaction, from being to having; and an ideology stressing personal fulfillment becomes dominant.

But the separation between these two types of explanations, the economic and

29. Arland Thornton, "Changing Attitudes towards Family Issues in the United States," *Journal of Marriage and the Family,* in press.

30. See Robert N. Bellah et al., *Habits of the Heart: Individualism and Commitment in American Life* (Berkeley: University of California Press, 1985), esp. chap. 4, "Love and Marriage."

31. Ron Lesthaeghe, "A Century of Demographic and Cultural Change in Western Europe," *Population and Development Review,* 9:411 (Sept. 1983).

32. Ronald Inglehart, *The Silent Revolution: Changing Values and Political Styles among Western Publics* (Princeton, NJ: Princeton University Press, 1977).

the cultural, is artificial. In fact, the great increases in industrial productivity have produced the affluence that Inglehart believes to be the stimulus toward an emphasis on self-fulfillment. Industrial development also has transformed the economies of the Western countries, producing a large expansion of the service sector, in which many of the jobs had come to be viewed as women's work. Thus, in the long run, industrial development in the West has acted to increase wages, expand labor market opportunities for women, and free individuals from the constraints of worrying about basic needs. On the other hand, as has been argued by various social scientists since Max Weber's *Protestant Ethic and the Spirit of Capitalism,* the emphasis on individualism in Western culture has helped bring about the high level of industrial development. Neither the more materialist nor the more ideological perspective provides much help in explaining the still puzzling period of 1945-65, but both perspectives seem essential to understanding what occurred before and has occurred since in this century.

APPROACHING THE YEAR 2000

The great recent changes of the postwar era are still in progress, despite the relative stability in the 1980s of rates of births, marriages, and divorces. As the past record of demographic forecasting amply demonstrates, it is hazardous to predict the future course of fertility and the family. Nevertheless, I will offer some speculations on the implications of current trends for the years ahead.

In the 1980s, birth rates did not continue the plunge that began in the mid-1960s; rather, they stabilized. In fact, by the end of the decade there were noticeable increases in the birth rates of women in their thirties.

It thus appears that the women of the baby-boom generation, having postponed marriage and childbearing while in their twenties, are trying to catch up. It is very unlikely that this late surge will produce large completed family sizes. On the other hand, it is likely that completed family sizes will be somewhat larger than had been feared early in the decade.

Consequently, the recent U.S. experience is inconsistent with the simple notion that contemporary fertility trends inevitably lead to extremely low birth rates. Whereas the TFR in some central European countries has dropped to the startlingly low level of 1.3 to 1.4, the TFR in the United State is currently at about 1.9, and further increases in the birth rates for older women could push it higher. Thus I would argue that the fear of an enormous shortfall of births in the United States is unfounded. To be sure, the TFR remains below the replacement level of 2.1. But a TFR in the neighborhood of 1.9 implies a shortfall of about 10 million persons over a generation of childbearing — about 25 years — and that shortfall could be compensated by an annual net flow of 400,000 immigrants.[33] In fact, recent levels of legal immigration have been about 600,000 per year, and illegal immigration is substantial.[34]

I would argue, therefore, that concerns about American fertility and the family in the 1990s and beyond are likely to focus less on the number of children than on whether their upbringing and education are adequate to meet the needs of our society. The circumstances of the average child's

33. There were about 50 million women of childbearing age in the late 1980s. A TFR that is 0.2 children below that replacement rate thus implies a shortfall of roughly 10 million births over a generation.

34. U.S. Department of Justice, Immigration and Naturalization Service, *Annual Report, 1987* (Washington, DC: Government Printing Office, 1988), tab. 1.

life are quite different from a generation ago. Children's family situations are much less stable, and it is likely that this level of instability will remain high or even increase. Our system of marriage now incorporates frequent cohabitation before and after formal unions, and these cohabiting relationships are even less stable than marriages. About half of all children are likely to spend time in a single-parent family before adulthood,[35] and it is likely that many of these single parents will form and dissolve cohabiting unions, thus further increasing children's experience of family disruption. Due in part to the changes in family structure and in part to poorly understood shifts in the economy, the economic circumstances of children deteriorated, on average, in the 1970s and 1980s; currently, one out of five children is living in a family with an income below the poverty line.[36]

The differences between blacks and whites in the characteristics of children are particularly striking. Here again the issue is not quantity: in recent years, the average family sizes of blacks and whites have been converging.[37] But black women tend to give birth at substantially younger ages than do white women, and the differential has been widening.[38] In 1987, 23 percent of all black mothers giving birth were teenagers, 9 of 10 of them unmarried. Among

whites, 10 percent of all mothers giving birth were teenagers, half of them unmarried.[39] Even at older ages, black women are far more likely to give birth out of wedlock than are whites, although the rates for whites have been rising more rapidly. Black women have higher rates of separation and divorce and lower rates of remarriage than do white women. As a result, only 39 percent of all black children in 1988 were living with two parents.[40] A number of observers have argued that the trends in family structure among blacks are an integral part of the problem of the growth of an underclass population of the persistently poor in central-city ghettos.[41]

More generally, as lower population growth produces tighter labor markets, business and government leaders are paying more attention to the skills that children are developing and the education they receive. Employers may not have the luxury in the early twenty-first century of ignoring the least-qualified segment of the labor force. As our society ages, the Social Security trust fund will need tax contributions from as many productive workers as possible. The more foresighted public and private leaders have already realized as much. Under these circumstances, ensuring an optimal level of development for children in poor families, children in immigrant families, and children in single-parent families will take on increasing importance. As recently as the early 1980s, few observers had noted these trends; now they are widely discussed. The current patterns of American fertility, marriage, and divorce will likely keep the issue of children's well-being on the public agenda in the 1990s.

35. Larry L. Bumpass, "Children and Marital Disruption: A Replication and Update," *Demography*, 21:71 (Feb. 1984).

36. For a discussion of trends in children's well-being, see Samuel H. Preston, "Children and the Elderly: Divergent Paths for America's Dependents," *Demography*, 21:435 (Nov. 1984); Nicholas Zill and Carolyn C. Rogers, "Recent Trends in the Well-Being of Children in the United States and Their Implications for Public Policy," in *The Changing American Family and Public Policy*, ed. A. J. Cherlin (Washington, DC: Urban Institute Press, 1988), pp. 31-115.

37. M.D.R. Evans, "American Fertility Patterns: A Comparison of White and Nonwhite Cohorts Born 1903-56," *Population and Development Review*, 12:275 (June 1986).

38. Ibid., p. 270.

39. National Center for Health Statistics, "Natality Statistics," tabs. 2 and 18, pp. 16 and 32.

40. Bureau of the Census, "Marital Status and Living Arrangements," p. 61.

41. William J. Wilson, *The Truly Disadvantaged: The Inner City, the Underclass, and Public Policy* (Chicago: University of Chicago Press, 1987).

ANNALS, *AAPSS,* **510,** July 1990

Growth and Diversity of the Population of the Soviet Union

By BARBARA A. ANDERSON and BRIAN D. SILVER

ABSTRACT: The most remarkable feature of the Soviet Union's demography is its ethnic diversity. More than 90 ethnic groups are indigenous to the territory of the Soviet Union. Ethnic Russians composed only 50.8 percent of the population according to preliminary 1989 census results. The article examines official Soviet statistics for the period 1959 to 1989 to illustrate some of the risks in describing Soviet demographic behavior. Is fertility in the Soviet Union high or low? Answer: both. Is the Soviet population growing rapidly or slowly? Answer: both. The changing ethnic composition of the population of the USSR as a whole reflects large differences in growth rates of ethnic groups; the changing composition of the USSR by region also reflects differences in migration by ethnic group. Differences in growth rates are reshaping the ethnic composition of the Soviet labor force. For the USSR as a whole between 1979 and 1989, three-fourths of the net increment to the working ages was contributed by the one-sixth of the population in 1979 that was traditionally Muslim in religion.

Barbara A. Anderson is professor of sociology at the University of Michigan and research scientist and associate director for training at the university's Population Studies Center. She holds a Ph.D. in sociology from Princeton University. She is the author of Internal Migration and Modernization in Late Nineteenth-Century Russia *and coauthor of* Human Fertility in Russia.

Brian D. Silver is professor and chairperson of the Department of Political Science at Michigan State University and a research affiliate of the Population Studies Center of the University of Michigan. He earned his Ph.D. from the University of Wisconsin. He is coeditor of Soviet Asian Ethnic Frontiers.

NOTE: The authors share equal responsibility for this article. The research was supported by NICHD grant nos. RO1 HD-19915 and P30 HD-10003.

THE Soviet Union has the third-largest population of any country in the world. The 1989 census counted 286.7 million people.[1] Developments in the Soviet population have been of great interest because of its size and because of the importance of the Soviet Union in world affairs. In addition, reports of unfavorable demographic features of the Soviet population, such as high rates of infant mortality and adult mortality, have been cited within the country and abroad as evidence of the low quality of life in the Soviet Union compared to other industrial countries. The infant mortality rate, for example, was 25.4 infant deaths per 1000 live births in 1987; life expectancy at birth for Soviet males was 65.0 years and for females, 73.8 years, in 1986-87.[2]

Perhaps the most remarkable feature of the Soviet Union's demography is not its size or the state of its public health but its ethnic diversity. Members of more than ninety ethnic groups that are indigenous to the territory of the Soviet Union were counted in the 1989 census. Twenty-two ethnic groups — "nationalities," in common Soviet usage — had populations of 1 million or more. Ethnic Russians composed 50.8 percent of the population in 1989 and they will fall below 50 percent of the Soviet population before the middle of the 1990s.[3] In addition to 145 million ethnic Russians in 1989, the Soviet population had 56 million members of other Slavic nationalities, 56 million members of nationalities whose traditional religion is Islam, and another 29 million people who are neither Slavs nor Muslims. Moreover, the Muslim population is growing rapidly. Though comprising only one-sixth of the population of the USSR in 1979, Muslims contributed 50 percent of the increase in the Soviet population between 1979 and 1989.

It should be difficult for observers of the Soviet Union today to ignore the multiethnic character of that country, as the non-Russian nationalities seek greater economic, cultural, and political autonomy, sometimes manifesting their feelings in large-scale public demonstrations. There have been many reported incidents of violence between ethnic groups — not only, as might be commonly supposed,

---

1. This is the total of the de facto or present (in Russian, *nalichnoe*) population in the USSR according to preliminary figures from the 1989 census. The de jure or permanent (*postoiannoe*) population is 1 million less: 285.7 million. The State Committee on Statistics of the USSR — formerly the Central Statistical Board — has changed the way in which it reports most population data in the censuses. Barbara A. Anderson and Brian D. Silver, "'Permanent' and 'Present' Populations in Soviet Statistics," *Soviet Studies*, 37:386-402 (July 1985). Accordingly, unless noted otherwise, all data in this article from the 1959 and 1970 Soviet censuses refer to the present population, and all data from the 1979 and 1989 censuses refer to the permanent population.

2. All of these reported figures are subject to error. Infant deaths appear to be underreported substantially, especially in the regions with high rates; and Soviet definitions of "infant death" and "live birth" differ from those proposed by the World Health Organization. We estimate that the reported infant mortality rates for the Soviet Union need to be inflated by at least 22 percent to make them comparable with World Health Organization definitions. Barbara A. Anderson and Brian D. Silver, "Infant Mortality in the Soviet Union: Regional Differences and Measurement Issues," *Population and Development Review*, 12:705-38(Dec. 1986). Life expectancy at birth is probably overestimated, due to underreporting of deaths, overstatement of age at death, and overstate-

ment of age in Soviet censuses. Idem, "The Changing Shape of Soviet Mortality, 1958-85: An Evaluation of Old and New Evidence," *Population Studies*, 43:243-65 (July 1989).

3. For further discussion of the changing ethnic composition of the Soviet population, see Barbara A. Anderson and Brian D. Silver, "Demographic Sources of the Changing Ethnic Composition of the Soviet Union," *Population and Development Review*, Dec. 1989, vol. 15.

between Russians and non-Russians, but also between members of non-Russian nationalities.

But even today one often reads of Soviet public health, Soviet mortality, and Soviet population growth, as if the range of demographic experience in the USSR were small. In this article we highlight the magnitude of the demographic differences associated with the ethnic diversity of the USSR, while describing trends in some of the main indicators of demographic change.

Our analysis is based on official Soviet population statistics.[4] Although ethnic differences in demographic behavior are very important in the Soviet Union, we cannot conduct our entire analysis on this basis, because very few data by ethnic group have been published. Thus part of our analysis relies on examination of regional patterns. The Soviet Union has a federal political system. Most major types of demographic data are published both for the Soviet Union as a whole and for the 15 major constituent union republics — also known as Soviet Socialist Republics (SSRs) — but not for ethnic groups. The 15 SSRs are listed in Table 1.

The SSRs are the traditional homelands of major ethnic groups. These ethnic groups are the titular nationalities of these regions in the sense that the areas are named after the ethnic group — Kazakhstan after the Kazakhs, Ukraine after the Ukrainians, and so on. But none of the areas is ethnically homogeneous. As shown in Table 1, the percentage of a republic's population that is of the titular nationality

4. These data have appeared in a variety of sources and are based either on Soviet censuses — of 1959, 1970, 1979, and 1989 — or on vital registration statistics. The data on ethnic groups for 1989 come from preliminary unpublished official data from the 1989 Soviet census.

ranges from a low of 39.5 percent in Kazakhstan to a high of 93.9 percent in Armenia. Consequently, statistics for the SSRs do not reflect only the demographic behavior of the titular nationality. Nevertheless, differences in the behavior of the titular nationalities are the main source of differences in most demographic behaviors of the populations of the SSRs. We shall use demographic statistics on ethnic groups when they are available.

SOVIET DEMOGRAPHIC BEHAVIOR
AS A COMPOSITE OF
THE BEHAVIOR OF ITS PARTS

Change in the behavior of a population often reflects different rates of change in different subpopulations. For example, from 1971 to 1976, the infant mortality rate (IMR) in the Soviet Union rose from 22.9 infant deaths per 1000 live births to 31.4, an increase of 37 percent. This increase was much larger in the rural areas: the IMR in rural areas rose from 24.3 to 37.8 — an increase of 56 percent — while the IMR in the urban areas increased 24 percent, from 21.6 to 26.7. By 1987, the IMR of the country as a whole had fallen to 25.4; in the urban areas it was 21.1, and in the rural areas it was 31.5. Thus the only reason the IMR in the USSR as a whole was higher in 1987 than in 1971 is that the rural IMR was higher in 1987 than it had been in 1971.

Social scientists sometimes use the term "compositional effect" to describe situations in which changes in the behavior of the whole population are a result of changes in the composition of that population rather than changes in the behavior of the constituent parts. For example, if a population consists of two subpopulations, one with a crude birth rate (CBR) of 20 live births per 1000 population and another with a CBR of 40, then the CBR of the

TABLE 1
CHARACTERISTICS OF SOVIET UNION REPUBLICS AND THEIR TITULAR NATIONALITY, 1989

Republic	Population (thousands)				Percentage Distribution			Characteristics of the Titular Nationality	
	Total	Titular	Russian	Other	Titular	Russian	Other	Traditional religion	Language group
RSFSR	147,386	119,807	119,807	27,579	81.3	81.3	18.7	Russian Orthodox	Slavic
Baltic									
Estonia	1,573	963	475	135	61.2	30.2	8.6	Lutheran	Finnic
Latvia	2,681	1,388	906	388	51.8	33.8	14.5	Lutheran	Baltic
Lithuania	3,673	2,924	344	406	79.6	9.4	11.0	Catholic	Baltic
West									
Belorussia	10,200	7,898	1,341	961	77.4	13.1	9.4	Russian Orthodox	Slavic
Moldavia	4,341	2,791	560	990	64.3	12.9	22.8	Russian Orthodox	Romance
Ukraine	51,704	37,370	11,340	2,993	72.3	21.9	5.8	Russian Orthodox	Slavic
Armenia-Georgia									
Armenia	3,283	3,082	52	150	93.9	1.6	4.6	Armenian Orthodox	Separate Indo-European
Georgia	5,449	3,789	339	1,321	69.5	6.2	24.2	Georgian Orthodox	Caucasian
Muslim SSRs									
Azerbaijan	7,029	5,801	392	836	82.5	5.6	11.9	Shiite Muslim	Turkic
Kazakhstan	16,538	6,532	6,226	3,780	39.5	37.6	22.9	Sunni Muslim	Turkic
Kirghizia	4,291	2,228	917	1,146	51.9	21.4	26.7	Sunni Muslim	Turkic
Tadzhikistan	5,112	3,168	387	1,557	62.0	7.6	30.5	Sunni Muslim	Iranic
Turkmenistan	3,534	2,524	334	675	71.4	9.5	19.1	Sunni Muslim	Turkic
Uzbekistan	19,906	14,124	1,652	4,130	71.0	8.3	20.7	Sunni Muslim	Turkic
USSR	285,689								

SOURCE: Population figures for 1989 are unpublished preliminary data from the 1989 Soviet census and are subject to correction. They refer to the "permanent" (postoiannoe) population. Figures for Azerbaijan and Armenia, in particular, may be less accurate because of the violence and mass migrations associated with the conflict over Nagorno-Karabagh and because of disruptions caused by the Armenian earthquake, both of which occurred in 1988.

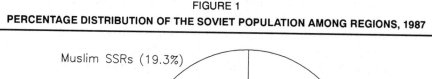

FIGURE 1
PERCENTAGE DISTRIBUTION OF THE SOVIET POPULATION AMONG REGIONS, 1987

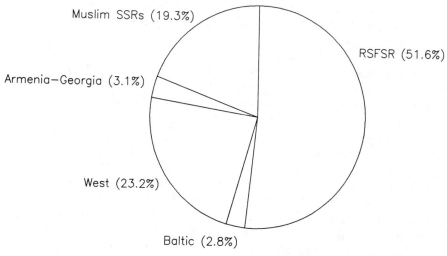

Muslim SSRs (19.3%)

RSFSR (51.6%)

Armenia—Georgia (3.1%)

West (23.2%)

Baltic (2.8%)

combined population would depend on the distribution of the population between the two groups. The CBR for the entire population would fall somewhere between 20 and 40. If the shares of the population that belonged to each group changed over time, while the CBRs of each subpopulation remained the same, then the change in the CBR of the entire population would be a compositional effect.

Of course, in real populations, change in the whole population usually involves both compositional changes and changes in the behavior of the separate subpopulations. In a population as diverse as that of the Soviet Union, the contribution of compositional changes to the changes in statistics for the population as a whole is often very large.

Regional components of
Soviet demographic behavior

Let us examine some data on the Soviet population in 1987.[5] Figure 1 shows the shares of the Soviet population that belong to each of five regional groupings of 15 SSRs: Russia, or the Russian Soviet Federated Socialist Republic (RSFSR); Baltic, composed of Estonia, Latvia, and Lithuania; the West, comprising Belorussia, Moldavia, and the Ukraine; Armenia-Georgia, comprising Armenia and Georgia; and the Muslim SSRs, which are Azerbaijan, Kazakhstan, Kirghizia, Tadzhikistan, Turkmen-

5. We use this year because it is the latest year for which we have data on all of the indicators for which the following comparison is to be made.

istan, and Uzbekistan.[6] A slight majority of the population, 51.6 percent, lived in the RSFSR. Only about 3 percent of the population lived in the Baltic or in Armenia-Georgia. Another 23 percent lived in the three republics of the Soviet West, and 19 percent lived in the six Muslim republics. Since these groupings exhaust the population of the USSR, the weighted average of the demographic behavior of the parts represents the demographic behavior of the USSR as a whole.

Now let us examine the share of births and deaths that occurred in each region in 1987. We pay particular attention to the shares contributed by the RSFSR and the six Muslim republics. Figure 2a shows that 45 percent of all births occurred in the RSFSR and 32 percent in the Muslim republics. Figure 2b shows that 55 percent of all deaths occurred in the RSFSR, and only 14 percent in the Muslim republics. Figure 2c shows that while 34 percent of all infant deaths occurred in the RSFSR, 51 percent occurred in the Muslim republics. Finally, Figure 2d shows that while 35 percent of the natural increase — births minus deaths — occurred in the RSFSR, 50 percent occurred in the Muslim republics.

The shares contributed by each of the population subgroups vary greatly from one demographic indicator to the next because of differences between the subgroups in fertility, mortality, and age structure. The shares of demographic events for the Muslim republics differ from their share for the Soviet population because the Muslim republics have high fertility, high infant mortality, and a young population compared to the rest of the Soviet Union.

This illustrates some of the risks in describing Soviet demographic behavior. Is fertility in the Soviet Union high or low? Answer: Both. It is low in the non-Muslim republics and very high in the Muslim republics. Is the Soviet population growing rapidly or slowly? Answer: Both. It is growing rapidly in the Muslim republics, at 2.0 percent per year, and slowly in the non-Muslim republics at less than 1 percent per year.

Therefore, when one speaks of Soviet demographic behavior, one is speaking of an average of behaviors that differ greatly across regions and ethnic groups. This average reflects the behavior of some of the parts better than others, depending on the demographic indicator referred to. Moreover, the average does not necessarily mainly reflect the behavior of the largest ethnic segments of the population, such as Russians or the Slavic groups taken together.

Ethnic components of Soviet demographic behavior

Data for Soviet regions are an imperfect surrogate for data on ethnic groups. Fortunately, for some demographic indicators we have direct data on ethnic groups. All Soviet citizens have a nationality (in Russian, natsional'nost').[7] After they receive their internal passport at age 16, Soviet citizens have an official nationality, which is listed on their identity papers, employment records, military records, and so forth. It is difficult or impossible for an individual to change this official national-

6. This is a conventional grouping of the Soviet republics, except for our placing of Azerbaijan with the other Muslim republics rather than with the two other Transcaucasian republics of Armenia and Georgia.

7. For a discussion of the terminology used in Soviet statistics on ethnic groups, see Brian D. Silver, "The Ethnic and Language Dimensions in Russian and Soviet Censuses," in Research Guide to the Russian and Soviet Censuses, ed. Ralph S. Clem (Ithaca, NY: Cornell University Press, 1986), pp. 70-97.

FIGURE 2
PERCENTAGE DISTRIBUTION OF VARIOUS DEMOGRAPHIC EVENTS AMONG SOVIET REGIONS, 1987

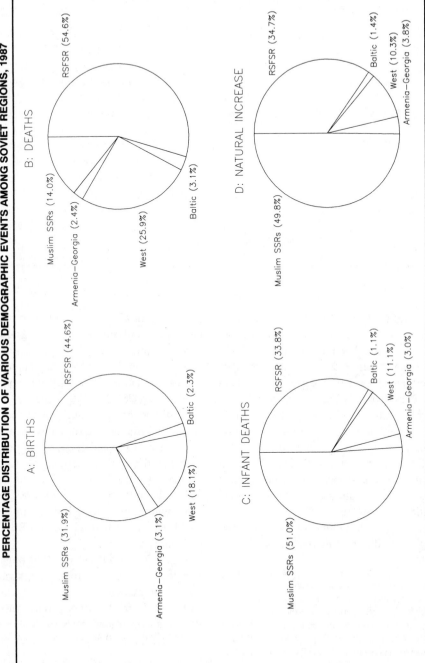

FIGURE 3
PERCENTAGE DISTRIBUTION OF THE SOVIET
POPULATION AMONG NATIONALITY GROUPINGS, 1989

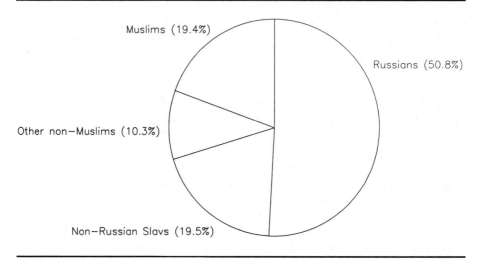

ity. Nationality in the Soviet censuses, however, is a subjective phenomenon, based on the self-report of the individual.

Even if there were no emigration from the Soviet Union, ethnic groups would not be closed populations, since people can migrate into or out of a given nationality by changing their self-reported ethnic identity from one census to the next. We refer to this process as ethnic reidentification. There is evidence of substantial ethnic reidentification among Soviet non-Russian nationalities in the past.[8]

Change in the number of people belonging to the different Soviet nationalities is

therefore not simply a result of fertility, mortality, and international migration. Based on projections of the population in 1989 from earlier data, whether ethnic Russians remained a majority of the population of the USSR in 1989 depended substantially on the extent of ethnic reidentification of the population between the censuses of 1979 and 1989. Some people who identified as a member of a non-Russian nationality in 1979 could have called themselves Russian in 1989, and some who identified as Russian in 1979 could have identified with a non-Russian nationality in 1989.[9]

Figure 3 shows the share of the population that belonged to four groupings of Soviet nationalities, according to preliminary data from the 1989 Soviet census: Russians constituted 50.8 percent; non-Russian Slavs, 19.5 percent; other non-

    8. For a summary of the evidence, as well as a discussion of methods of measuring ethnic reidentification, see Barbara A. Anderson, "Some Factors Related to Ethnic Reidentification in the Russian Republic," in *Soviet Nationality Policies and Practices* (New York: Praeger, 1978), pp. 309-33; Barbara A. Anderson and Brian D. Silver, "Estimating Russification of Ethnic Identity among Non-Russians in the USSR," *Demography,* 20:461-89 (Nov. 1983).

    9. For further discussion, see Anderson and Silver, "Demographic Sources."

Muslims, 10.3 percent; and Muslims, 19.4 percent. The number of people that this represents is given in panel A of Table 2. These figures are based on the entire Soviet population, not only the titular nationalities of the 15 union republics.[10]

In 1989, Russians remained a bare majority of the Soviet population. We think the number of Russians is somewhat smaller than might have been expected, due to a decrease in the tendency of non-Russians to change their identification to Russian and perhaps to a return by some self-declared Russians to an earlier non-Russian ethnic identity. But with the available data, we cannot measure the extent of ethnic reidentification between 1979 and 1989.[11]

Panel B of Table 2 shows that Russians compose a decreasing share of the Soviet population between the last four census dates, from 54.7 percent in 1959 to 50.8 percent in 1989. Muslims, on the other hand, constitute an increasing share, from 11.8 percent in 1959 to 19.4 percent in 1989. Non-Russian Slavs decreased their share from 22.5 percent to 19.5 percent, while other non-Muslims decreased from 11.0 percent to 10.3 percent. All four groupings, however, grew in absolute size in each intercensal period.

Panel D of Table 2 shows how much each of the four groupings of nationalities contributed to the overall population growth of the Soviet Union between the

last four census dates. Most noticeable are the relative contributions of Muslims and Russians. Between 1959 and 1970 Muslims contributed 31.7 percent of the population growth of the USSR and Russians contributed 45.4 percent, but by 1979-89 this contribution had reversed: Muslims contributed 49.7 percent and Russians, 32.6 percent. This reversal reflects the continuing high fertility rates of Muslim nationalities and the low fertility rates of Russians, other Slavs, and other non-Muslims.

The differences in the growth rates of nationalities underlie the differences in the natural increase of Soviet regional populations depicted in Figure 2d.[12] But a comparison of growth rates by region and by nationality—compare panel C of Table 2 with panel C of Table 3—also makes clear that use of regional data in place of ethnic group data often reduces the magnitude of the differences in demographic behavior.[13] In the period 1979-89, for example, the Muslim population grew at an average annual rate of 2.4 percent, while the population of the six Muslim republics grew at an annual rate of 2.0 percent. Similarly, the number of Russians grew at an average annual rate of 0.5 percent, while the population of the RSFSR grew at a rate of 0.7 percent. The regional difference is smaller

10. The Muslim population of the USSR, for example, consists of—in addition to the titular nationalities of the six Muslim SSRs—the Volga Tatars, with 6.6 million people in 1989; the Peoples of Dagestan, with 2.1 million; the Chechens, with 1.0 million; and 21 more Muslim nationalities.

11. Estimation of the amount of ethnic reidentification requires data on the age distribution of the population by nationality. To date—Dec. 1989—no data on age by nationality have been published for either the 1979 or 1989 Soviet censuses.

12. In Figure 2d, we are able to depict rates of natural increase—births minus deaths—by region, because birth and death rates are reported for SSRs. In Table 2, we are not able to depict rates of natural increase of ethnic groups because birth and death rates are not reported for nationalities. But the growth rates given in the table's panel C closely approximate the rates of natural increase, since only a few nationalities have experienced substantial international migration in recent decades.

13. For further illustrations of this general point, see Brian D. Silver, "Levels of Sociocultural Development among Soviet Nationalities: A Partial Test of the Equalization Hypothesis," *American Political Science Review,* 68:1618-37 (Dec. 1974).

TABLE 2

SOME CHARACTERISTICS OF THE FOUR ETHNIC GROUPINGS USED IN THE ANALYSIS

		Russians	Non-Russian Slavs	Other Non-Muslims	Muslims	Total USSR
A. Population size (thousands)	1959	114,114	46,910	23,027	24,699	208,827
	1970	129,015	51,357	26,102	35,107	241,720
	1979	137,397	53,352	27,508	43,809	262,085
	1989	145,072	55,700	29,336	55,533	285,689
B. Percentage of USSR population	1959	54.7	22.5	11.0	11.8	100.0
	1970	53.4	21.3	10.8	14.5	100.0
	1979	52.4	20.4	10.5	16.7	100.0
	1989	50.8	19.5	10.3	19.4	100.0
C. Average annual growth rate (percentage)	1959-70	1.1	0.8	1.1	3.2	1.3
	1970-79	0.7	0.4	0.6	2.5	0.9
	1979-89	0.5	0.4	0.6	2.4	0.9
D. Percentage of total Soviet population growth occurring in the grouping	1959-70	45.4	13.5	9.4	31.7	100.0
	1970-79	40.9	9.7	6.9	42.5	100.0
	1979-89	32.6	10.0	7.8	49.7	100.0

SOURCE: Data from 1959, 1970, and 1979 are published official statistics derived from Soviet censuses conducted in those years. Data from 1989 are from unpublished preliminary statistics from the 1989 census. Population counts for 1959 and 1970 are the "present" (*nalichnoe*) population; counts for 1979 and 1989 are the "permanent" (*postoiannoe*) population.

TABLE 3
SOME CHARACTERISTICS OF THE FIVE REGIONAL GROUPINGS USED IN THE ANALYSIS

		RSFSR	Baltic	West	Armenia-Georgia	Muslim SSRs	Total USSR
A. Population size (thousands)	1959	117,534	6,002	52,809	5,807	26,674	208,827
	1970	129,941	6,825	59,618	7,167	37,884	241,720
	1979	137,410	7,359	63,092	8,030	46,194	262,085
	1989	147,386	7,944	66,245	8,732	56,410	285,689
B. Percentage of USSR population	1959	56.3	2.9	25.3	2.8	12.8	100.0
	1970	53.8	2.8	24.7	3.0	15.7	100.0
	1979	52.4	2.8	24.1	3.1	17.6	100.0
	1989	51.4	2.8	23.1	3.1	19.7	100.0
C. Average annual growth rate (percentage)	1959-70	0.9	1.2	1.1	1.9	3.2	1.3
	1970-79	0.6	0.8	0.6	1.3	2.2	0.9
	1979-89	0.7	0.8	0.5	0.8	2.0	0.9
D. Percentage of total Soviet population growth occurring in the grouping	1959-70	38.1	2.5	20.9	4.2	34.4	100.0
	1970-79	36.2	2.6	16.8	4.2	40.2	100.0
	1979-89	40.5	2.4	12.8	2.9	40.5	100.0

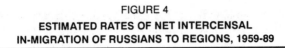

FIGURE 4
ESTIMATED RATES OF NET INTERCENSAL
IN-MIGRATION OF RUSSIANS TO REGIONS, 1959-89

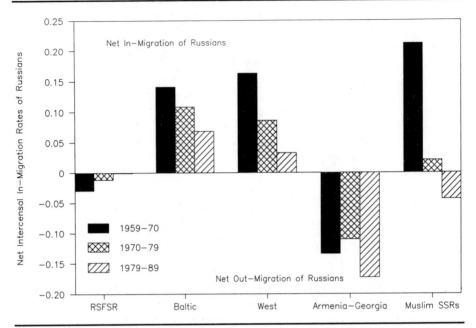

NOTE: This figure shows the estimated amount of Russian net in-migration to the region between censuses divided by the number of Russians in the region at the first census.

than the ethnic group difference because regions are not ethnically homogeneous and because of different migration patterns by ethnic group. In particular, between 1979 and 1989, on balance, Russians migrated out of the Muslim republics and the net migration of Russians out of the RSFSR was close to zero.

Figure 4 shows the estimated net number of Russian migrants into each region between recent census dates divided by the number of persons in the region at the initial date. Thus it shows the proportion by which the population of the region would have increased or decreased in the period due to the migration of Russians.[14]

14. Russians experienced very little international migration. Thus their growth in the Soviet Union as a whole is primarily the result of natural increase. The

We can refer to this as a net migration rate.[15]

Between 1959 and 1970, as well as between 1970 and 1979, there was net migration of Russians into the Muslim republics. Most of this migration was to the Virgin Lands territory of Kazakhstan,[16] but there

net number of Russian migrants into a region was estimated as the difference between the number of Russians in the region at the second date and the number of Russians there would have been in the region if the Russian population had grown between censuses proportionately to the Russian population in the entire Soviet Union. For more discussion of these estimates, see Anderson and Silver, "Demographic Sources."

15. Strictly speaking, there can be no net migration rate because there is no population at risk of net migration; however, such a measure is conventionally referred to as a net migration rate.

16. In 1959-70, an estimated 69 percent of the net Russian migration to the Muslim republics was to

was a net influx of Russians into five of the six Muslim republics in both the 1959-70 and 1970-79 intercensal periods — the exception was Azerbaijan, from which there was net out-migration of Russians in both periods. Between 1979 and 1989, however, there was net out-migration of Russians from all six Muslim republics.[17]

Figure 4 also shows that there was net out-migration of Russians from Armenia and Georgia in all three intercensal periods as well as net in-migration of Russians to both the Baltic and the Soviet West in all three periods. Russians were not the only internal migrants; however, Russians, Ukrainians, and Belorussians composed the bulk of those Soviet citizens who moved across union-republic boundaries in response to new jobs.

In the 1950s and 1960s, a policy of the intermixing of different nationalities was endorsed openly by central authorities, and relocation of labor was one method of achieving such mixing. This policy has long been controversial in the non-Russian republics. The net result of the migration patterns by different ethnic groups in recent decades has been the increasing ethnic homogenization and, one might say, indigenization, of the Muslim republics, Armenia, and Georgia, and the decreasing homogenization — increasing Russianization — of the Baltic and the Soviet West. In September 1989, the Central Committee of the Communist Party of the Soviet Union for the first time formally acknowledged

the adverse consequences of this policy — in particular, its threat to the preservation of ethnic distinctiveness and its exacerbation of interethnic tensions.[18]

DIFFERENCES IN REGIONAL AND
ETHNIC DEMOGRAPHIC PATTERNS

In the remainder of this article, we explore several dimensions of Soviet demographic behavior by region and by ethnic group. We turn now to infant mortality.

Infant mortality

The IMR is often interpreted as an indicator of the quality of life in a society. It reflects the effects of personal health and hygiene, diet, public health and sanitation programs, and the quality and availability of medical services. Figure 5 shows the differences in the average IMRs for the republics in each group at five-year intervals from 1960 to 1985. The IMR for the USSR as a whole in 1985 was about the same as it was in 1965. This contrasts with the trend toward improvement in infant mortality in most other countries of the industrial world.

The data for separate regional groupings show different levels and trends in infant mortality. In the RSFSR and the Baltic, the IMR declined in each five-year interval except 1970-75. In the West also the IMR rose between 1970 and 1975 and was lower in 1985 than in 1960 and 1965, but between 1965 and 1985 there was little decline. The pattern in Armenia and Georgia is similar to that found in the West, except that the IMR in 1985 was much lower than the IMR in 1965. In general, the patterns of change in the IMRs in the

---

Kazakhstan; in 1970-79, an estimated 44 percent of the net Russian migration to these republics was to Kazakhstan.

17. For further details on the ethnic patterns of migration, see Brian D. Silver, "Population Redistribution and the Ethnic Balance in Transcaucasia," in *Nationalism and Social Change in Transcaucasia,* ed. Ronald G. Suny (Ann Arbor: University of Michigan Press, 1983), pp. 376-96; Anderson and Silver, "Demographic Sources."

18. See "Party's Draft Platform on Nationalities Policy," *Current Digest of the Soviet Press,* 13 Sept. 1989, pp. 1-8.

FIGURE 5
INFANT MORTALITY RATE FOR USSR AND SOVIET REGIONS, 1960-85

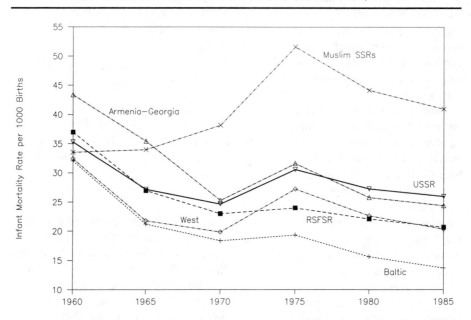

RSFSR, Baltic, West, and Armenia-Georgia were similar to one another between 1960 and 1985.

The most distinctive pattern appears in the Muslim republics. There the reported IMR in 1960 was, on average, lower than that found in the USSR as a whole and in the other four regions. It then rose to a peak in the mid-1970s and subsequently declined. The average IMR in 1985, however, was substantially higher than the IMR in 1960, 1965, and 1970, and it was much higher than the IMR in the other Soviet regions.

Why the distinctive pattern among Muslim republics? The figures for 1960 tell part of the story. Medical services, health care, and public sanitation are of lower quality and more limited availability in the Muslim republics, especially those in Central Asia, than in most other regions

of the USSR.[19] That the IMR in 1960 reported for the Muslim republics was lower than the IMRs reported for other regions undoubtedly reflects underreporting of infant deaths in the Muslim republics. This does not mean that all infant deaths were reported in other regions, but the extent of the underreporting was probably much greater in the Muslim areas.[20] The rise in

19. We have heard reports of IMRs of over 100 for some remote parts of Siberia, within the RSFSR. No IMRs that high have been officially published for any region of the Soviet Union in recent years, however.

20. Elsewhere we estimated the IMRs for the indigenous nationalities of the Muslim republics. We found that in 1959, the IMRs of people belonging to the indigenous nationalities were lower than the IMRs of the European-background population—such as Russians and Ukrainians—living in the Muslim republics. This is implausible. See Barbara A. Anderson, Brian D. Silver, and Jinyun Liu, "Mortality of Ethnic Groups in Soviet Central Asia and Northern

the IMRs in the Muslim republics in later years probably reflects mostly improvements in the reporting of infant deaths, not worsening actual infant mortality. In other words, the actual IMRs in the Muslim republics in 1960 were probably higher than the rates reported in the mid-1970s and later.

Elsewhere we have argued that the rise in reported infant mortality in the Soviet Union in the early 1970s was mostly an artifact of improvements in statistical record keeping and the completeness of reporting of infant deaths, especially in Soviet Central Asia. Both in Central Asia and elsewhere in the Soviet Union, new procedures introduced in the early 1970s for tabulating infant deaths, along with increasing incentives for registering infants who were at high risk of dying in infancy, could have raised the reported IMRs even if the actual IMRs remained the same or declined.[21] We think these new procedures and incentives would have had this effect not only in the Muslim republics but also in other parts of the Soviet Union.

This does not mean that all increases in mortality reported in the 1960s and 1970s in the Soviet Union were an artifact of improved reporting. The increase in reported mortality of working-age males beginning in the mid-1960s probably reflected real worsening of the health of Soviet males.[22] Moreover, it is possible that

some of the increase in infant mortality was also real. There are many reports, for example, of poor water quality in Central Asia, perhaps intensified by the increasing population density in rural areas.

Fertility rates

Part of the explanation of the high rates of infant mortality among Soviet Muslim populations may be high fertility. When women have many children, especially in the context of limited availability of prenatal care or limited possibility of using the available services, then newborns are likely to be at high risk of dying. Among some Muslim populations, such as Tadzhiks and Turkmenians, the frequency of marriages between cousins is also a special risk factor for infant mortality.

Figure 6 shows the average total fertility rate (TFR) for the titular nationalities of the five regions of the USSR at three dates, 1958-59, 1969-70, and 1978-79, as reported by Soviet demographers.[23] The TFR is the number of children that a woman would have in her reproductive life if she followed a given age-specific fertility schedule, such as that of all women in a given year. Figure 6 shows that the TFR of the Muslim groups is much higher than that of the others. On average, as late as 1978-79, Muslim women could expect to bear 5.6 children, while non-Muslim women could expect to bear between 1.8 and 2.3 children.

The comparatively low fertility of non-Muslim women is not a result of a high incidence of childlessness; in fact, very high proportions of non-Muslim women marry and have at least one child. High

China," *Research Reports* (University of Michigan, Population Studies Center), Sept. 1989, no. 89-158.

21. See Anderson and Silver, "Infant Mortality in the Soviet Union."

22. For further discussion, see Barbara A. Anderson and Brian D. Silver, "Sex Differentials in Mortality in the Soviet Union: Regional Differences in Length of Working Life in Comparative Perspective," *Population Studies,* 40:191-214 (July 1986); idem, "Changing Shape"; idem, "Patterns of Cohort Mortality in the Soviet Population," *Population and Development Review,* 15:471-501 (Sept. 1989).

23. G. Bondarskaia and L. Darskii, "Etnicheskaia differentsiatsiia rozhdaemosti v SSSR" (Ethnic differentiation of fertility in the USSR), *Vestnik statistiki,* Dec. 1988, no. 12, pp. 16-21.

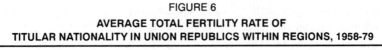

FIGURE 6
AVERAGE TOTAL FERTILITY RATE OF
TITULAR NATIONALITY IN UNION REPUBLICS WITHIN REGIONS, 1958-79

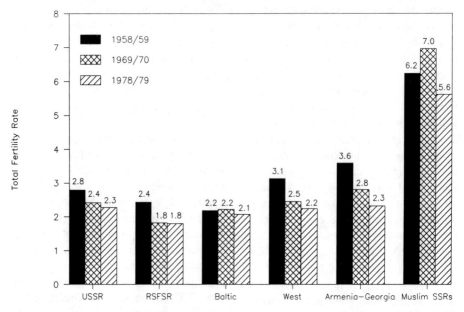

fertility of Soviet Muslim women has persisted despite their high levels of education compared to Muslim women in other countries. For example, in the rural population of Tadzhikistan in 1979, 48 percent of females aged 10 or over had at least seven years of education; and of the six Muslim republics, the population of Tadzhikistan had the lowest level of educational attainment in 1979. In contrast, in Egypt in 1976, only 15 percent of females aged 10 or over had at least primary education.

The rise in the reported TFR among Muslims between 1958-59 and 1969-70 was probably the result of a combination of some real increase in fertility and an artifactual increase in fertility resulting from more complete reporting of births.[24] It has been estimated, for example, that in Tadzhikistan 23 percent of the births in the latter 1950s were not reported.[25] Un-

24. A real increase in fertility between 1959 and 1970 could have occurred as a result of a reduction in the proportion of women of childbearing ages who are married to much older men. See Barbara A. Anderson, "Male Age and Fertility: Results from Ireland prior to 1911," *Population Index,* 41:561-66 (1974).

25. See Ansley J. Coale, Barbara A. Anderson, and Erna Härm, *Human Fertility in Russia since the Nineteenth Century* (Princeton, NJ: Princeton University Press, 1979); Anderson and Silver, "Estimating Russification." For indirect evidence of improvement in registration of births, see idem, "The Effects of the Registration System on the Seasonality of Births: The Case of the Soviet Union," *Population Studies,* 42:303-20 (July 1988).

derregistration persisted into the 1960s and 1970s but probably diminished in prevalence.[26]

The strong ethnic differences in the TFRs illustrate why the answer to the question, Is fertility in the Soviet Union high or low? is, Both. At the same time, it is clear that the rates are changing. As shown in Figure 6, they declined for all ethnic groupings between 1969-70 and 1978-79. In later years, for which we have data by region but not by ethnic group, the TFRs of Muslim areas continued to decline through the 1980s, but they rose slightly in the non-Muslim areas. As a result, the TFR of the USSR population in 1986-87 was 2.51, compared to 2.27 in 1978-79.

High-order births

Another indicator of differences in fertility behavior within the Soviet Union is the prevalence of high-order births. Figure 7 shows the percentage of births that are of fifth or higher order for various years for which data are available for Soviet republics.

If any single measure could testify to the sharp difference in the life situations of women, and the comparative risks of infant mortality between regions and ethnic groups, it is this one. In the 1960s and early 1970s, more than 30 percent of all births were of fifth or higher order in the Muslim republics. Even in 1986, one of every six

births in the Muslim republics was fifth order or higher.[27]

The percentage of high-order births has dropped at successive dates in every region, except for the increase between 1965 and 1970 in the Muslim SSRs. This is consistent with the pattern of change in the TFRs during the same time span.

Distribution by age

A major consequence of the differences in fertility between regions and ethnic groups is differences in the age distributions of the population as well as differences in the growth of segments of the age structure. Of special interest is the size of the working-age population, as well as the population below and above the working ages. By convention in Soviet labor statistics, the working ages are 16-59 for men and 16-54 for women, although this does not mean that all people enter the labor force exactly at age 16 and retire at age 55 or 60.

Panels A through C of Table 4 show for each regional grouping the number of persons in the three age categories at the time of the censuses of 1959, 1970, and 1979, as well as in 1987, which is not a census year.[28] The data from these panels are summarized in Figure 8. We use data on regions

26. Coale, Anderson, and Härm, *Human Fertility in Russia;* Barbara A. Anderson and Brian D. Silver, "Estimating Census Undercount from School-Enrollment Data: An Application to the Soviet Censuses of 1959 and 1970," *Demography,* 20:461-89 (Nov. 1983); W. Ward Kingkade, *An Evaluation of Selected Soviet Population Statistics,* CIR Staff Paper no. 9, U.S. Department of Commerce, Bureau of the Census, Center for International Research, Nov. 1985.

27. This measure actually understates the difference between Muslim and non-Muslim fertility, because it does not take into account differences in the age structures of the regional populations. Since the age distribution of women in the Muslim republics is much younger than the age distribution of women in other regions, proportionately fewer Muslim women would be near the end of their childbearing years.

28. The latest date for which age data for the Soviet population have been published is 1987, a noncensus year. Age distributions in Soviet censuses are subject to error caused by undercounting of young children, older adolescents, and young adults, as well

FIGURE 7

**PERCENTAGE OF BIRTHS THAT WERE
ORDER FIVE OR HIGHER FOR USSR AND SOVIET REGIONS, 1965-86**

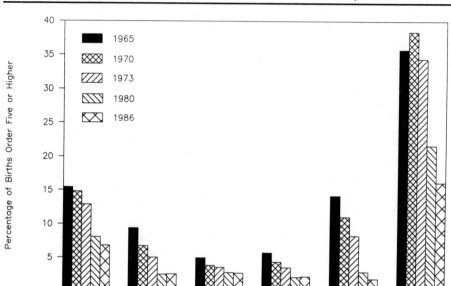

rather than ethnic groups because statistics on the age distributions of ethnic groups have not been published since the 1970 census.

Four of the regions—RSFSR, Baltic, West, and Armenia-Georgia—experienced little change between 1959 and 1987 in the number of persons under the working ages. The dip between 1970 and 1979 in the RSFSR is an echo of the small size of the cohort of women born during World War II, which resulted in a small cohort being born during the 1970s. A similar, though weaker, pattern appears also in the West and the Baltic.

In the fifth region—the Muslim SSRs—the number of persons below working ages more than doubled between 1959 and 1987, from 10.1 million to 21.1 million. This is not surprising in light of the differentials in fertility observed earlier. Moreover, the Muslim populations of Soviet Central Asia did not suffer losses in World War II as severe as those suffered by the Russians, Balts, Ukrainians, and Belorussians and hence do not show a decline between 1970 and 1979 in the number of people below the working ages.[29]

All of the regions experienced growth in the number of persons in the working

as age misstatement, including age exaggeration, by old people. For further discussion, see Anderson and Silver, "Estimating Census Undercount"; Lea Keil Garson, "The Centenarian Question: Old Age Mortality in the Soviet Union 1897-1970" (Ph.D. diss., Princeton University, 1986). We do not have enough information to correct the age distributions for each region.

29. For further discussion of the demographic impact of World War II on Soviet nationalities, see Barbara A. Anderson and Brian D. Silver, "Demographic Consequences of World War II on the Non-Russian Nationalities of the USSR," in *The Impact of World War II on the Soviet Union* (Totowa, NJ: Rowman & Allanheld, 1985), pp. 207-42; idem, "Patterns of Cohort Mortality in the Soviet Population."

TABLE 4
DISTRIBUTION OF AND INCREMENTS TO DEPENDENT AND WORKING-AGE POPULATIONS BY REGION, 1959-87 (Population in thousands)

		RSFSR	Baltic	West	Armenia-Georgia	Muslim SSRs	Total USSR
A.	Number below working ages						
	1959	35,094	1,549	14,851	1,887	10,114	63,496
	1970	37,145	1,762	16,569	2,552	16,795	74,822
	1979	31,974	1,739	14,974	2,410	18,505	69,602
	1987	34,723	1,850	15,721	2,475	21,149	75,918
B.	Number in working ages						
	1959	68,609	3,443	30,923	3,190	13,656	119,822
	1970	72,751	3,751	32,759	3,660	17,180	130,101
	1979	82,959	4,253	36,624	4,577	23,471	151,884
	1987	83,859	4,459	36,684	4,908	28,099	158,008
C.	Number above working ages						
	1959	13,827	1,009	7,032	730	2,903	25,501
	1970	19,987	1,309	10,260	948	3,873	36,377
	1979	22,437	1,365	11,477	1,036	4,197	40,511
	1987	26,589	1,510	12,888	1,280	5,145	47,412
D.	Region's percentage increment to population below working ages						
	1959-70	18.1	1.9	15.2	5.9	59.0	100.0
	1970-79	—*	—*	—*	—*	—*	—*
	1979-87	43.5	1.8	11.8	1.0	41.9	100.0
E.	Region's percentage increment to population in working ages						
	1959-70	40.3	3.0	17.9	4.6	34.3	100.0
	1970-79	46.9	2.3	17.7	4.2	28.9	100.0
	1979-87	14.7	3.4	1.0	5.4	75.6	100.0
F.	Region's percentage increment to population above working ages						
	1959-70	56.6	2.8	29.7	2.0	8.9	100.0
	1970-79	59.2	1.3	29.5	2.1	7.8	100.0
	1979-87	60.2	2.1	20.4	3.5	13.7	100.0

*For 1970-79, because there was a net decrease in the number of persons below working ages, we do not show the percentage distribution of the net increment to this number.

FIGURE 8

**POPULATION BELOW WORKING AGES, IN WORKING AGES,
AND ABOVE WORKING AGES FOR SOVIET REGIONS, 1959-87**

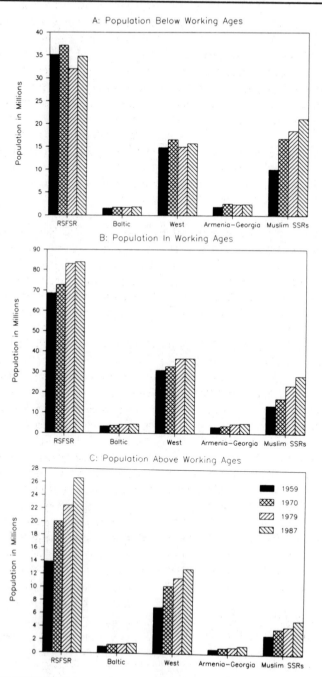

ages in each interval. The largest absolute growth occurred in the RSFSR — 15.2 million. The sharpest rise in the RSFSR occurred between 1970 and 1979. The increase in population in the working ages in the Muslim republics between 1959 and 1987 — 14.4 million — nearly equaled that of the RSFSR. In relative terms, the growth of the working-age population in the Muslim republics — 105.8 percent — far outstripped the growth in the RSFSR — 22.2 percent.

Every region experienced growth in the number of persons above the working ages. In both absolute and relative terms, the largest increase — 12.8 million, or 92.3 percent — occurred in the RSFSR. But the relative growth was quite substantial in all regions except the Baltic. Even in the Muslim republics the number of persons above working age increased by 77.2 percent between 1959 and 1987. The growth of this number in the Baltic was probably held down by the fact that its population was relatively old even in 1959.

The Muslim republics are the only region to experience substantial growth in all three age segments between 1959 and 1987. As a result, they are becoming an increasingly large contributor to the net increments to the Soviet population in the working ages and above the working ages. As shown in panel E of Table 4, in the 1959-70 and 1970-79 intercensal periods, the Muslim SSRs contributed about a third of the net additions to the working-age population of the USSR. Between 1979 and 1987, however, the Muslim SSRs contributed three-fourths of the net increment to the working-age population of the USSR.

This does not mean that three of every four workers first entering the labor force comes from a Muslim republic. Only about one-fourth of new entrants to the working

ages between 1979 and 1987 lived in a Muslim republic.[30] The net increment to the working ages from a given region is the difference between the number of people in that region entering the working ages and the number leaving the working ages, whether through reaching pension age or through death. The relatively young age composition of the populations of the Muslim republics means that they account for a very substantial share of the new entrants plus survivors in the working ages, even larger than their contribution of 50 percent of the net increment to the Soviet population as a whole between 1979 and 1989.

Another source of the increasing contribution of the Muslim republics to the working ages and to the population over the working ages is high and increasing adult male mortality in the European part of the USSR, especially between age 40 and 60. Adult male mortality was especially high in the RSFSR. In 1969-70, a male in the RSFSR who had survived to age 40 had only a 75 percent chance of surviving to age 60. In Soviet Central Asia and Transcaucasia, a 40-year-old man in 1969-70 had an 86 percent chance of living to age 60. The level of adult male mortality in the RSFSR in 1969-70 was higher than in any other developed country. In 1985-86, the chance that a 40-year-old male in the RSFSR would live to his sixtieth birthday was still only 75 percent; however, the earlier worsening of adult male mortality in the RSFSR had stopped.

In contrast, in 1985-86 males in Armenia experienced the lowest mortality of any republic population in the 40-60 age range. In that year, a 40-year-old male in Armenia

30. Recall that, as shown in Figure 2a, only 32 percent of births in 1987 occurred in the Muslim republics. Moreover, only 25 percent of the 15- to 19-year-olds in 1987 resided in the Muslim republics.

had an 86 percent chance of living to age 60. The reported mortality in Armenia for adult males between the ages of 40 and 60 was comparable to that in the Federal Republic of Germany in 1981-82 or Japan in 1969-70, although it was lower than that of American men in 1981-82.[31]

CONCLUSION

One lesson from this analysis is that the study of Soviet demographic behavior requires sensitivity to differences in behavior between regions and ethnic groups. These differences must be an important aspect of any attempt to explain the trends in the behavior and composition of the Soviet population.

The ethnic differentials in rates of population growth that we have shown make clear why so many issues in social policy in the Soviet Union have different implications for different ethnic groups. Pronatalist policies in the USSR, aimed primarily at the non-Muslim groups, exist alongside programs to reduce fertility among Muslim women. School enrollments are holding steady or increasing moderately in much of the USSR but growing rapidly in the Muslim areas. Increasing shares of conscripts to the armed forces and of new entrants to the labor force come from the Muslim populations; decreasing shares come from Russians and other non-Muslims.

Furthermore, a majority of the net increment to the labor force comes from the

31. For further discussion, see Anderson and Silver, "Sex Differentials"; idem, "Changing Shape." The Central Asian republics report fairly low adult male mortality. We think that this is partially a result of underreporting of mortality and overstatement of age in Central Asia. See Anderson and Silver, "Changing Shape."

Muslim republics. This presents certain problems for the development of the Soviet economy. The main problem is not the education and skill levels of population from these republics. New entrants to the working ages from the Muslim republics are probably, on average, better educated than the workers who are leaving the labor force through retirement or death. Instead, the problems relate to the location and mobility of the indigenous populations of the Muslim SSRs. The populations show little inclination to move from their traditional regions of settlement to areas that are experiencing labor shortages, and they usually have poor command of the Russian language and hence cannot move to just any job for which their technical or other skills qualify them. Moreover, since nonindigenous populations seem to be departing from the Muslim republics, there is even less incentive for the members of the titular nationality to leave their home republic in search of work or career opportunities or to improve their facility in the Russian language.

The changing ethnic composition of Soviet regions—toward greater Russianization of the European republics and greater indigenization of the non-European ones—is also important for understanding the ethnic politics of the Soviet Union. In the Baltic republics and Moldavia, leaders of the Communist Party and of popular-front movements have sought to limit the in-migration of Russians in order to preserve the culture and language of the titular nationality and to assert greater local control over the future economic and political development of their republics. If the policy of economic and political *perestroika* ("restructuring") continues to evolve toward greater local autonomy, then these non-Russian republics are likely to become less hospitable to in-migrants from nontitular nationalities than they have been in the past. In most non-European republics, out-migration of Russians and other non-indigenous nationalities was under way well before Mikhail Gorbachev came to power in 1985. Further implementation of *perestroika* is likely to help sustain that tendency.

Book Department

INTERNATIONAL RELATIONS AND POLITICS

BEITZ, CHARLES R. *Political Equality: An Essay in Democratic Theory.* Pp. xviii, 253. Princeton, NJ: Princeton University Press, 1989. $25.00.

This essay sets forth an interesting theory of political equality that turns on procedural fairness. Beitz explicitly rejects results-oriented theories, on grounds that these do not and indeed cannot provide an adequate account of political fairness as it applies to the individual. Similarly, he dissents from social choice and other rarefied formulations because, whatever else such fare may do for those who dish it up, it turns out not to be very appetizing for others who worry about the creation, operation, or reform of actual political institutions. Beitz ventures considerably beyond his initially contractualist framework, in that nothing in such philosophic postures requires that one be concerned with procedural equality. He aptly cites examples from Mill to Rawls.

Fairness in modes of political participation, in Beitz's view, is the single most important characteristic the egalitarian ideal should demand of political institutions. As he sees it,

fairness involves three normative considerations that, taken together, constitute the superior "regulative interests" he imputes to individual citizens. These are recognition, equitable treatment, and deliberative responsibility. In specifying them — and their empirical meaning — Beitz creatively addresses the problem, raised by Dahl and others, that some interests are held so much more intensely than others that no simple procedural mode, or other extant theory of social choice or decision making, can hope to take them adequately into account.

If decision rules and procedures are arguably the central problem of democratic theory, it is evasive to claim, as some do, that any procedure is acceptable that registers the general will, or produces the best results for the collectivity. As a practical matter, citizens rightly worry about the content of policy, the nature of the process — including the quality of debate and openness of decision points — that brings policies into being, and the administrative and political consequences of one set of policies over another. In order to take proper account of such concerns, recognition requires equality of opportunity of each citizen to influence policy outcomes; equitable treatment necessitates that citizens be spared faits accomplis and be permitted to defend their interests; and deliberative responsibility prescribes the greatest possible open public discussion and debate of alternative policy options.

Where these regulative interests inform decisional procedures, individuals interested in reaching agreement with others may reasonably be expected to accept the latter as fair. Where any one of them is clearly obscured or deeply threatened, the individual citizen should be expected to reject procedures, irrespective of what might be the nature of the policy outcomes they produce. In short, the institutions of democratic participation should be justifiable to each citizen, taking careful account of him or her as both maker and matter of government. Indeed, it is precisely because democratic institutions are capable of satisfying such requirements that they are preferable to others.

The Beitz system, dubbed "complex proceduralism," is informal — and a far cry from the arid, deductive formulations of Rawls and others. It is also pluralistic, in the sense that it both recognizes the existence of conflict in society and suggests that the institutional means of dealing with it, even as the means pay due respect to the regulative interests, may vary. Variation may be compelled by the historical, cultural, or existential context in which the institutions themselves are to be located. It is only when these contextual factors are brought into play that one can give due weight to the moral side of political participation. Deterministic models that mechanically produce decisions, solutions, outcomes, and so on are largely alien to considerations of this kind.

The volume's second half is devoted to the application of complex proceduralism to basic issues like representation, the formation of political agendas, and the use of finance in electoral competition. Not everyone will agree with Beitz's specific conclusions, for example, about the relative merits of proportional representation versus district voting. These chapters nevertheless provide an empirical basis for gauging the attractiveness of his argument. They also drive home a major point about regulative interests: far from constituting a conceptual straitjacket, they turn out to be susceptible to a variety of combinatory forms, none of which would necessarily vitiate their status as acid tests of the acceptability of democratic decision-making institutions as fair.

Political scientists who live on this planet, and who believe that theories of this kind should have reasonably palpable implications for the here, now, and tomorrow, will welcome this book.

JOSEPH LaPALOMBARA

Yale University
New Haven
Connecticut

NACHMIAS, NITZA. *Transfer of Arms, Leverage, and Peace in the Middle East.* Pp. 196. New York: Greenwood Press, 1988. $39.95.

Nitza Nachmias's *Transfer of Arms, Leverage, and Peace in the Middle East* is a book that promises much more than it delivers. The premise of the book, that arms transfers are an increasingly important — if not the most important — aspect of U.S. foreign policy and that this gives the United States leverage — as opposed to influence — over the recipients of arms, promises to be an interesting change from the more traditional studies of U.S. involvement in the Middle East. Unfortunately, the premise, and indeed the study itself, fails to live up to expectations.

The basis of the study is that U.S. involvement and indeed leverage over its allies is crucial if the Middle East is to ever experience some sort of peace. Traditionally, American involvement in the region has been of all sorts — diplomatic, military, and economic — though since 1967 the transfer of arms from the United States to Israel has become an increasingly important U.S. policy tool.

Theoretically, this transfer of arms, Nachmias explains, should give the United States leverage over Israeli policy formulation and actions. This leverage is brought about by the two defining features of leverage: coercion, or the withholding of benefits, and inducement, or the giving of benefits. Nachmias is adamant that leverage, while a form of power, is a concept that differs in kind and degree from power and influence in that it "excludes the application of brute force and assumes two cooperating actors in a relationship of dependency." In regard to the United States and Israel, the dependence of Israel on U.S. military aid should produce a situation where Israel is a U.S. client.

In such a situation, the United States would theoretically exert tremendous leverage over Israeli policy and would be able to influence this policy through threats of coercion or inducements. The conclusion of the book, however, is that U.S. arms transfers have not resulted in the expected dependency relationship, and Nachmias indeed concludes by stating that it is the United States that is in many ways an Israeli client. Nachmias's purpose in the bulk of the book is to explore why this is the case. She concludes that leverage has failed not because of U.S. domestic politics, as is usually assumed, but because of changes in the international and regional environments — changes that have continuously caught the United States by surprise and unprepared.

Nachmias begins her study with an examination of the Rogers peace plan of 1969 in a chapter that she subtitles "The Wrong Idea at the Wrong Time for the Wrong Actors." Her main argument against the plan was that Rogers attempted to impose a settlement on Israel concerning the occupied territories by threatening to withhold arms from Israel if it did not comply with U.S. demands. Moreover, the plan assumed a variety of conditions that did not exist, including a belief in the willingness of the Soviet Union to abandon its advances in the Middle East and a willingness among Arab states to recognize Israel. Israel was also not willing to bend to U.S. demands because it would mean, as the Israelis saw it, giving up territory for arms, a tradeoff they were not willing to make.

Leverage similarly failed to work in expected ways with the disengagement agreements that Nachmias discusses in the next chapter. It was not arms transfers that finally pushed Israel to negotiate with the Egyptians over the Sinai but a combination of economic and strategic consideration and the willingness of Sadat to bend considerably on important issues. Leverage through arms transfers, therefore, proved to be less of a factor in influencing Israeli policy than the more traditional interests of international relations. Leverage was used more by the United States to influence events surrounding the Camp David Accords, as discussed in chapter 4. The leverage included delays — rather than the withholding — of transfers and the restriction of military credits. In addition, Israel was also promised rewards after the process was successfully concluded, rewards that included F-16 jets, infrared weapon systems, and cluster bombs. Here, U.S. leverage did achieve a U.S. policy goal, but it was, again, not the primary reason why Israel acted the way that it did. Traditional interests — assessments of economic, strategic, and domestic political requirements — played the most important role.

The dangers inherent in leverage are dealt with in a discussion of the Lebanese crisis and the U.S. response to it. Again, U.S. misperceptions of regional and international realities meant that the United States had little — here, indeed no — leverage over even its allies. As Nachmias states, "Faced with a fait accompli (after the Israeli invasion which the U.S. could do nothing to stop) the United States, albeit reluctantly, accepted most of Israel's military actions." In the end, despite its status as a global superpower, the United States found itself a mere onlooker in Lebanon with no power, no influence, and no leverage with which to affect events.

In conclusion, then, it becomes evident that the United States, despite shipping enormous amounts of military goods to Israel, has experienced little, if any, benefit from these shipments vis-à-vis leverage over Israeli policy. This calls into question the entire concept of leverage, which Nachmias leads us to believe is so crucial to the understanding of international relations. In the final analysis, Nachmias fails to show that leverage is an entity distinct from power and influence. Her definition of leverage is not much different from definitions of influence that have been common through the years.

Therefore the premise of the book, that leverage is some kind of misunderstood and understudied concept in international relations, is an odd one given that it does not emerge as a separate entity from power and influence. In the end, what determines the actions of any political actor is myriad considerations of which access to arms is but one. It is only in very specific instances that such access is a key element in a decision on whether to act or not, and it is much more common that other considerations — such as economic, diplomatic, or strategic considerations — play a greater and more constant role. Despite increasing arms transfers to Israel from the United States, U.S. influence and leverage over Israel have declined.

T. Y. ISMAEL

University of Calgary
Alberta
Canada

AFRICA, ASIA, AND LATIN AMERICA

BESTOR, THEODORE. *Neighborhood Tokyo.* Pp. xvi, 347. Stanford, CA: Stanford University Press, 1989. $35.00.

Theodore Bestor's *Neighborhood Tokyo* is essentially an ethnographic case study of an eight-square-block Tokyo neighborhood presented under the pseudonym Miyamoto-cho. The urban neighborhood, chosen for its "ordinariness," is not a formal administrative division of the city but has nevertheless a logic and cohesion drawn from the network of obligations and interdependencies that link its households. Similar cohesion within such neighborhoods has been seen heretofore as the remnant of traditional village culture reasserting itself in a new urbanized

society. Bestor argues convincingly that those very features long held to be traditional survivals are rather the results of social change brought on by the peopling of Miyamoto-cho by urban exiles, particularly those driven from the center of the city by the 1923 earthquake. Those "survivals," he holds, are in fact recent constructs of new and essentially urban origin.

Bestor notes the difficulty of an outsider penetrating Japanese institutions, and indeed his method of settling quietly into the neighborhood and being slowly absorbed into what he studied seems the only way to come to grips with the essences of Japanese neighborhood life. His descriptions of that life are perceptive and penetrating and his presentation felicitous.

The one jarring note in this excellent work is the cover of anonymity with which Bestor cloaks both his neighborhood and its citizens, for they are all given pseudonyms. While this may save the researcher potential embarrassment in the future if he should study the neighborhood anew, it leaves the reader with a vague and disturbing sense of viewing the whole through a filter — of not being let in completely to share the truth. And it will certainly make it difficult for new and revising generations to test change in Miyamoto-cho. This, however, is a rather minor consideration in a work of real excellence that should demonstrate amply the dangers in easy and pat explanations of the Japanese people and what moves them.

R. KENT LANCASTER

Goucher College
Towson
Maryland

CAMP, RODERIC A. *Entrepreneurs and Politics in Twentieth-Century Mexico.* Pp. 306. New York: Oxford University Press, 1989. $35.00.

The private sector in Mexico has long been an elusive element in the chemistry of Mexican development. Such elusiveness is largely traceable to the power matrix established in the 1917 Constitution, where the state co-opted organized labor and the peasants but left the private sector a weak outsider. The Constitution established an executive supremacy, placing it in a commanding position to guide Mexican industrialization and to control the form that the public-private relationship would assume. No one has yet offered as comprehensive an analysis of this previously mostly invisible public-private relationship as Roderic Camp presents.

Camp argues that the dependency status of the private sector, established by the state in the first decades of this century, has never been fully overcome. That has been as much due to the nature of the relationship as to the composition of the private sector. Family control and ownership of Mexican industries have changed less than one would expect of a nation struggling to enter an internationally interdependent world economy, and they have allowed old notions of public-private relations to persevere.

The state has maintained its supremacy, at some cost to development, by a series of presidential acts that have increased the public role in business. The nationalization of oil by President Cárdenas in 1938 is most often cited, but of additional significance in his term was the reformation of the PRN (now PRI) to exclude the private sector. Although the Alemán and Ávila Camacho administrations in the 1940s and 1950s favored the private sector, achieving perhaps the apogee of positive public-private feeling in this century, Presidents Echeverría and López Portillo were less comfortable with the private sector. The latter's nationalization of banking in 1982 drew into the public sphere an industry with a strong public-private interrelationship. Camp's historical development briefly but skillfully establishes the limited Mexican public-private interchanges, and contrasts the U.S. experience as creating fewer barriers to such interchanges, the latter being less affected by kinship.

The Mexican entrepreneur is effectively presented by Camp's attention to place of birth, socioeconomic background of parents, and education. He views each characteristic as important in establishing the private sector as a closed elite that has missed opportunities to absorb working-class Mexico into and strengthen the private sector. The public sector, in contrast, has more effectively drawn upon the working class for future leaders. But, more recently, there has been some fusion as an increasing number of public officials have been educated abroad or by private Mexican universities, where the government has less ability to mold them into the traditional pattern of state attitudes toward the permissible role of the private sector. This fusion is affirmed by recent developments in Mexico, occurring after Camp's writing. The government is more willing to risk state supremacy by allowing electoral reforms and, more important, opposition success. For me, schooled in Mexican events from the perception of its legal history and the regulation of foreign investment, Camp has filled an enormous gap of ignorance of the nature of the private sector and its relations with the state. If I could ask more of him, it would be to use his talents to postulate on the public-private relationship and the future of Mexican development.

MICHAEL W. GORDON

University of Florida
Gainesville

DOMÍNGUEZ, JORGE I. *To Make a World Safe for Revolution: Cuba's Foreign Policy.* Pp. viii, 365. Cambridge, MA: Harvard University Press, 1988. $35.00.

Nobody writes about Cuba with greater authority and intelligence than Jorge Domínguez. In the past ten years his numerous publications have probed the political and social structure of contemporary Cuba with rare industry and skill.

The work under review carefully and reliably examines the nature and process of Cuban foreign policy. It offers a convenient historical overview of the genesis in the 1960s and traces the sometimes difficult and uneven relationship with the Soviet Union, the enduring conflict with the United States, and the erratic diplomacy with the neighboring Caribbean and Latin American states, including the unfortunate episode of Grenada. It concludes with an insightful analysis of the complex operational procedures of Cuban foreign policy. Domínguez insists that "Cuba accepted Soviet hegemony because Cuban leaders came to value it"; "that Castro was not pushed into Soviet arms by the United States or by domestic conflicts"; that Cuban and Soviet aims have frequently diverged both in Africa and Latin America; that Cuban military aims have been more constrained in the Americas than Africa owing to the primacy of the United States in the hemisphere; and that "Cuban foreign policy would not be what it is without Castro, but it would also not be what it is if only Castro were responsible for it." While these observations are not surprising to specialists — or those familiar with Domínguez's earlier writings — they are copiously substantiated and contextualized here with extensive interviews and reviews by highly informed and highly placed Cuban scholars and specialists.

There are a few minor shortcomings. Although well written, the work lacks a bibliography. Domínguez does not discuss the rift between Barbados and Cuba over the transshipment of Cuban troops to Angola in 1976 or the notorious public exchanges between Maurice Bishop of Grenada and Tom Adams of Barbados in the early 1980s. There is no source given for the assertion that "on October 21 [1983] the Organization of Eastern Caribbean States met in Barbados to request U.S. and British intervention in Grenada"; and the description of the Caribbean support to the U.S. invasion of Grenada is misleading. In some cases, the analysis has been overtaken by events. The warm relations between Cuba and the Soviet Union have chilled since the introduction of *perestroika* and *glasnost*. The Interior Ministry has fallen considerably further from political grace in 1989 as a result of possible implications in narcotics trafficking that claimed the life by execution of the brilliant and popular Division General Arnaldo Ochoa. In addition, the Castro brothers may be a bit more isolated and a bit more powerful within the structure of decision making than before.

FRANKLIN W. KNIGHT

Johns Hopkins University
Baltimore
Maryland

KUCZYNSKI, PEDRO-PABLO. *Latin American Debt.* Pp. xv, 258. Baltimore, MD: Johns Hopkins University Press; New York: Twentieth Century Fund, 1988. $32.50. Paperbound, $12.95.

MARICHAL, CARLOS. *A Century of Debt Crises in Latin America: From Independence to the Great Depression: 1820-1930.* Pp. xiv, 283. Princeton, NJ: Princeton University Press, 1989. $45.00. Paperbound, $16.50.

During the past seven years, Latin America has suffered the most intense economic crisis since the Great Depression of the 1930s. Following two decades in which the region's gross domestic product grew at an annual rate of close to 6 percent (1960-80), virtually all Latin American nations have experienced economic contraction, intense inflation, and serious declines in mass living standards. In retrospect, it is clear that the earlier period of economic growth and the current crisis are inexorably linked. Huge external debts, incurred by the public and private sector in order to cover current-account deficits or to invest in future growth, fueled the earlier period of expansion and ultimately produced the debt crisis of the 1980s.

The books reviewed here represent differing perspectives by two distinguished Latin American scholars on the root causes of the region's debt problems. Carlos Marichal, a historian, examines a series of Latin American debt crises from the time of independence through the Great Depression (1820-1930). Only in his epilogue does he offer brief, and somewhat disappointing, comparisons with the current situation. Marichal's analysis, very much in the tradition of dependency theory, suggests that

Latin America's boom and bust economic cycles were "the result of phases of expansion of the world economy, which tended to stimulate the . . . export of excess capital . . . to Latin America [followed by] . . . widespread downswings of the economies of industrialized nations, which provoked a sharp reduction of the outward flow of financial resources."

The book extends beyond most *dependista* analysis by examining loan patterns, rather than concentrating exclusively on foreign investment and trade between center and periphery. By differentiating between the causes of various debt crises and distinguishing the policies of major debtor nations, Marichal adds nuance to the dependency literature. While he examines the domestic factors that led Latin American political leaders repeatedly to incur loans, he clearly blames the cycle of debt crises not on Latin American policymaking but on the region's relationship to the world economic system.

Pedro-Pablo Kuczynski, an economist, bank official, and former Peruvian cabinet minister, examines only Latin America's current economic plight. His far more conservative analysis attributes the current crisis to excessive spending and borrowing by populist and military regimes that "wanted [their] economies to grow at a substantially higher rate than their resources allowed." Latin American economies, he argues, suffer from inadequate rates of savings, inefficient import-substitution industrialization, noncompetitive manufactured exports, nonprofitable state enterprises that subsidize politically significant consumer groups, populist monetary and exchange policies, which feature artificially low interest rates and overvalued currencies, and hostility toward foreign investment. Public-sector current-account deficits and easy credit in the 1970s and early 1980s led to "uneconomic investments and the postponement of difficult austerity measures."

In looking at possible solutions to the crisis, Kuczynski generally favors fairly orthodox stabilization policies and emphasizes monetarist,

rather than structuralist, remedies. At the same time, however, he notes that Latin America will not be able to resume economic growth and exit the current crisis without some form of debt relief. "The biggest obstacle to interest relief," he argues, "is not institutional or economic. . . . The obstacle is primarily political." Ultimately, he feels that banks must "reflow" interest payments coming out of Latin America back into the region. Regardless of who is to blame for the current crisis—and Kuczynski does fault the banks for excessive, indeed foolish, lending—the solution to the crisis must come from the international community coupled with more sensible economic policies within Latin America.

Kuczynski's book will undoubtedly become a core reading for the nonspecialist seeking a better understanding of the current debt crisis.

HOWARD HANDELMAN

University of Wisconsin
Milwaukee

MONTANER, CARLOS ALBERTO. *Fidel Castro and the Cuban Revolution: Age, Position, Character, Destiny, Personality and Ambition.* Pp. 214. New Brunswick, NJ: Transaction, 1989. $29.95.

If you believe that Jeane Kirkpatrick is brilliant and that the government of Cuba is as evil as that of Chile's General Pinochet, then this is the book for you. This is especially the case if you have not read Montaner's earlier *Secret Report on the Cuban Revolution* (1981), the vast bulk of which has been clumsily borrowed for this present volume.

Montaner left Cuba in 1981 for political reasons, and it is clear that his traumatic experiences in prison there—movingly noted on page 111—act as a filter through which he sees the Cuban revolutionary process and in particular its *líder máximo*, Fidel Castro. He is a skilled writer, with an established reputation as a novelist and short-story writer. Unfortunately, while *Fidel Castro and the Cuban Revolution* is well written, and indeed has some brilliant insights into Cuban society as a whole and Castro's role in particular, it fails as an interpretive essay — largely because Montaner's prejudices frequently cloud his analysis.

The bitterness and frustration so deeply felt by Montaner are encountered throughout the book, as he resorts to a battery of techniques — anger, scorn, and sarcasm being the most commonly encountered — to underscore Fidel's vile ways: "Mirror, mirror, on the wall, who's the most beautiful tyrant of them all?" A fiery polemicist, Carlos Alberto Montaner sees hardly any saving graces in *Castroismo:* Vice-President Rodríguez "dares not raise his voice" to Fidel; degradation and vulgarity are the order of the day; Cuba's intellectuals are "mediocre personalities only capable of writing Cuban peasant rhymes." Castro's Cuba is summed up by him in this lament for bygone days, one of many emotional outbursts: "That country of obedient and solicitous marionettes used to be a land of proud and rebellious people until fear ate their guts away."

This idealized view of the prerevolutionary past is annoying. True, downtown Havana seemed a developed city in 1959, much as the area around Mexico City's Paseo de la Reforma did in 1910. The Third World, however, clearly began on the outskirts of Havana, with tar-paper shacks, sweeping unemployment, and the litany of the ills of underdevelopment. Montaner seeks to juggle statistics to prove his point, noting that "the slaughter of cattle and hogs in 1957 gave an annual per capita of 34 kilograms of meat" and that Cuba was in third place in the world in regard to the ratio of kilometers of roads per thousand of vehicles. Such data pose the obvious question, however: meat and highways for whom? Indeed, all that these figures may demonstrate is that some privileged Cubans ate an enormous amount of meat and had an excellent road system at their disposal. A better understanding of socioeconomic conditions, and one that provides a very different picture of rural life,

can be found in Lowry Nelson's *Rural Cuba* or the disturbing surveys undertaken by the Agrupación católica universitaria in the mid-1950s.

Montaner clearly lives in the past, longing for days of yore. For example, he writes, "One of Cuba's biggest accomplishments was its large and open middle levels" — despite abundant evidence to the contrary. Indeed, he even goes so far as to intimate that the 1962 rationing was far inferior to food rations given slaves in 1842. He gives the impression, for instance, that slaves ate four times as much meat per person as did Cubans in the early 1960s.

This fixation with the past is seen in some blatantly incorrect information given in the book. In part this is due to Montaner's conclusions that the golden past before 1959 was far better than the present, but it is also due to the shift in East-West relationships and to developments behind the now rusting Iron Curtain. One example of the latter will perhaps suffice to illustrate the dated nature of this phenomenon. Montaner writes, "Cuba is fundamentally a satellite. She does not digress even one inch on the key issues from the (adopted) Mother Country." This in a country where Gorbachev's 1989 visit revealed the great differences of opinion over *perestroika* and where in August 1989 the Soviet publications *Sputnik* and *Moscow News* were banned by the Cuban government.

Whatever the origin for his lament for a bygone era, there are numerous errors in Montaner's study: the ratio of blacks and women in positions of power has increased quite dramatically in the last five years. The Catholic Church — despite his claims — is not dying off: church attendance is increasing, and, as the archbishop of Havana told me three years ago, some 50 percent of burials are accompanied by a religious service. Indeed, some 30 percent of all babies born in Havana are now baptized. Newspapers and magazines do give coverage to religious news. In recent years the Cuban government has — albeit belatedly — allowed international human rights organizations to inspect Cubans — in September 1988 a U.N. delegation headed by a Senegalese representative did precisely that.

In sum, this book — despite its occasional flash of brilliant insight into the role of Fidel Castro and Cuba and Montaner's correct observations that "Fidel is his government's only serious critic" and that "Fidel is more of a Papist than the Pope. It is he who has discreetly pulled the Russians' ears when the Soviets have deviated from Marxist-Leninist orthodoxy" — is disappointing. In part it is due to Montaner's own bitterness, accompanied by his fond memories of prerevolutionary times. There is also a lack of solid scholarship, as well as a desire to be shocking. This is unfortunate because Carlos Alberto Montaner is a skilled writer who, if he could better focus his observations, would have some useful — and needed — criticisms.

JOHN M. KIRK

Dalhousie University
Halifax
Nova Scotia
Canada

STOLCKE, VERENA. *Coffee Planters, Workers and Wives: Class Conflict and Gender Relations on São Paulo Plantations, 1850-1980.* Pp. xviii, 344. New York: St. Martin's Press, 1988. $55.00.

From the perspective of ordinary people's lives, the proletarianization of the rural work force is the most significant change going on in developing countries today. Curiously, the models of social change that prevail in North American social sciences give little attention to this phenomenon. The reason, in Charles Tilly's view (*As Sociology Meets History* [New York: Academic Press, 1981], pp. 179-87), has less to do with poor data than it does with the persistent adherence to theories of differentiation and integration that ignore the qualitative transformation at hand.

Verena Stolcke's book on coffee plantations in São Paulo, Brazil, is a welcome corrective to

this tendency, and much more to boot. Drawing on historical records and in-depth interviews with farm workers, she presents a detailed analysis of the processes by which the family-based *colonato* system, begun in the 1870s, has been increasingly replaced by wage labor since the 1960s. She further shows how changes in productive relations were embedded in, and interacted with, family structure and cultural definitions of gender roles.

In Stolcke's view, the *colonato* system was made obsolete not by purely economic or technical developments but by the political changes in the 1950s and 1960s that reorganized the structure of domination in the rural economy, including the conditions for surplus labor appropriation. Stolcke documents the fact that the shift to casual wage labor did not go uncontested. Despite the workers' acute class consciousness, the balance of power in the countryside so favored landlords that the protests that occurred were more often individual acts of resistance at work rather than full-blown collective movements.

Stolcke's analysis of women's fate in the transition to wage labor is textured and insightful. Using their own voices to good effect, she shows how women's lower labor-market commitment and their higher work standards were the result of a process by which women's subordinate position in the home was extended to the work site. Because their social identity as wives and mothers remained intact, the move to wage work meant increased responsibilities for women, causing them to reduce their fertility expectations.

Stolcke treats none of the topics she takes up as independent of one another. In her explanations of the *colonato* system, and its replacement by wage labor, Stolcke consistently refers to the two-way — and historically specific — interactions between broad politicoeconomic processes, the worker's family structure, and the gender consciousness held by men and women. If the study specifically concerns coffee plantations in southern Brazil, the findings as well as the theory and method presented in this book are of general value to anyone investigating the human consequences of social change.

CHARLES H. WOOD

University of Florida
Gainesville

ZEITLIN, MAURICE and RICHARD EARL RATCLIFF. *Landlords and Capitalists: The Dominant Class of Chile.* Pp. xxiv, 288. Princeton, NJ: Princeton University Press, 1988. $45.00. Paperbound, $12.95.

Landlords and Capitalists undertakes two tasks. The first is to provide a thorough and systematic analysis of the "concrete ensemble of social relations" within the dominant class in Chile in the mid-1960s. The second task is to bring the empirical findings to bear on several theoretical issues.

The empirical task is carried out admirably. Zeitlin and Ratcliff identified four sets of individuals with economic power in Chile: the officers and directors of 37 top nonfinancial corporations; the officers and directors of six major banks; the owners of the largest landed estates in the country; and the investors with the largest aggregate shareholdings in a still broader set of corporations and banks. The landholdings, stockholdings, managerial positions, kinship relations, and political offices of these individuals were then exhaustively analyzed. The purpose of the analysis was to reveal the extent to which these individuals were in fact bound together in an intricate network of relations. Ties that range from combined ownership interests and interlocking directorates through intermarriage were persuasively documented. One key finding was the existence of a set of finance capitalists, men who sat simultaneously in the managements of major banks and the largest nonfinancial corporations. These individuals were far wealthier than ordinary corporate executives and more likely to personally own capital or to belong to a principal capitalist family. Another finding

was that more than 40 percent of bankers and more than a third of corporate executives either owned landed estates themselves or had close relatives who did. Alongside property ties, Zeitlin and Ratcliff found extensive kinship relations. Indeed, perhaps the most striking finding was the identification of one huge kinship network to which almost 40 percent of the individuals in the banking, corporate-executive, and landowner universes belonged.

These empirical findings inform discussions of theoretical issues throughout the book. For example, the findings validate Zeitlin and Ratcliff's view that a focus on individuals and firms in class analysis is too narrow. This point is made most clearly in an extended rebuttal to the theory of managerial capitalism, with its attendant notion that the capitalist class was disappearing. By looking beyond individuals' personal holdings to the families', and by taking into account connections between firms, two key propositions were refuted. First, many fewer firms were found to be controlled by management than expected. Second, the class situation of managers was frequently indistinguishable from that of individuals identified independently as capitalists. A second example addresses those development theorists who posit the existence of a national bourgeoisie in contradistinction to the landowning oligarchy. The extent of interpenetration between land and capital ownership in Chile suggests that, at a minimum, the existence of such sectors must be treated as an empirical question, not as a theoretical assumption.

These examples illustrate Zeitlin and Ratcliff's strong commitment to a mutual engagement between theoretical and empirical work. They explicitly criticize the "penchant for theorization, and even 'investigation,' by postulation" that has afflicted sociological conceptions of the dominant class. Thus it is ironic that the greatest difficulty with their study is a tendency to read action off of structure. The empirical analysis is structural: the reader is provided with a detailed description of the internal relations of a dominant class at a certain point in time.

Zeitlin and Ratcliff are careful not to claim that they can comment on the process of class formation; they say little about how the internal class structure they found came into existence.

Instead they err on the other end, with frequent references to structurally imposed imperatives for action. Although these may be intended as hypotheses, more often they simply have the status of assertions. For example, the authors write, "The principal capital-owning families must strive to place their members at the helms both of the banks and the corporations." Another example: "The self-contradictory ... interests ... of landed capitalists [give] special impetus to their search for class leadership and direct political representation, so that they can shape state policy to harmonize these recalcitrant interests." While the internal class structure Zeitlin and Ratcliff have documented is surely consistent with such behavioral imperatives, virtually no information other than structural location is provided to support the claims. On the one hand, such information would have required more research on top of what was already clearly a massive project. On the other, without such evidence, competing explanations of outcomes cannot be evaluated. Perhaps state policies were always carefully crafted compromises that balanced inherently contradictory interests. But perhaps state policies instead reflected a tug of war, in which landed interests sometimes prevailed, and manufacturing interests won out other times. Perhaps kinship relations were not always sufficient to prevent serious material conflicts. The research on structure, exhaustive as it is, must be supplemented with research on the mechanisms by which that structure is translated into action. Clearly dominant classes within capitalism have not disappeared. But their capacity for action cannot be deduced from their internal structure.

KIMBERLY STANTON

University of Chicago
Illinois

EUROPE

DUGGAN, CHRISTOPHER. *Fascism and the Mafia.* Pp. xiii, 322. New Haven, CT: Yale University Press, 1989. $27.50.

There is one term that sends *frissons* of fear mingled with sardonic pride running through Sicilian hearts, whether in Palermo or Brooklyn. In recent years several motion pictures, made in Hollywood, have further sensationalized and cashed in on these feelings. It is the word "Mafia."

Seemingly standing in direct opposition to the outside-of-the-law, individualistic bravado and buccaneering life-style of the *mafiosi* was the Italian movement that took its name from the ancient Roman symbol of total state authority, rigid discipline, and idealistic self-sacrifice for Senate and people, the *fasces.* What actually happened when these two forces met head-on during the 1920s and 1930s?

Christopher Duggan, a fellow of All Souls', Oxford, attempts in this work to answer the question. In accord with the traditions of his college, Duggan has done an extremely good job of research. His description of the *latifondi,* the huge agricultural estates, their wealthy owners, and their impoverished workers serves as a realistic backdrop for the dramatic events he recounts.

Duggan seeks to define the term "Mafia" and trace its origins. Here he runs into a labyrinth. After a while his attempts at definition remind one of the saying, "Now you see it, now you don't." Again and again he adduces strong evidence that no such organization has ever existed. It is simply a term for the image Sicilian men have felt obliged to project in order to secure their standing among their fellows. But the thought keeps nagging at the reader's mind: is this denial of real existence merely a supreme example of the traditional response to questions about the Mafia, "I don't know," "I was not there," and the like? *Omertà.*

Into his highly detailed narrative, which

moves somewhat slowly at times, Duggan has managed to insert a fascinating and illuminating story of two contrasting figures who led the fight of Fascism against the Mafia during the 1920s. Both men were strongly opposed to the Mafia and wanted to see it eliminated from the island. Here the similarities between them ended.

Alfredo Cucco, a native Sicilian, was an oculist whose hobby was wrestling. He became a *fasciste della prima hora* and *federale* (regional head) of the Fascist Party in Palermo. He believed that the island could only be redeemed by an idealistic and patriotic intransigence that would sweep away the corruption and self-seeking of the past. A typical petit bourgeois, Cucco inevitably offended big business, the Church, the large landowners, and the crown.

In line with the promise of the *fascisti* to restore law and order everywhere, and by eliminating regionalisms to unify the nation, Mussolini was under strong pressure to "do something about Sicily." He decided to appoint as *prefetto* (state administrator) of Palermo Cesare Mori, to whom he also entrusted the supreme command of the entire island's police. Mori was a Northerner from Pavia and a career police commander who had spent many years in Sicily. He had distinguished himself by the pursuit and capture of bandits and by suppressing strikes by the agricultural workers. He was a conservative monarchist who came late to Fascism, after the March on Rome. The Duce felt that Mori was an excellent policeman but was not too sure of his Fascism.

The duel between Cucco, the idealist, and Mori, the realist, as recounted by Duggan, is exciting and informative. It ended as most such duels between highly placed administrators end. After several years Mori succeeded in getting Cucco expelled from the party only to be himself stabbed in the back several years later. Mori never regained a position of power and he died a decade later.

Cucco succeeded in being readmitted to the party, served in Mussolini's government at Salò, was condemned to death after 1945, and was given refuge in the Vatican until his death sentence was commuted. Thereafter he helped to found the neofascist Movimento sociale italiano

(MSI) and served from 1953 until his death, in 1968, as an MSI deputy in the parliament of the new Italian Republic.

The different approaches and views of Cucco and Mori with respect to the task of destroying the Mafia are highly instructive. Did the contrasting efforts of these two different but strong administrators really succeed in destroying the Mafia as promised by the Duce, however much the latter used them for propaganda purposes? To the impartial observer considering subsequent developments in Sicily, this seems unlikely. Duggan concludes, "As in the past, the idea of a criminal conspiracy seemed to mask a more complex political, social and cultural reality."

Was there and is there a Mafia? *Io non so.*

H. F. MACKENSEN

Fairleigh Dickinson University
Teaneck
New Jersey

LE TISSIER, TONY. *The Battle of Berlin 1945.* Pp. xiii, 290. New York: St. Martin's Press, 1988. $29.95.

The destruction of the Third Reich and Hitler's suicide in his Berlin bunker remain fascinating subjects. Tony Le Tissier's *Battle of Berlin 1945* is another addition to the literature concerning these events.

Le Tissier's contribution lies in his analysis of the political motives that drove the Soviet war machine. His contention that Stalin attempted to discredit Marshal Zhukov by encouraging a race to Berlin with Marshal Konev is illogical, however. If the general secretary had wanted to injure Zhukov's reputation, he would have sent him to another front where fewer opportunities for glory existed. Also, there were tactical considerations that necessitated a division of command between the two men.

Le Tissier's narrow research base is the major weakness of the book. He uses only published sources, primarily in English with a few in German. *The Battle of Berlin 1945* suffers from the same deficiency as most popular, and many scholarly, histories of the Eastern Front:

the omission of Russian sources. Le Tissier should have made better use of Soviet military journals. In addition, his tone is often polemic. He denies the efficacy of Soviet claims that 20 million Soviets were killed in the war and presents no concrete basis for his argument. He consistently underestimates the capabilities of the Red Army, a mistake that cost Hitler and his minions dearly.

This is not to suggest that the book is without its merits. Le Tissier's knowledge of the geography of Berlin and his practice of giving current place names when place names have changed are of great utility. Numerous maps enable the reader more easily to follow the flow of events. Excellent illustrations as well as lengthy quotations from eyewitness accounts further enhance the value of the work. Most important, readers will find *The Battle of Berlin 1945* a well-written and interesting book.

RUSSEL LEMMONS

Miami University
Oxford
Ohio

MAIER, CHARLES S. *The Unmasterable Past: History, Holocaust, and German National Identity.* Pp. xi, 227. Cambridge, MA: Harvard University Press, 1988. $22.50.

Herein we encounter a historicophilosophical meditation on the antecedents and future of contemporary Germany. Scholarly and temperate, Charles Maier probes the *historikerstreit,* the at times fierce controversy raging between German historians respecting the quiddity of the nation. This people's frantic quest after self-identity entails a working through of a guilt-burdened past. Were the monstrous atrocities committed by the Third Reich an inexplicable aberration or an almost predictable function of the German national character? Embedded in this conundrum lurks a tantalizing irony: the denouement of the Final Solution — the colossal Nazi striving to purge itself of a Jewish excrescence — demands a coming to terms with the Holocaust in order to alchemize a German self-definition.

Maier perforce finds himself taking up the related issue of *sonderweg:* whether German evolution exhibits a uniqueness — in a pejorative sense — setting it apart from Western democratic development. If there are differences, are these attributable to Germany's *Mitteleuropa* location — its geopolitical vulnerability vis-à-vis a Franco-British aggressive alliance and a menacing Russia? Was the Prussian developmental experience, culminating in Bismarck's "Caesarist" regime, with heavy emphasis upon militarism, expansionist politics, and suffocating bureaucracy, decisive for an emergent Germany? Then again, the subject may be pursued along socioeconomic lines, with clarification sought by appeal to lingering feudalism in the Germanies and the prevalence of oppressive social inequalities. While acknowledging limited merit in these and other theories, Maier fails to find irresistible explanatory power in any of them.

Maier firmly repudiates the "comparability" tu quoque argument — that other peoples have committed wholesale slaughter. After examining "parallels," Maier concludes that only in the case of the Jewish Holocaust was the full state apparatus, in keeping with deliberate public policy, systematically directed to ruthless extirpation of a people. Indeed, let one brood upon all deaths as undifferentiated evil and what emerges is a banality culminating in President Reagan's Bitburg gaucherie.

Does remembering obsessively obstruct therapeutic reconstruction? In confronting this morbidity, Maier draws upon Jurgen Habermas's "life forms." The latter holds that illiberal institutional structures and invidious collective attitudes, when transmitted to the younger generation, exert a malign potency capable of metastasis into a recrudescent totalitarianism. Maier finds Habermas's preference for a German constitutional democracy within a Western community too passionlessly rationalistic to galvanize popular emotional allegiance.

The specific landscape upon which Maier works his craft is West Germany. Yet he engages his subject to launch broad historiographical inquiry, transcending time and place. He is sufficiently secure intellectually to weave an eclectic methodological synthesis of social philosophy and the sociology of history. Heidegger, Kant, Marx, Nietzsche, Max Weber are grist for his mill, as well as the more likely Meinecke and Von Ranke. He discerns within the vaunted immaculateness of strict methodology a tilting in favor of neoconservatism or social democratic political ideology. Regarding the writings of today's German historians, he is intimately familiar, and he provides a full critical section of German-language documentation. Indeed, he is so thoroughly saturated in his sources as to dizzy an uninformed reader with the convolutions of point-counterpoint polemic.

It is challenging to conjecture what impact the current upheavals in central and Baltic Europe — and especially the massive exodus from East Germany — are having upon Maier's assessments. Be that as it may, this volume, even without revision, should survive as a valuable contribution toward interpreting the unmasterable past.

ELMER N. LEAR

Pennsylvania State
    University
Middletown

UNITED STATES

DAVIS, SUE. *Justice Rehnquist and the Constitution.* Pp. x, 247. Princeton, NJ: Princeton University Press, 1989. $19.95.

LUBAN, DAVID. *Lawyers and Justice: An Ethical Study.* Pp. xxix, 440. Princeton, NJ: Princeton University Press, 1989. $55.00. Paperbound, $12.95.

Sue Davis writes that there are three types of Supreme Court biography: (1) book-length, full-life studies; (2) "scientific" analyses empirically examining votes as a function of values; and (3) focused studies limited to a justice's work on the Court. She places her own study of

William Rehnquist's work as an associate justice from 1971 to 1986 squarely into the third category. Taken on its own terms, a study analyzing Rehnquist's legal philosophy by utilizing his judicial opinions and papers — "with the goal of understanding his methods and values" — this book is a helpful addition to the public law literature. The typology of judicial biography, however, is nominal, or in any event, simplistic. True, various existing biographies can be fitted into the typology, but the typology does not derive from nor does it tell us anything about methodology. Amazingly, there is no mention in this book — in the body, index, or references — of the work of J. Woodford Howard, who not only wrote one of the best Supreme Court biographies — of Mr. Justice Murphy — but who also explicated in a path-breaking article in the *American Political Science Review* the methods and uses of judicial biography as a research vehicle. Even allowing for this omission, one wonders why an author attempting to understand a justice's decisions would not at least include possible explanations available in the empirical research literature. Knowing what we know, for example, it is just not possible to believe that Justice Rehnquist's votes are wholly unaffected by such variables as bloc activity.

Davis does a good job of describing Rehnquist's formal role as an associate justice. Her descriptions of his opinions are detailed and thorough. Her survey of his philosophical positions is comprehensive. And she does identify a hierarchy of values that inhere in his votes and opinions. Especially early in the book, Davis does a good job of pointing out the inconsistencies in various characterizations of Rehnquist by off-the-court commentators and critics. Some say he is an activist, others say he is restrained. Some consider him a strict constructionist, others find him loose. She kindly attributes this confusion to the preliminary nature of the assessments. But she then proceeds to present her principal thesis, which is that Rehnquist is not a right-wing, result-oriented ideologue but a legal positivist whose hierarchy of values places federalism — state autonomy — first, property rights second, and individual rights third.

She does fine work in laying out this conclusion. Of course, "right-wing" is not just one thing. And it may well be that her conclusion is entirely compatible with the description of Rehnquist that she argues it rejects.

As the first book-length study of Rehnquist, this volume is quite useful — but as a source of information, not as a piece of analysis. As legal scholarship, this is a good book. As political science — and Sue Davis is a political scientist at the University of Delaware — it lacks a certain context and coherence that a broader methodology would have almost certainly produced.

David Luban's new book, *Lawyers and Justice,* differs markedly from the Rehnquist biography in both substance and quality. It is perhaps the best book I have ever read on lawyers' ethics. Luban is a former chair of the professional responsibility section of the Association of American Law Schools and the editor of the highly acclaimed *Good Lawyer.* A law professor and philosopher, Luban's basic jurisprudential assumption is that lawyers are the law, that is, law cannot be different from what lawyers do or better than lawyers make it. On one level, Luban's critique is pedestrian, well known, and overworked — lawyers are concerned with their clients and not with justice. As one would expect, then, he deals throughout the book with lawyers' professional roles and social responsibility and presents a moral philosopher's analysis of lawyers' ethics. But one of the many things that make this a both superb and provocative book, different from most others on the same subject, is that Luban analyzes the link between legal ethics and political theory.

The critique consists of several interrelated parts. Lawyers are governed by a "role morality" that takes precedence over "common morality," for example, a lawyer helps a man convicted of incest to regain custody of his children because the duty of the lawyer's station in life is extreme partisan zeal on behalf of his client. In turn, the "advisory system," at the heart of Anglo-American law, justifies that extreme partisan zeal and excuses the lawyer from any moral responsibility for the client's goals and methods. The result is an "institutionalized immunity

from the requirements of conscience." In a polity that is "extraordinarily lawyer-intensive," lawyers' ethical problems become public difficulties not adequately addressed by self-regulation. The proposal consists of a Brandeis-like plea that lawyers seize "the opportunity in the law" — and defend it against the professional norm of client service and the bottom-line ethic, thus not only making the law more just but making the client more public spirited.

Best of all, this book is accessible to the average reader. Though both philosophical and profound, it is written in a manner easily understood by the reasonably educated.

WILLIAM C. LOUTHAN

Ohio Wesleyan University
Delaware

EDWARDS, GEORGE, C., III. *At the Margins: Presidential Leadership of Congress.* Pp. xiv, 233. New Haven, CT: Yale University Press, 1989. $24.00.

FOREMAN, CHRISTOPHER H., Jr. *Signals from the Hill: Congressional Oversight and the Challenge of Social Regulation.* Pp. x, 214. New Haven, CT: Yale University Press, 1989. $27.50.

In the American system of government the opportunities for interaction between the legislative and executive branches are truly varied and great. In these books, *At the Margins: Presidential Leadership of Congress,* by George C. Edwards, and *Signals from the Hill: Congressional Oversight and the Challenge of Social Regulation,* by Christopher H. Foreman, the diversity of legislative-executive relations is presented. The Edwards book deals with the interaction between the president and the Congress, focusing on the question of presidential influence on congressional floor votes. In contrast, the Foreman book deals with the interaction of the federal bureaucracy and the congressional committees that play the major role in congressional oversight. Since these books deal with such fundamentally different aspects of legislative-executive relations, it is extremely difficult to review them as a pair. I have therefore decided to review them separately.

Foreman examines an important question about the nature of policymaking in the United States. He asks what effects congressional oversight has on the behavior of federal regulatory agencies and ultimately the impacts of regulatory efforts. Using material drawn from several regulatory agencies, including the Environmental Protection Agency, the Occupational Safety and Health Administration, the Federal Trade Commission, and the Food and Drug Administration, he argues that many previous studies have underestimated the quantity of congressional oversight. After examining congressional involvement in the confirmation and nomination of agency personnel, the supply of funds to regulatory agencies through the appropriations process, and the continual monitoring of agency decisions by the relevant committees and subcommittees, Foreman debunks the myth that regulatory agencies are autonomous actors operating in a sea of congressional indifference.

But showing that Congress does engage in a great deal of oversight activity is not the same as saying that congressional oversight improves public policy. The last half of the book, in which he attempts to analyze why congressional oversight does not necessarily improve policy outcomes, makes his book an important contribution for students of public policy, congressional behavior, and public administration. Especially interesting is the discussion of why Congress often focuses its attention on the means of regulatory policy rather than on the ends of such policy.

The book by George Edwards continues a line of research in which the concept of presidential leadership is used as the focus of analysis. Building on Richard Neustadt's work, Edwards is explicitly concerned with sources of influence that are "centered on the presidency." He identifies and analyzes three potential sources of influence, namely, political party, public support, and leadership skill. His analysis indicates that these sources of influence are

marginal. The basic argument is that the president is not a dominant actor in the legislative process but rather operates "at the margins of coalition building to exploit opportunities presented by a favorable configuration of political forces in his environment." In analyzing the effect of presidential skills, Edwards argues that the "examination of legislative skills has failed to reveal systematic evidence of their impact on presidential support." Even though I agree with the basic tone of his argument, I believe that his analysis will ultimately be unpersuasive to presidency scholars who believe that presidential activity makes a difference. The reason is that Edwards does not — and cannot — observe and analyze influence; he can only analyze members' support for the president.

In addition, Edwards has modified his position on the impact of presidential popularity. Where he previously argued that "research provides evidence that members of Congress do respond to . . . the president's current popularity among their supporters" and that presidential popularity "must be added to the list of variables that have been found useful in explaining roll call behavior," he now argues that "presidential approval is not a resource that in most instances will dominate executive-legislative relations . . . it works at the margins."

Finally, in his discussion and defense of his measure — presidential support scores — Edwards argues that individual support scores are better than box scores and success-on-votes measures because support scores can be disaggregated. But, as should be clear to anyone who has studied these measures, they all involve some type of aggregation. Presidential support scores aggregate individual behavior over a period of time — a calendar year, in Edwards's case. Furthermore, it is silly to argue that analyzing success on roll-call votes cannot be disaggregated. One can use the vote as the unit of analysis to study whether or not the president's position prevails and how different collections of individuals behave on each vote. In addition, given Edwards's strong pitch for disaggregation to the individual-member level, it is surprising that he fails to report any individual-level analysis, that is, relationships between characteristics of individuals and levels of support for the president. Instead, all of his tables present summaries of aggregations of individuals. Thus he fails to exploit the major advantage of using an indicator of individual behavior. For example, with his research design he could have analyzed the effects of members' constituency characteristics—how well the president ran in the district, whether the member was electorally marginal, seniority, and so on. Unfortunately, he did not record any of these potentially important variables. The only individual-level variable he has is members' party, and even here he does not present an analysis that relates an individual's party to that individual's level of support for the president.

In sum, these books represent significant scholarly efforts that students of executive-legislative relations will find well worth reading.

RICHARD FLEISHER

Fordham University
Bronx
New York

FAIRBANKS, ROBERT B. *Making Better Citizens: Housing Reform and the Community Development Strategy in Cincinnati, 1890-1960.* Pp. xii, 243. Champaign: University of Illinois Press, 1988. $24.95.

Because the idea of decent and affordable housing as a guaranteed right to each and every individual has never firmly rooted itself in the American value structure, efforts by local activists, voluntary groups, and philanthropists to press for low- and middle-income housing have been frequented.

Making Better Citizens chronicles and assesses the housing-reform movement in one of the nation's major cities, Cincinnati, Ohio. Underscored is the fact that Cincinnati had earned national recognition as an advocate for progressive housing-reform policy long before the Fed-

eral Housing Act was legislated in 1949. The book examines two periods: first, the early period of tenement reform, from the late nineteenth century to the time immediately after World War II, and, second, the period from the mid-1940s to 1960.

Fairbanks concurs that both periods were undermined by internal contradictions and that these combined with other factors led to the decline of the reform movement. The initial period, while committed to the principle of building an ideal metropolitan social atmosphere as the foundation for good citizenship, also embraced the idea of separate but equal housing for black and white Cincinnatians. The housing that was provided for blacks was often inadequate compared with housing for whites. Dependent persons or the very poor who were unprotected by a functional family and became wards of the state were overlooked. The second period brought about an ideological shift. The vision was one that downplayed the life-shaping impact of neighborhood community while emphasizing the importance of individual needs and the individual as the functional unit of society. As for planners during this era, the concept of revitalization of the urban arena became synonymous with developing industrial parks, constructing sprawling sports complexes, and modernizing central business districts. It suggested a diminishing commitment to low-cost housing.

Fairbanks's study of the movement for low-cost housing and community development in Cincinnati is timely, as it has emerged at the very juncture when the housing problem and homelessness have reached crisis proportions across the nation, particularly in the urban centers. It is also insightful and penetrating. What this study offers is an opportunity to place the problem in its historical context and approach a clearer understanding. It does not, however, offer any earthshaking solutions. In addition, the impact of American capitalism is not clearly defined or sufficiently integrated into the analysis. Specifically, reference is made to capital and capital formation as a basic ingredient in shaping the housing industry and to their role in shaping the values of professional planners, activists, housers, and philanthropists. When linked to the American economic system, racism, which Fairbanks addresses as responsible for segregated housing arrangements for blacks, could be better understood.

Making Better Citizens is informative, well researched, and written for a wide audience. While the book focuses on Cincinnati, its relevance is much broader. Housing activists, planners, scholars, and all persons who are expressly concerned with America's urban housing dilemma would find this book interesting.

CHARLES GREEN

Hunter College
New York City

FOWLER, LINDA L. and ROBERT D. McCLURE. *Political Ambition: Who Decides to Run for Congress.* Pp. xiii, 247. New Haven, CT: Yale University Press, 1989. $25.00.

For members of Congress, 1989 began with a firestorm engulfing the issues of a pay raise and limits on honoraria. It continued with the slow agony of Speaker Jim Wright's demise and the swifter but no less devastating departure of House leader Tony Coelho of California. Interspersed were a number of other stories that included allegations of fraud, abuse, and misconduct on the part of several more members. Given these, and the increasing scrutiny focused on public officials, one might wonder why anyone would want to serve in the Congress of the United States.

Fortunately, Linda L. Fowler and Robert D. McClure have combined their talents to study how people decide whether or not to run for Congress. In *Political Ambition* they seek to understand more about the incentives and disincentives that bring men and women in and out of public life. In particular they look at a wide range of "unseen candidates," those who could have run for Congress but did not do so.

To provide focus, they chose to concentrate their attention on New York's Thirtieth Con-

gressional District during the elections of 1984 and 1986. Their story begins on 6 February 1984, when longtime incumbent Barber Conable announced that he would not seek reelection. From this point the goal is "to track the thinking of every political insider who played a significant role in determining who would be the 30th district's congressional representative." Because what was expected to be a bitterly fought wide-open contest never really materialized in 1984, the story continued on to 1986 when a major confrontation actually took place.

As the 1984 race evolved, a number of unanticipated developments occurred. With the exception of Fred Eckert, the early front runner and eventual victor, none of the perceived strongest candidates entered the fray. Even among local politicians, virtually no one fully appreciated the significance of the 1982 redistricting, which shifted the balance of power in the Thirtieth District. Also, a number of prospective challengers concluded that the possibility of a career in the Congress did not outweigh the advantages of a secure seat in the state legislature. Snapshots of prominent nonpoliticians in the district provided ample evidence that intense political ambition could have outlets other than elective office. Moreover, in combination with other factors, the personal costs of leaving the community had considerable impact on the decision-making process, particularly for those most successful in business, professional, or family pursuits outside politics.

The 1984 election itself offered no great surprises. Republican Party insiders eased Eckert's way by discouraging primary opponents. The Democrats' failure to persuade the national party and political action committees that Doug Call could win doomed his effort. Barber Conable's sweeping public endorsement of Eckert overshadowed the candidate's weaknesses and thus was critical to his success. The result was an Eckert victory, but by a smaller margin than expected. This finally showed the Democrats how competitive the district had become and paved the way for Louise Slaughter's tough, expensive, high-profile campaign in 1986.

Although the search for Barber Conable's successor did not follow the course of conventional wisdom and, in fact, led Fowler and McClure through more unlikely twists and turns than they could have invented, it nevertheless drove home their basic premise that election-day results depend on decisions made by prospective candidates months or even years beforehand. Such recruitment decisions emerge from a combination of individual motivations and district circumstances. As they noted, "modern House campaigns required both an extraordinary level of personal political ambition and a local environment that allowed those aspirations to be directed toward Congress." The winnowing process severely limits voter choice and, as in the case of New York's Thirtieth District, often leads to bizarre results — replacement of conservative Conable first with ultraconservative Eckert, then just two years later with liberal Slaughter. The key remains the burning desire to be a member of Congress. The high costs, complex organizational requirements, and heavy personal toll ensure that only the most committed and ambitious survive.

Fowler and McClure have performed an outstanding service in *Political Ambition*. The decision to use one congressional district as a case study was truly inspired as it offered an opportunity to test hypotheses against actual events. They appear to have spoken with every significant actor in the drama and in so doing provide a range of vantage points from which to view the decision-making process. While not all of their conclusions are new or radical, all are well documented. The special effort to focus on the recruitment of women, which leads to the view that an aggressive strategy to increase the number of women in Congress may drain the reservoir of talent for future races, may in itself contribute to the loss of potential female candidates during the winnowing process. Moreover, it does not seem consistent with the sense that a Slaughter candidacy in 1984, complete with strong party and political-action-committee support, might well have prevailed over Eckert given his relatively weak showing against Doug Call.

Political Ambition is a rare commodity — a scholarly work that is fun to read. It will appeal both to the specialist and to the general observer of the political scene. While not a primer for those who may be running for Congress someday, it certainly provides many useful insights, not the least of which is that such an effort is difficult if not impossible "if a politician has not already got on the fast track and been warming up for the big race for a long time."

JOSEPH A. IMLER

Arlington
Virginia

KOHL, LAWRENCE FREDERICK. *The Politics of Individualism: Parties and the American Character in the Jacksonian Era.* Pp. xii, 266. New York: Oxford University Press, 1989. $29.95.

School children in America are taught to honor and cherish the Founding Fathers. The Founders are heroes to be viewed with considerable reverence, almost mystical characters, who could do no wrong. But when Andrew Jackson is studied, the reverence and mystical qualities are replaced by understanding, for Jackson appears much more human, certainly more modern, and he is easily understood as the champion of the masses, who brought government within reach of everyone.

Most historians recognize this shift in attitude from Washington and Jefferson to Jackson and reckon with it in various ways. It is treated as a shift from the traditional to the modern and accounted for largely because of the vast transformations taking place in American life. Population quadrupled, the country more than doubled in size, and the industrial revolution gained momentum, dramatically changing the modes of transportation, communication, and methods of production. Some describe the change as one from an agrarian communal-based society to a liberal capitalistic entrepreneurial society, from a self-sufficient economy to one that contended with market forces.

In his new book on Jacksonian politics, Lawrence Kohl argues that the political manifestations of these changes can only be understood through the context of individualism. Through a careful study of the political rhetoric of the period, he analyzes the divergent reaction to the emergence of this individualistic social order. His primary interest is to explain how the great political parties, Whigs and Democrats, reacted in the Jacksonian era to this new individualist social order. He disagrees with the historians writing during the cold-war period after World War II, who found little difference between these parties and who maintained that their heated and antagonistic rhetoric only marked their real similarities. In principles and values, they argued, there was little difference between these pragmatic parties. They existed primarily to elect their leaders to political office. Kohl, on the other hand, finds the differences real and significant. Those who were comfortable "with the personal, self-interested relationships which characterize an individualist society, became Whigs; and . . . those who still felt bound to others in more personal ways, became Jacksonians."

The significance of Kohl's work lies in this psychological explanation for political-party affiliation. The intense party loyalty that characterized these early political parties, according to Kohl, was due to the new individualistic social order sweeping the nation in the second quarter of the nineteenth century. While many will question Kohl's interpretation, most will find it stimulating and challenging, if not totally convincing. Others, for example, have found the Whigs politically more tradition bound in their strong antiparty rhetoric than the Democrats. Similarly, considerable evidence exists, and not only rhetorical, that the Democrats were quite satisfied and adept in the new individualistic capitalistic environment and that, indeed, the Whigs were far more burdened and inhibited by traditional values and morality than the greedy and more grasping Democrats. Even so, this is

a good book and worthy of serious consideration by all those interested in American politics.

GENE D. LEWIS

University of Cincinnati
Ohio

LINK, ARTHUR S. et al., eds. *The Papers of Woodrow Wilson.* Vol. 59. Pp. xxiv, 674. Princeton, NJ: Princeton University Press, 1988. $52.50.

LINK, ARTHUR S. et al., eds. *The Papers of Woodrow Wilson.* Vol. 60. Pp. xxiv, 674. Princeton, NJ: Princeton University Press, 1989. $52.50.

The conferences that led to the final peace treaty with Germany and the creation of the League of Nations are so evidently in history that they can be read as expressions of old hopes and anticipations. These failed to materialize, and this failure raises questions of how they might have been better posed, considering the emotionalism then dominating the major nations. In any case, the meetings helped set up conditions that affected the future.

The volumes under review necessarily focus on the debates of the key participants, and first of all Wilson himself. Our editors have perused diaries and accounts from others involved in the peace-making process. These materials affect our views of David Lloyd George, Georges Clemenceau, and Vittorio Emanuele Orlando, but there seems always something left obscure. Thus wars on the Continent continued while the Council of Four debated and discussed, and the latter were as important as the decisions at which they arrived.

Interspersed between major arguments as to what to do with defeated Germany are numerous issues affecting millions of people that could have tilted one way or another. Thus Admiral Kolchak, a major White Guard opponent of the Bolsheviks, claimed to have set up a Russian government that would soon complete its victory over Red Army forces. He promised to call a democratic Constituent Assembly to create a regime dedicated to serving justly the Russian peasantry, as well as Poles, Baltic people, and others. Hindsight shows the futility — and probable insincerity — of Kolchak partisans, but, with military aid, they could have won the field. The Council's withholding of troops proved strategic.

Czechs, Hungarians, Romanians, and others mobilized military forces and engaged in actions intended to augment their borders or serve ethnic interests. Their progress was watched closely by the would-be peacemakers who had armies to throw in any direction but who were faced with dilemmas on every side. Lloyd George and Clemenceau were clearly bent on securing dominant positions for their nations; Wilson stands out among them as having no borders to defend and as evidently seeking justice so intensely as to affect his health. Yet he, no less than his partners, could not avoid personal attitudes that, under the pressures of world upheaval, seem all but bizarre.

Thus the Council agrees that armies must be ready for possible action, considering, for example, that the Austro-Hungarian Empire has been shattered. But how should the armies perform? Lloyd George fears that Marshal Foch still cherishes old French imperialist dreams. He is too much influenced by his colleague General Weygand: "I saw him speaking nonstop into the ear of the Marshal, indicating what he should say." Lloyd George found Foch changed: "His face has a firm expression."

With such vagarious notions determining attitudes, little that is definite can be expected from the Council of Four. Its Preliminary Conditions of Peace treats Germany harshly, so much so that no German government can be found that would accept its onerous terms. German leaders agree to disarmament and, indeed, hope, as accepted members of the League of Nations, to foist disarmament on all the participants. Immediate, too, are the ambitions of Orlando, one of the Council, who hopes to see Italy a power in the Mediterranean and Near East once more.

Wilson works his way as best he and his advisers — and first of all Colonel House — can, but the materials for justice are sparse. History is brought into the discussion of Upper Silesia, to determine whether it is more German than Polish. Its very information makes it evident that history can as readily be marshaled on one side as the other. Germany must accept responsibility for the war. There is more history. But the Council's simple reference to the "peace-loving nations of Western Europe" makes it evident that the major assumptions that determine decisions will be self-serving, though not necessarily the best.

LOUIS FILLER

The Belfry
Ovid
Michigan

LONGLEY, LAWRENCE D. and WALTER J. OLE-SZEK. *Bicameral Politics: Conference Committees in Congress.* Pp. xiv, 361. New Haven, CT: Yale University Press, 1989. $50.00. Paperbound, $16.95.

Longley and Oleszek have written the standard reference on congressional conference committees. *Bicameral Politics* is a comprehensive account of the rules conference procedure, the tactical considerations associated with conference politics, and the scholarly and journalistic literature on the subject. All students of congressional politics will turn first to Longley and Oleszek when they begin their own studies of the conference process in Congress.

Bicameral Politics is not organized formally into parts, but its chapters come in three sets. Because of the distinctiveness of each set, it is convenient to comment on each set separately.

The first set of chapters — 1 through 6 — concerns the history, scholarly treatment, and context of conference politics. Useful introductions to bicameralism and the use of conference committees to resolve interchamber differences, changes in rules governing conference deliberations, the "who wins in conference" literature, and the relations between conferees and their parent chambers and committees can be found in these chapters. Generally, these chapters constitute a high-quality textbook treatment of these subjects—they are not definitive but do outline the considerations that a more rigorous treatment of each of the many subjects would have to take into account.

The first set of chapters is enticing but not very satisfying. A major theme of these chapters, change in conference politics in recent decades, is convincing, but it is not adequately developed. Key propositions about changing conference politics are illustrated with examples but are not tested, even when systematic evidence could easily be marshaled. A central discussion in recent political science, the importance of conferences for committee power, is relegated to a footnote. Longley and Oleszek are fully aware that they raise more questions than they answer and rightly encourage their readers to pursue some of the issues they note.

The second set of chapters—7 through 10—constitutes the best available examination of the procedures and tactics surrounding conference committees. Organized into four components—the players, preconference stages, the conference stage, and postconference stages—these chapters should be assigned to every undergraduate and graduate seminar on Congress, and all professional students of Congress will start with these chapters in developing their own research on conference politics. Indeed, many instructors will use these chapters as the core material on the mechanics of the legislative process. As in the first set of chapters, these chapters are well illustrated, demonstrating that Longley and Oleszek are the champion self-appointed archivists of congressional politics. No one can match them for their collection of appropriate examples and pointed quotes from public sources.

The third set, the final two chapters, tells the story of eight conferences and, in doing so, illustrates the wide variety of procedural routes taken by legislation, even for those measures taken to conference. The cases bring to life the procedures and tactics described in the previous set of chapters. They do not add up to much, however, because Longley and Oleszek draw few general lessons from the cases, leaving the cases to speak for themselves—as they seldom do. In fact, the book ends with a whimper.

A footnote about the design of this book, directed as much at the publisher as the authors, is in order. The design is very weak, particularly in the first set of chapters, where each chapter and section is introduced by at least one quotation. Several pages include nothing more than a chapter or section title, one or two quotes, half a page of footnotes, and no or just one or two lines of text. Some of the quotations are not effective and some footnotes could be abbreviated. In two cases, I noticed that footnotes commented on matters discussed in other footnotes but not addressed in the text. All these problems substantially reduce the viability of this book for classroom use.

Even with its weaknesses, this book is much more than the "introductory stab at analysis and understanding" that Longley and Oleszek claim in their last paragraph. It provides a good feel of the interplay between preferences, policies, and procedures in conference politics. Few books make the strategic use of procedure more vivid than this one. In addition, while intended to be a theoretical treatment of conference committees, it is a complete and balanced examination of a vital subject and will be the primary source on the subject for decades to come. Everyone, including the most experienced members of Congress, will learn a great deal from Longley and Oleszek.

STEVEN S. SMITH

University of Minnesota
Minneapolis

SINCLAIR, BARBARA. *The Transformation of the U.S. Senate*. Pp. 233. Baltimore, MD: Johns Hopkins University Press, 1989. $28.50.

BACH, STANLEY and STEVEN S. SMITH. *Managing Uncertainty in the House of Represen-*

tatives: Adaptation and Innovation in Special Rules. Pp. xii, 140. Washington, DC: Brookings Institution, 1988. Paperbound, $8.95.

The titles of these books accurately suggest the themes that they explore. Sinclair's examination of the contemporary U.S. Senate delineates major change in the political style, distribution of power, and adherence to the Senate norms described by Donald R. Matthews in *U.S. Senators and Their World* (1960). Bach and Smith's study reveals that changes and reforms in the House of Representatives during the 1970s have resulted in the majority party's pursuit of procedural innovation in Rules Committee special rules to evolve a strategy for managing uncertainty on the floor of the House. Both books are tightly written using quantitative measurements rather than impressionistic data. Their common themes stand out — democratic impulses and more openness have made both bodies more responsive to the sentiments of majorities and rank-and-file members. Significant differences in procedure and political viewpoint still exist between the bodies.

The audience for these books consists of those who want to get a feeling for the manner in which the contemporary House and Senate have adjusted their goals, procedures, and power structures to accommodate such forces as the importance of the national mass media, the decline of political parties, the emergence of a more heterogeneous membership, and the consequences of the legislative reforms of the 1970s. Both books provide one with an appreciation of the complexity, richness, and intricacy of wielding political influence in the 1980s.

Sinclair dramatically shows how the Senate no longer can be described as structured and hierarchical or characterized as a club where adherence to the rules and norms result in a relatively unequal distribution of influence. Today, the Senate is described as a body that provides an effective forum for interest articulation and agenda setting where influence is much more equally distributed and members' behavior is accorded a very wide latitude. The norms and other informal arrangements have been modified where they hamper the pursuit of a senator's goals. Sinclair concludes that the Senate is now better able to perform the interest-representation function but less efficient as a decision-making body. The contemporary Senate, Sinclair summarizes, is more staff dependent, more reflective of the preferences of the entire membership, and more responsive to public opinion.

A key chapter explores the current vitality and efficacy of the norms delineated by Matthews. Sinclair concludes that many stifled the goals of new members elected during the 1960s. Significant modification has occurred: the apprenticeship norm died quickly; those of specialization, legislative work, reciprocity, and institutional patriotism "became defunct or drastically changed their form." Courtesy is still a norm but is violated more frequently.

Legislative activism on a wide range of issues without membership on the relevant committee has become a Senate style that has profound consequences, such as making the Senate floor a more active decision-making arena. There are more frequent attempts to alter committee decisions through proposing amendments. Greater resort to filibuster, threats to filibuster, and calls for holds on pending proposals as well as burdensome quorum calls occur. The Senate is now a "more participatory and less committee-centered institution" responsive to a far wider range of policy issues and multiple arenas than in the 1950s. Sinclair documents these changes with a quantitative analysis using floor amendment proposals and the number of bills sponsored by a senator to define legislative activism by generalist and specialist senators.

Bach and Smith's book examines adaptation and innovation in special rules devised by the House Rules Committee between 1975 and 1986 as a means of reducing unpredictability during floor consideration of legislation. This book's subject matter is more technical and of narrower range. Its overarching conclusion is that the disruption and unpredictability of conducting business on the floor during the 1970s plus the redistribution of power to subcommittees created a less stable setting for floor debate. The majority party and the Speaker of the House have come to rely much more heavily on restrictive special rules to inhibit amending activity on the floor, especially by the minority party and those who are not committee members.

Totally gone are the old days when the Rules Committee was the traffic cop of the House that issued either open or closed rules, that is, rules defining the conditions of debate as well as whether amendments from the floor were permissible or not. Now the Speaker and the committee chairs depend upon the Rules Committee to devise an extraordinary range of special — sometimes unique — rules that are categorized as open, organizing, expansive, closed, restrictive, or complex. Such intricacy has occurred in part due to multiple committee referrals of legislation, increased reliance upon subcommittees, and the inability of majority-party floor managers to approach floor debates with the confidence that they can anticipate amendments and produce the votes to defeat them. Special rules restrict amending activity and help reduce unpredictability in floor consideration.

The variety in special rules is notable — some permit amendments only to specified provisions of measures; some require advance publication in the *Congressional Record;* others prohibit all or almost all amendments to certain provisions or to committee-sponsored amendments; and, finally, others restrict amendments to those specifically printed or otherwise designated in the special rule. Some special rules are written with a strong bias toward the majority party and/or committee interests and result in suppressing floor amendments or restricting the minority to offering only one amendment, which amounts to an alternative measure to the one being considered. Other features have to do with king-of-the-mountain rules, under which the House votes on several versions of a measure, but, if the majority approves more than one of the alternatives, only the last of them wins. Another innovation concerns self-executing rules, under which the House, by adopting a special rule, agrees to adopt Senate amendments.

The creativity of the House Rules Committee, of course, is aimed at influencing political and policy outcomes by defining alternatives for members to choose from while maintaining a balance between open deliberations and reasonably prompt final decisions. All this intricate strategic procedural ingenuity must be accomplished in a way that is politically acceptable to the House membership, not simply in a way that the Speaker may desire. Bach and Smith conclude that "by promoting the Speaker's party program, protecting Democratic leaders and their bills, and making floor proceedings more manageable for the members at large," the reliance on restrictive special rules has increased. The House has had to adapt to greater decentralization of committees, reinvigorated party caucuses, and the new budget process. The consequence of these transformations in special rules has been Democratic approval but Republican resentment and opposition to the restrictions that limit amendments from the floor.

The trend toward restrictive rules can be summarized as a partnership between the Speaker and his party leadership and Rules Committee Democrats who now serve as an adjunct to the majority-party leadership. The Rules Committee is no longer an independent power center, as is illustrated by the discussion of Representative Claude Pepper's ill-fated attempt to get House consideration of his long-term home health care bill in 1987 with a special rule that bypassed both the Ways and Means and Energy and Commerce Committees, which had jurisdiction over the subject.

JAMES R. KERR

Southern Illinois University
Edwardsville

SOCIOLOGY

BAUMGARTNER, M. P. *The Moral Order of a Suburb.* Pp. x, 172. New York: Oxford University Press, 1989. $19.95.

This study of the management of conflict in a suburb is a thought-provoking contribution to the sociology and anthropology of law. Prior theory about the role of law in society has emphasized active negotiation and resolution of conflicts, whether by formal or informal means. Empirical research has usually examined everyday dispute resolution in less developed societies or formal dispute resolution in modern industrial societies. This book is novel in at least two respects. Its theoretical focus is on avoidance of conflict and its setting is the suburbs, a largely neglected arena for the study of informal dispute resolution.

The research centered on a single suburb of New York City, referred to as Hampton. Ethnographic field work took place over a 12-month period during 1978-79. The participant observation covered Hampton's middle class — largely of northern European extraction — most intensively, but it also included the town's working class, predominantly of Italian background. In all, Baumgartner's conversations yielded over 200 reported instances of conflict with family members, friends, neighbors, and strangers. These conflicts and their management are the book's focal point.

Baumgartner concludes that the social conditions of life in suburbia — transience, privacy, individuation, material independence, and freedom from authority — lend themselves to what she terms "moral minimalism": aversion to confrontation or conflict and preference for weak forms of social control. It is "possible to speak of the suburb as a culture of avoidance."

The reader may agree with this conclusion without agreeing with the further implications that are drawn. For example, Baumgartner argues that there is more avoidance on the part of the middle class than the working class in Hampton. Yet her data speak to absolute numbers of conflicts, not to the proportion of all interchanges that become open conflicts. It is possible that the closer networks of the working class generate many instances of avoidance that were inaccessible to the participant observer. Further, Baumgartner argues that the dominance of avoidance "contrasts sharply with claims that American society is particularly violent or litigious." But perhaps it is true both that a large proportion of American suburban conflicts are handled by avoidance and that a larger proportion or absolute number of American conflicts end in violence or litigation than is the case elsewhere. Full answers to such questions require a further look at both conflict in the suburbs and avoidance in other settings. This book is the first, not the last, word in what promises to be an important debate.

V. LEE HAMILTON

University of Maryland
College Park

DeSWAAN, ABRAM. *In Care of the State: Health, Education and Welfare in Europe and the USA in the Modern Era.* Pp. ix, 339. New York: Oxford University Press, 1988. $39.95.

AARON, HENRY J., BARRY P. BOSWORTH, and GARY BURTLESS. *Can America Afford to Grow Old? Paying for Social Security.* Pp. xiv, 144. Washington, DC: Brookings Institution, 1988. Paperbound, $7.95.

In the Care of the State is an outstanding comparative treatment of three areas of recurring community concern: popular education, social welfare, and health care. *Can America Afford to Grow Old?* is a Brookings Institution study of the immediate budgetary issues surrounding Social Security in the United States.

Abram DeSwaan has based his study on secondary, specialized works; the notes are copious and the extensive bibliography is excellent. His approach is historical-sociological: he treats of the collectivizing of poor relief, education, and health care in the Netherlands, Germany, France, Britain, and the United States, and the chronology ranges from early modern times to the present. Representative is his account and analysis of social welfare.

During the late Middle Ages, aid to the poor came primarily from monasteries, towns, and, later, cities. One central motive was to restrain assistance sufficiently to prevent a flood of indigent to a given area that might overrun limited resources. On the other hand, it was widely feared that too limited sustenance would cause the poor to become roving predatory bands. Thus the felt need was to reach some level of assistance that would satisfy the desire for stability and, at the same time, alleviate the fear of brigandage. From this situation regional arrangements emerged, but they were easily upset by any untoward event, such as a crop failure, that generated large numbers of peasants searching for the means of survival. Eventually, a national collectivization of efforts to ease the most severe effects of destitution and disease resulted.

The major landmarks in the emergence of generalized responsibility for education, poor relief, and health care represented an emerging elite consensus in which "collective charitable arrangements were formed, at the parish level first, later at the level of cities and, finally, at the national level." While this progression appears logical enough today, it occurred at different rates over time and was uneven in scope. It was certainly not inevitable.

With the growth of industrial capitalism, the machinery of the state itself became part of the dynamic of change; that is, some security resulted not so much from class struggle or planned efforts by capitalists to quiet workers but from the exertions of activist elites — politicians, bureaucrats, and union leaders. The narrative account of these developments is engaging and includes some useful conceptualizations such as figuration, or the human interdependencies that change and develop over time — and the judicious and effective use of game theory.

This is a first-rate, analytical work that is invaluable as a basis for thinking about social welfare.

Of a much more specific, policy-oriented character is the study by economists Henry Aaron, Barry Bosworth, and Gary Burtless. It is a thoroughly researched argument for a national savings policy for Social Security surpluses. Theirs is a tightly reasoned, scholarly analysis of three basic alternatives: first, surpluses may be borrowed to augment current federal income, which is the current policy; second, rather than accumulating large surpluses, revenues could be reduced to equal annual costs; or third, revenues could be kept at the current or higher level and used for national savings and capital development. The authors argue that the latter policy would reduce "consumption . . . to increase savings, raise the rate of growth in the stock of capital, and boost future production." It is this third option for which the authors argue most cogently.

Both of the books under review demand the attention of Americans.

DON LeFAVE

Yuba College
Marysville
California

JOHNSON, MIRIAM M. *Strong Mothers, Weak Wives: The Search for Gender Equality.* Pp. xii, 347. Berkeley: University of California Press, 1988. $25.00.

Miriam Johnson sets out to return feminism to an earlier clarity and focus regarding the cause of woman's oppression. In doing so, she hopes to "bring into balance and perspective two concerns within feminism: the desire for greater equality and the desire that values more associated with maternal attitudes should govern the behavior of both women and men." To achieve this aim she makes a series of interlocking points. The full complexity of her argument and the varied points she makes along the way cannot be done justice in such a short space; thus I will focus on her major points.

First, Johnson argues that it is important to focus on male dominance as the crucial causal agent in the oppression of women. Further, in understanding the cause of male dominance it is necessary to focus on the male peer group as the central socializing agent for men. This perspective is proposed in contradistinction to trends in feminism that are represented by the work of Dorothy Dinnerstein and Nancy Chodorow. These authors theorize that the oppression of women partly emanates from the unconscious psychological consequences of people's being nurtured in early childhood exclusively by women.

Second, Johnson proposes that we distinguish between the social roles of mother and wife. She argues that it is the role of the wife, within marriage, that organizes women's oppression. It is here that those negative characteristics associated with the female sex role — for example, subservience, passivity, living for and through another — are located and perpetuated. The role of mothering, on the other hand, is one that embodies and perpetuates life-affirming and positive values such as relatedness, nurturance, and helping other people to define "and sort out legitimate and illegitimate needs." Further, it is within the institution of marriage that husbands subjugate wives and, perhaps even more important, take the lead in facilitating the sex-role differentiation of children that prepares their daughters to take on the role of wife.

Her recommendations for social action flow from these arguments. She argues that involving men to a greater degree in child care — as Dinnerstein has proposed — is dangerous since it will provide them with greater opportunity to facilitate sex-role stratification. Instead, she suggests that men and women "grow up" and abandon their irrational, infantile thought patterns, a process in which women are uniquely suited to take the lead. In addition, she advocates a more widespread adoption of "maternal values." Johnson does not advocate an abandonment of the institution of marriage, because, she notes, this is unlikely to occur, because marriage can protect women from even more exploitative relationships with men, and because marriage "offers women an opportunity to 'socialize' men." Instead, she advocates increased egalitarian relationships, both within and outside of mar-

riage, where the model of women's friendships is the prevailing paradigm.

The book has some important strengths. Johnson provides a lucid summary of trends within feminist thought, such as the relative emphasis on difference versus sameness in relation to men and women. She also provides an interesting discussion of the oedipal stage of Freud's theory and what she argues is the relatively greater taboo against mother-son incest. Throughout, her attempts to have us look more closely at, and piece apart, intertwined concepts provide a helpful counterpoint to the tendency to take various constructs for granted. In addition, her assertion of the value of mothering is a valuable counterweight to trends — within and outside of feminism — that devalue both the act of mothering and the values historically associated with it.

The book is at its weakest in its presentation of information and in its method of supporting its main arguments. For example, the distinction between mothers and wives is simply asserted and then supported by describing negative characteristics or behaviors of women as "wifely" and positive ones as "motherly." The argument that it is the male peer group that accounts for men's socialization into a role characterized by the need for dominance is supported by an assortment of observations and research, some of which are taken out of the context of their field and presented in a way that gives no credence to alternative or more complex explanations. Her conclusions, valid or invalid, are not always supported by the material that has preceded them. For example, she writes, "Many studies indicate that teachers are concerned with teaching children how to be 'good students.' This parallels my argument that mothers are concerned with teaching children how to be 'good human beings.'" Both statements may well be true, but it is not clear how the former may reasonably be used as a support for the latter.

At the beginning of her book, Johnson suggests that we use the social sciences, particularly the tool of empiricism, to critique and analyze the status quo and to help us understand our perceptions. Indeed, her book is full of references to psychological, sociological, and, to a lesser extent, anthropological theory and research. Unfortunately, the way she makes use of this information often violates many widely held premises of scientific inquiry. She distorts important theories, takes research out of the context of its field, and at times changes the meaning of terms from other fields to suit her purposes. One example will have to suffice. She rides roughshod over the work of Dinnerstein and in the process misses her main point. She lambastes Dinnerstein for blaming the ills of the world on women's mothering—which is a distortion in that Dinnerstein is saying that it is the fact of single-sex parenting that is problematic—and then offers as an alternative hypothesis the view that "the basic problem here is not so much women's mothering but the nonrational, 'unprocessed' or primary process thinking that continues to influence the adult's responses in certain triggering situations." Johnson's alternative hypothesis is precisely the point that Dinnerstein uses her entire book to elaborate. Later, after dismissing Dinnerstein, Johnson interprets the relatively greater taboo on mother-son incest as arising from its unique inverse of customary male dominance—an important and interesting observation. She then goes on to note that "from a developmental standpoint, male shows of dominance over women as wives is a method of minimizing males' incapacity to dominate women as mothers," which also happens to be one of the main points that Dinnerstein makes throughout her book. Although she refers, at different points in the book, to unconscious processes, her treatment of Dinnerstein does not leave the reader confident that she appreciates them.

Some of the best work in the book is done in the disembedding of various constructs from one another. Unfortunately, this is a one-sided practice, and concepts are only disembedded when the process enhances the overall thrust of her argument. Thus she separates the concepts of gender identity from sexuality and sexual orientation, an important distinction, but at the same time she collapses the categories of the female sex and the mothering role. These two

identities are used interchangeably throughout the book, yet it is never clear what the exact relationship is between the mothering role and femaleness. Do the maternal values that emanate from women flow from their biological capacity to have children, or do they result from the act of mothering? If the former, how can one be so sure that the negative features so long associated with mothering—self-sacrifice, passivity, constraint to the domestic sphere—are not also linked to the same biological source? If the latter, what about men who mother and women who do not? Are men who mother maternal and women who do not masculine?

A similar problem arises in the context of her important point that we stop assuming that passivity is inherently connected to so-called maternal values such as relatedness. She thereby creates a useful distinction between qualities typically associated with the feminine sphere of life, yet she performs no such service for the masculine sphere. Thus masculine qualities of separation and autonomy are invariably linked with dominance and control, whereas self-sacrifice and passivity are strenuously separated from any inherent connection with femaleness. At no point does she acknowledge that some of the virtues ascribed to mothers—such as recognizing another's needs while maintaining an awareness of one's own—are capacities that probably rest on a psychological base of both separation and relatedness. There is, in fact, a considerable psychological literature that bears on this issue. Similarly, she assumes that female sexuality can be both diffusely erotic and relational, as well as genitally sexual and agenetic, but she pigeonholes men into a sexuality that "[denies] relationality in general and connect[s] sex with aggression and degrading the object."

In sum, the book makes a contribution by stressing the values embodied in the mothering role and by raising some interesting questions, such as the distinction between the role of wife and the role of mother, and how men are socialized to become dominant. On the other hand, Johnson's argument is considerably weakened by her presentation of material. Specifically, the book is biased in its presentation of theory and data as well as in the application of its analytical tools. In general, the book tends to make women complex — appropriately; however, it unduly simplifies men. In a book about women this might not be a problem, but Johnson's book is about women and men, and she makes many statements concerning the psychological and behavioral qualities of men as a group. The tone of the book and some of its arguments seem to substitute the all-too-common treatment of women as not men with a treatment of men as not women. The book communicates that positive human values are inherently female and maternal, and if men are to develop into more reasonable human beings, they will have to adopt these inherently maternal values. In addition, the lack of clarity in the book about whether certain qualities are inherently female or whether they are human virtues more frequently manifested in this culture by women raises certain problems. Notions of inherent female virtue that is tied to the capacity to mother has long been used to unduly restrict women, both literally and psychologically. Although Johnson is aware of the risk of her material's being interpreted this way, she does not resolve this problem in the way that she makes her argument.

LESLIE LEBOWITZ

Duke University
Durham
North Carolina

LONG, LARRY. *Migration and Residential Mobility in the United States.* Pp. xviii, 397. New York: Russell Sage Foundation, 1988. $42.50.

FREY, WILLIAM H. and ALDEN SPEARE, Jr. *Regional and Metropolitan Growth and Decline in the United States.* Pp. xxix, 586. New York: Russell Sage Foundation, 1988. $70.00.

Migration and Residential Mobility and *Regional and Metropolitan Growth and Decline*

are two books in the ambitious series planned, commissioned, and monitored by the National Committee for Research on the 1980 Census, a committee appointed by the Social Science Research Council and sponsored by the Council, the Russell Sage Foundation, and the Alfred P. Sloan Foundation, in collaboration with the U.S. Bureau of the Census. The goal of the series is to convert the statistics of the 1980 census into authoritative analyses of major changes and trends in U.S. life, a primarily descriptive picture enriched by both a historical perspective and a concern with the future. The books look at ethnic groups, status groups, and spatial dimensions. Specific attention is given to social forces such as black-nonblack changes, Hispanic and Asian migration patterns, and women's life-style changes. The discussions are broad, from general topics to numerous specific concepts such as gentrification, rural renaissance, and urban public transportation.

Migration and Residential Mobility analyzes trends and patterns of geographical mobility within the United States, using the decennial censuses since 1940 and other major national surveys. This volume presents a picture of U.S. geographical mobility for the last half century, shows how policy has been affected by available knowledge, and shows where more research is needed. The book follows recent literature in putting greater reliance on micro-level models in an attempt to explore behavioral bases for migration. For example, the book presents the first data for the United States as a whole on the numbers of reasons for moving reported by interstate migrations, and presents international comparisons to affirm the notion of considerable geographical mobility in the United States. The book also emphasizes analyses that improve population projections for subnational areas and pushes strongly for more attention in general to program planning and evaluation. Larry Long gives special attention to the consequences of migration and stability, recognizing this as a complex issue.

Regional and Metropolitan Growth and Decline uses detailed data to present a picture of the fundamental redistribution of population in the United States in the 1970s and early 1980s, using 1980 census data and later data where available. The major explanations and theories to explain these patterns are critiqued. The first part of the book evaluates patterns across regions and metropolitan areas, and the last part evaluates patterns within large metropolitan areas. The book documents that the 1970s can be regarded as a transition decade in U.S. population redistribution and in historical trends in the industrial world. In the United States, the westward redistribution became a southward and westward redistribution, the largest metropolitan areas had population losses, nonmetropolitan areas gained at the expense of metropolitan areas—modified since 1980—and the pace of suburbanization declined. Frey and Speare conclude that we are likely never again to be able to look as closely to past trends as a guide for the future and that it is too soon to forecast which metropolitan areas and regions will dominate U.S. settlement patterns in the coming decades. They do an admirable job, however, of examining significant changes in race relations, family-formation patterns, the nature of work, and other factors that are now operating.

Each of the volumes does an outstanding job of presenting and interpreting the data. The analyses are thorough, interdisciplinary, insightful, and recognizable of shortcomings. The concern with examining the consequences as well as the causes of change gives a welcome push to the move for more attention to policy and planning.

ABRAHAM D. LAVENDER

Florida International University
Miami

LUEPNITZ, DEBORAH ANNA. *The Family Interpreted: Feminist Theory in Clinical Practice.* Pp. xii, 349. New York: Basic Books, 1988. $22.95.

The revolution in thought ushered in by modern feminism has steadily expanded its zone of influence until even psychotherapy has begun to take notice. I say "even" because while the pioneering work of Freud and the more explicit prefeminist work of Karen Horney or Clara Thompson proposed new and challenging hypotheses about gender and patterns of distress, the field as a whole was slow to change. Not only did traditional conceptions of gender and family persist, but until quite recently, an androcentric yardstick prevailed.

Nowhere has this been more apparent than in the relative newcomer to the healing profession, family therapy. And nowhere has the utility of feminist theory been more ably demonstrated than in Deborah Anna Luepnitz's book, *The Family Interpreted: Feminist Theory in Clinical Practice.* Although this is a book about psychotherapy with families, with three case studies presented at the end, it is really a book about theory. The argument developed points to the need for family therapy to become better grounded in systematic theory in general and in feminist theory in particular. Techniques of therapy, in which the field abounds, will not provide that theory.

Accordingly, Luepnitz has a twofold aim: (1) to link social theory and family therapy, and (2) to connect family therapy with feminist thought. Although this link cannot be fully forged at this time, the foundation for a theoretically grounded synthesis is possible now, and this book is offered as a step in that direction.

A brief historical overview of the family's evolution helps Luepnitz to locate the contemporary family in a changing cultural and sociological context, which adds an oft-neglected—and illuminating—dimension to current writing in the field. This is supplemented by an examination of the ideologies that infuse our conceptions of the normal family and the value of judgments embedded in contemporary clinical practice.

As regards layout, the book consists of an introductory chapter that provides a carefully crafted framework for the analysis, followed by seven chapters, each a critical appraisal of a leading school or approach to family therapy today—including those of Ackerman, Bowen, Minuchin, Satir, Whitaker, and others—as well as the philosophical underpinnings proposed by the influential Gregory Bateson. Luepnitz felicitously combines reverence and critique. She meticulously builds toward her main conclusion to the effect that however creative and original their unquestionable contributions, most of these luminaries remained relatively unenlightened about the basic patriarchal assumptions about gender that inform their work. In addition, they are typically uninformed about or dismissive of feminist theory and feminist therapy, a deficiency Luepnitz seeks to remedy.

If the proposed additions of feminist concepts to traditional therapy are persuasive, they remain, at this stage, of promising rather then proved utility. Nonetheless, simply to counteract traditionalist ideas by the infusion of a new worldview is bound to generate the intellectual ferment and debate needed for growth. It is hoped that this will raise the level of contemporary discourse as well as improve the quality of therapy. All of this is offered in a collaborative rather than contentious spirit, one that stresses the addition, not the substitution, of feminist therapy to teaching, research, and clinical practice.

In what is perhaps the most brilliant chapter of the book, Luepnitz explores the potentially fruitful collaboration between classic psychoanalytic theory and feminist therapy, encouraging their future alliance for the benefit of both.

The final chapters of the book present three necessarily selective case histories of families actually treated by Luepnitz. These are designed to illustrate the application of feminist concepts to existing family therapy. Such a therapy, by paying critical attention to gender issues, strives to empower families by reducing their sense of isolation, enlarging their zones of respect and empathy for each family member, and eliminating the unbalanced and destructive rank order of gender within families. The latter, it is argued, results all too often in father absence and mother devaluation within a patriarchal family framework that is perpetuated from generation to generation.

As Luepnitz is quick to acknowledge, these illustrations cannot as yet demonstrate the validity of feminist over other therapies, but they can expand intellectual horizons and therapeutize aims. If she holds out a rather ambitious agenda for feminist therapy, it is one infused with historic awareness, critical acumen, wide learning, and intellectual rigor.

The book is beautifully written, cogently argued, conceptually sophisticated, and penetrating in its import—in short, an impressive achievement to be savored by theorists and therapists alike.

SUZANNE KELLER

Princeton University
New Jersey

PERLMANN, JOEL. *Ethnic Differences: Schooling and Social Structure among the Irish, Italians, Jews, and Blacks in an American City, 1880-1935.* Pp. xi, 327 New York: Cambridge University Press, 1988. No price.

The field of ethnic studies has gained increasing stature in the social sciences in the past three decades. Of particular interest is the topic of ethnic differences in schooling and in standing in the economic opportunity structure in complex societies. I must note that this is no longer a uniquely American preoccupation. For example, European scholars are increasingly turning to scrutinize questions of comparative ethnicity as Europe contends with the issue of the future fate of second-generation immigrants —such as Turks, Moroccans, southern Italians, and Spaniards—in northern Europe. This book takes on the complex and delicate problem of the gap in academic achievement and socioeconomic standing among the Irish, Italians, Russian Jews, and blacks in Providence, Rhode Island, in the years 1880-1935. Throughout, Perlmann also compares the ethnic experience with Yankee norms. Is class background, as Marxist-oriented scholars have been advocating, the prime mover in the educational achievement and eventual economic attainment of children? Or, conversely, is culture, particularly its shaping of a work ethic—or a "culture of poverty"—the most basic sufficient reason to explain measured ethnic differences?

The book is divided into an introduction, five substantial chapters, a conclusion, and an appendix. The introduction and the first chapter explain the goals of the study: an inquiry into the possible causes of the "dramatic differences in the school achievements of ethnic groups," and the complex relationships between educational outcomes and economic attainment across groups. The introduction and chapter 1 present basic information as to the nature of the exquisitely detailed historical data on ethnicity, schooling, and social structure in the city of Providence. The five substantial chapters contain statistical and other data comparing the nature of the ethnic experience in schools and in the job market. The conclusion is a measured interpretation of the meaning of ethnic differences. The appendix discusses various issues of research methodology.

The Russian Jews and the black immigrants fall at opposite ends of a continuum of ethnic educational achievement and economic attainment, with the Irish and the Italians falling somewhere in between. The children of Russian Jews did comparatively very well in schools. They were "more likely to receive relatively extended education than were those of other immigrant groups" and were able to improve their economic standing more rapidly than the children of other groups. The striking features of the Russian Jewish experience include the comparatively high level of literacy upon arrival to the United States—only one-fifth of the males and two-fifths of the females were illiterate—and their quick entry into commerce, as opposed to the more usual immigrant route into the U.S. opportunity structure: through manual labor. By 1915 Russian Jewish children were more likely to enroll in high school—54.3 percent of all native-born sons of Russian Jews entered high school compared to 17.0 percent of the native-born sons of Italians—they were more likely to receive better grades and more likely to graduate and go on to college than any other of the groups considered. Contrary to what Russian Jewish cultural tradition may have led us to predict, there were no important gender differences in the education of boys and girls, at least not until college: both Russian Jewish boys and girls were more likely to enter high school and to graduate. Of critical importance is the fact that even after controlling for family characteristics associated with class—such as father's occupation, family's property value, number of siblings, and single-parent household—the Russian Jewish standing in academic performance remained the highest. Clearly, something other than class was operating. The cultural reverence for the written word—the talmudic tradition of study and interpretation, the honorable and desirable role of the scholar in the culture—surely contributed to shaping the standing of this immigrant group in the U.S. educational system. As Perlmann notes, although class is certainly an important variable in the schooling outcome and economic standing of the children of immigrants, it certainly does not explain the entire picture.

If class and culture are both important in understanding the immigrant journey, including some of the specific problems the Irish and Italians encountered in the New World, a full discussion of the poisonous effects of discrimination must be taken into account if we are to understand the relatively poor educational performance of blacks in schools. Most striking is the fact that whereas black children were almost as likely as Yankees to be enrolled in schools, their progress through the grades and their high school entry rates were consistently low. In 1915 and 1925 theirs was the lowest high school entry rate in the city. Was this to be accounted for by class, by culture, or by family structure? Black single-parent households were not uncommon in the 1880-1925 period. According to Perlmann's calculations, "the most critical of these aspects of family background was social class: Blacks were overwhelmingly concentrated among the poor. Family structure exerted a much weaker influence on schooling." Yet, again, class alone does not explain the entire picture. Blacks in Providence faced a job ceiling above which they could not rise regardless of their educational credentials. In the year 1915, whereas 68 percent all of high school graduates found employment in the white-collar sector, only 18 percent of the black high school graduates were able to find white-collar employment. Note that even after controlling for class differences between these high school graduates the residual black-white difference remains enormous. Even those blacks with higher grade point averages than whites were unable to compete fairly for jobs: the cards were stacked against them, regardless of educational effort and earned credentials.

The treatment of the notion of culture and its relation to schooling and the incorporation of immigrants into American life is beneath the stature of the book as a whole. Perlmann often reduces culture to a somewhat arbitrary list of traits—"fatalism," "familism," "individualism," among others—that hardly constitute a culture in the modern anthropological use of the term. Incidentally, the book fails to consider the possible influence on schooling of linguistic and discourse discontinuities between the English language of the schools and the children's home language. How did the fact that children came from households where Yiddish, Italian, or black English was spoken relate to educational experience and outcome? Nor are the linkages between schooling outcome and experience in the economic opportunity structure, so critical to understanding the black case, well articulated theoretically. Curiously, Perlmann does not weigh the relation of a transatlantic migration experience versus an internal migration—blacks versus all other ethnic groups—to schooling problems and outcomes.

Still this book is a carefully crafted work that I predict, will become a classic in the study of ethnicity, class, and schooling in modern American history. The book is full of fascinating analysis of historical detail on ethnic differences—such as on why blacks were far less

likely to send their children to work than any of the other groups; why the Irish middle class was more likely to enroll their children in Catholic schools; and why the daughters of Italian *contadini* were most likely to be employed as textile workers—and their relation to educational outcome. Reading the book from the perspective of the late 1980s and early 1990s, one is struck by the unmistakably equivocal performance of the American educational system. The pages of the *New York Times* routinely report accounts—often sensationalist—of the spectacular achievements of Asian youths in American high schools and most prestigious universities. At the same time, blacks, American Indians, mainland Puerto Ricans, and Mexican Americans continue to fail in schools at alarmingly high rates. The point is that ethnic differences and ethnic inequalities are historically enduring problems in this country; yet, with the exception of alarmingly few serious anthropological and sociological studies, contemporary ethnic differences are still simplistically attributed to the overworked idea of a culture of poverty or to some form of unreflective pop class analysis or, even worse, to some alleged innate biological differences. Joel Perlmann's meticulous work is a sober reminder of the complexities—and potential rewards—involved in studying and understanding ethnic differences.

MARCELO M. SUAREZ-OROZCO

University of California
San Diego

ECONOMICS

ETZIONI, AMITAI. *The Moral Dimension: Toward a New Economics.* Pp. xv, 257. New York: Macmillan, 1988. $24.95.

One way to proceed in the social sciences might be called the simplifying approach. In order to create internally consistent general theories, simplifiers ignore whole aspects of reality that do not fit with their presuppositions. In addition to the natural sciences, this method is used in economics, and that is what the author of this comprehensive book does not like. Amitai Etzioni criticizes economics for what he believes to be its unrealistic and immoral psychology.

Its simplicity makes this psychology unrealistic. Yet because they assume only that individuals choose the most efficient means to maximize a primary end, economists can ignore psychological complexities and build a parsimonious set of deductive explanations for the behavior of large numbers of people. Much of Etzioni's book concentrates on findings showing that this primitive psychology is inaccurate. The problem is with the model put forward as an alternative. Even though relationships between measures of norms, values, personalities, and how people behave generally are negligible, Etzioni wants us to return to the older social science that relied on these explanations. In spite of their faults, economic models have done better than mental models when they have been tested, in part because economists focus on behavior and largely ignore mental processes.

Etzioni argues that the psychology of economics is immoral because it encourages people to seek selfish ends. While many students probably take this vulgarized lesson from their economics classes, the charge is almost unfair. Economists do not attempt to explain the selection of ends, so the pursuit of unselfish goals is completely consistent with their formulations. Etzioni realizes this, but he worries about the effects of this vulgarized lesson.

There also is a vexing dilemma inherent in ethical critiques of honest efforts to understand human behavior. Suppose in our search for the truth we find that theories based on unpalatable assumptions yield the most understanding. While no one should ignore moral considerations, which should come first in the social sciences, getting people to do the right thing or finding the truth no matter where that search leads? Etzioni eschews an individualistic stance for ethical reasons, but perhaps economic assumptions will help us to understand much more about human affairs.

In a book that will be valuable to critics of economics, Etzioni has amassed much evidence

that contradicts economic assumptions, but the conceptual apparatus he advocates is not a good replacement for what he dislikes about that discipline.

DAVID JACOBS

University of Oregon
Eugene

KOOPMAN, GEORG, KLAUS MATTHIES, and BEATE RESZAT. *Oil and the International Economy: Lessons from Two Price Shocks.* Pp. 451. New Brunswick, NJ: Transaction Books, 1989. Paperbound, $24.95.

GELB, ALAN. *Oil Windfalls: Blessing or Curse?* Pp. x, 357. New York: Oxford University Press, 1988. $32.50.

Energy is at the trough of Anthony Downs's "issue attention cycle." For consumers this is good news: oil prices, as I write, hover between $17 and $18 per barrel and prices at the pump fluctuate around the $1 level. For producers the situation is far more troubling. The wealthy producers of the Gulf can sit back and wait for the next price spiral. The poorer exporters are in far more dire circumstances; they are burdened with debt that they incurred in the high-rolling days of the 1970s and teeter on the brink of insolvency.

What is to be done? Koopman et al. suggest that the industrialized nations provide development assistance to debt-ridden poor nations—be they oil importers or exporters—in order to reduce pressure on energy markets. Gelb and associates offer no specific proposal but hint at a radically disturbing conclusion: eliminating political instability is the only way for less well-off exporters to garner the will to resist demands by groups for huge expenditures such as public-works projects. Such enterprises are typically marked by great cost overruns, long delays, and excessive work forces. The projects feed on themselves during inflationary periods, leading to spiraling foreign debt and foreign-exchange imbalances. Governments subject to such pressures are likely to make the wrong investment decisions initially, emphasizing infrastructure development rather than savings, and cannot adjust wages and domestic oil prices to meet changing economic circumstances.

The problem, however, is more severe than would be suggested by instability alone. After all, who wants governmental instability? Rather, the implication — unstated — is that the real culprit, aside from the case of Nigeria, is democracy. Is, then, democracy the real villain in the search for a coherent energy-development policy? It is not surprising that Gelb and his associates do not make the argument directly, since this study was written under the auspices of the World Bank, which, after all, is funded largely by the Western democracies.

Democracy is a messy political system. As Theodore Lowi (*The End of Liberalism*) and Mancur Olson (*The Rise and Decline of Nations*) have argued, open polities lead to the proliferation of interest groups. These actors push politicians to enact policies that might differ from what economists find optimal. Political machines, in either urban America or Venezuela and Ecuador, must provide potential supporters with tangible benefits. On the other hand, noncompetitive regimes — even if formally democratic — such as Trinidad and Tobago, Algeria, and Indonesia have greater freedom to pursue policy initiatives that might mitigate the impact of the bust cycles.

The Gelb volume raises important questions, albeit with only passing references to these political issues. It is a study of what happened to six developing oil exporters in the wake of the oil bust of the 1980s. Following eight comparative chapters, there are six country chapters — on Algeria, Ecuador, Indonesia, Nigeria, Trinidad and Tobago, and Venezuela — coauthored by Gelb with specialists on each country. There is a forgettable second chapter introducing a variety of theories and models that do not recur in the book. The bulk of the analysis, however, is fascinating, even if the prose is turgid. The heart of the argument is that the developing countries made their own choices on how to handle their new-found wealth and they all did rather poorly. The more stable were able to reverse course when prices began to slide and

pursue more economically efficient policies, while Nigeria, which has been marked by a series of coups, military governments, and democratic eras, and the two Latin American democracies could not curb their citizens' tastes for high levels of public spending.

The volume by Koopman et al., on the other hand, has no central theme. I could not even find any overall logic underlying the chapter sequence. Nevertheless, there is a lot of interesting material herein, even if the book, a reprint of a 1984 West German publication, is somewhat out of date. For example, Table 1.4 on page 45 reports a prediction that the U.S. domestic supply of oil would run out by 1991.

Oil and the International Economy seems modeled after such volumes as *Energy Future*. The authors argue that oil-price increases in the 1970s had marked effects on exchange rates, the inflationary impact of the price spikes were long-term as well as short-term, low energy prices may ultimately be destabilizing, and price increases have highlighted competitiveness between consuming nations.

Most of the arguments are unobjectionable, although it is unclear what undergirds them. Did Koopman and his coauthors employ any econometric techniques, as Gelb did? Aside from a few simple regression equations, there is no indication of how the supporting data are derived. Moreover, the regression showing that increasing oil prices had no significant effect on the overall consumer price index in the United States ignores a great deal of evidence to the contrary. The authors argue that thinly populated countries with large oil reserves, such as those in the Gulf, will be moderate in pricing and producing behavior, neglecting Kuwait's role as a violator of production quotas of the Organization of Petroleum Exporting Countries. They maintain that protectionism is largely traceable to the increase in oil prices, ignoring past histories of tariffs in the West and other equally significant changes in the international political economy, especially the shift from manufacturing to services. There are minor irritants as well: in Table 3.5 Iran is misclassified as an Arab country, and the list of oil importers among developing countries curiously excludes, among others, Taiwan, Chad, Mali, Grenada, Guinea, Mozambique, Belize, and Tunisia.

The Koopman et al. volume is produced by photo-offset from what seems to be a typewriter or an off-center computer printer. It has no index. The Gelb volume is far more attractive. It has an index. Its margins are justified. When underlining with a ruler, one does not draw a line through any words. But when one arrives at page 255 — at least in my copy — there is a gap of eight pages. The stubs are there, but that is about all.

ERIC M. USLANER

University of Maryland
College Park

OTHER BOOKS

ALEXANDER, HERBERT and BRIAN HAGERTY. *Financing the 1984 Election.* Pp. xvi, 430. Lexington, MA: Lexington Books, 1987. $45.00.

AMBROSE, STEPHEN E. *Rise to Liberalism: American Foreign Policy since 1938.* 5th ed. New York: Penguin, 1988. Paperbound, $8.95.

ARBENA, JOSEPH L., ed. *Sport and Society in Latin America: Diffusion, Dependency, and the Rise of Mass Culture.* Pp. ix, 162. Westport, CT: Greenwood Press, 1988. $29.95.

BAILEY, SYDNEY D. *The Procedure of the UN Security Council.* 2d ed. Pp. xiii, 499. New York: Oxford University Press, 1988. $85.00.

BALDWIN, ROBERT E., CARL B. HAMILTON, and ANDRE SAPIR. *Issues in US-EC Trade Relations.* Pp. xii, 397. Chicago: University of Chicago Press, 1988. $49.00.

BARBER, WILLIAM. *From the New Deal Era: Herbert Hoover, the Economists, and American Economic Policy, 1921-1933.* Pp. xii, 237. New York: Cambridge University Press, 1985. $39.50.

BARLOW, J. JACKSON, LEONARD W. LEVY, and KEN MASUGI, eds. *The American Founding: Essays on the Formation of the Constitution.* Pp. xxii, 341. Westport, CT: Greenwood Press, 1988. $45.00.

BERG, RAISSA L. *Acquired Traits: Memoirs of a Geneticist from the Soviet Union.* Pp. xi, 483. New York: Viking, 1988. $19.95.

BOCK, JOSEPH. *The White House Staff and the National Security Assistant: Friendship and Friction at the Water's Edge.* Pp. xii, 215. Westport, CT: Greenwood Press, 1987. $35.00.

BOCK, JOSEPH G. *The White House Staff and the National Security Council: Friendship and Friction at the Water's Edge.* Pp. xii, 215. Westport, CT: Greenwood Press, 1987. No price.

CALHOUN, FREDERICK S. *Power and Principle: Armed Intervention in Wilsonian Foreign Policy.* Pp. xi, 333. Kent, OH: Kent State University Press, 1986. $28.00.

CAMMACK, PAUL, DAVID POOL, and WILLIAM TORDOFF. *Third World Politics: A Comparative Introduction.* Pp. xi, 308. Baltimore, MD: Johns Hopkins University Press, 1988. $38.50. Paperbound, $14.95.

CARROLL, PETER and DAVID W. NOBLE. *The Free and the Unfree: A New History of the United States.* 2d ed. New York: Penguin Books, 1988. Paperbound, $7.95.

COHEN, STANLEY. *Against Criminology.* Pp. xii, 310. New Brunswick, NJ: Transaction Books, 1988. Paperbound, no price.

DAVID, JOHN. *Libyan Politics: Tribe and Revolution.* Pp. xii, 297. Berkeley: University of California Press, 1987. No price.

DAVIS, REED M., ed. *Moral Reasoning and Statecraft.* Pp. xiii, 193. Lanham, MD: University Press of America, 1988. $26.50. Paperbound, $12.75.

DE MESQUITA, BRUCE BUENO, DAVID NEWMAN, and ALVIN RABUSHKA. *Forecasting Political Events: The Future of Hong Kong.* Pp. x, 198. New Haven, CT: Yale University Press, 1988. Paperbound, $12.95.

DENNIS, NORMAN and A. H. HALSEY. *English Ethical Socialism: Thomas More to R. H. Tawney.* Pp. xiv, 282. New York: Oxford University Press, 1988. $57.00.

DINNERSTEIN, LEONARD. *Uneasy at Home: Antisemitism in the American Jewish Experience.* Pp. xi, 281. New York: Columbia University Press, 1987. $25.00.

DRUCKER, HENRY et al., eds. *Developments in British Politics.* Revised ed. Pp. xvi, 432. New York: St. Martin's Press, 1988. Paperbound, $14.95.

DUNCAN, HUGH DALZIEL. *Culture and Democracy.* Pp. xxx, 616. New Brunswick, NJ: Transaction Books, 1989. $24.95.

EDMONDS, ROBIN. *Setting the Mould: The United States and Britain, 1945-1950.* Pp. xxx, 349. New York: W. W. Norton, 1986. $22.95.

EDSFORTH, RONALD. *Class Conflict and Cultural Consensus: The Making of a Mass Consumer Society in Flint, Michigan.* Pp. xvi,

294. New Brunswick, NJ: Rutgers University Press, 1986. $40.00.

FEATHERSTONE, KEVIN. *Socialist Parties and European Integration: A Comparative History.* Pp. xiii, 366. New York: St. Martin's Press, 1988. $49.95.

FELD, WERNER J. and ROBERT S. JORDAN with LEON HURWITZ. *International Organizations: A Comparative Approach.* 2d ed. Pp. xxii, 330. New York: Praeger, 1988. No price.

FORD, GERALD R. *The Ford Presidency.* Edited by Kenneth Thompson. Pp. xviii, 361. Lanham, MD: University Press of America, 1988. $31.75. Paperbound, $17.50.

FORSYTH, MURRAY and MAURICE KEENS-SOPER, eds. *A Guide to the Political Classics: Plato to Rousseau.* Pp. 205. New York: Oxford University Press, 1988. $39.95.

FRY, MAXWELL J. *Money, Interest, and Banking in Economic Development.* Pp. xx, 522. Baltimore, MD: Johns Hopkins University Press, 1988. $37.50. Paperbound, $14.95.

GARTMAN, DAVID. *Auto Slavery: The Labor Process in the American Automobile Industry, 1897-1950.* Pp. xv, 348. New Brunswick, NJ: Rutgers University Press, 1986. $42.00. Paperbound, $20.00.

GERT, BERNARD. *Morality: A New Justification of the Moral Rules.* Pp. xxx, 317. New York: Oxford University Press, 1988. $34.00.

GLEECK, LEWIS E., Jr. *Dissolving the Colonial Bond: American Ambassadors to the Philippines, 1946-1984.* Pp. x, 403. Quezon City: New Day, 1988. Distributed by the Cellar Book Shop, Detroit, MI. Paperbound, $16.00.

GOLDWIN, ROBERT A. and ART KAUFMAN, eds. *Slavery and Its Consequences: The Constitution, Equality, and Race.* Pp. xvi, 181. Washington, DC: American Enterprise Institute for Public Policy Research, 1988. Paperbound, no price.

GOLEMBIEWSKI, ROBERT T. *Men, Management, and Morality: Toward a New Organizational Ethic.* Pp. xvi, 320. New Brunswick, NJ: Transaction Books, 1989. No price.

GRANA, CESAR. *Meaning and Authenticity: Further Essays on the Sociology of Art.* Pp. xxiii, 188. New Brunswick, NJ: Transaction Books, 1989. No price.

GREENFELD, LIAH and MICHEL MARTIN, eds. *Center: Ideas and Institutions.* Pp. xxii, 282. Chicago: University of Chicago Press, 1989. $39.95.

GRETHER, DAVID M. et al. *The Allocation of Scarce Resources: Experimental Economics and the Problem of Allocating Airport Slots.* Pp. xviii, 333. Boulder, CO: Westview Press, 1989. Paperbound, $34.95.

GREY, JEFFREY. *The Commonwealth Armies and the Korean War.* Pp. xii, 244. New York: Manchester University Press, 1988. Distributed by St. Martin's Press, New York. $45.00.

HALL, JOHN A. *Powers and Liberties: The Causes and Consequences of the Rise of the West.* Pp. vi, 272. Berkeley: University of California Press, 1986. $19.95.

HOLMES, JOHN and JOHN KIRTON, eds. *Canada and the New Internationalism.* Pp. xii, 164. Toronto: Canadian Institute for International Affairs, 1987. Paperbound, $14.00.

HONIG, EMILY and GAIL HERSHATTER. *Personal Voices: Chinese Women in the 1980s.* Pp. vii, 387. Stanford, CA: Stanford University Press, 1988. $42.50. Paperbound, $12.95.

HOPE, MARJORIE and JAMES YOUNG. *The Faces of Homelessness.* Pp. xv, 318. Lexington, MA: Lexington Books, 1986. $25.00.

KATZ, MICHAEL B. *Reconstructing American Education.* Pp. viii, 212. Cambridge, MA: Harvard University Press, 1987. $22.50.

KELLERMAN, BARBARA and JEFFREY Z. RUBIN, eds. *Leadership and Negotiation in the Middle East.* Pp. x, 299. New York: Praeger, 1988. No price.

KETTL, DONALD F. *Leadership at the Fed.* Pp. xiii, 218. New Haven, CT: Yale University Press, 1988. Paperbound, $11.95.

KHALIDI, RASHID. *Under Siege: PLO Decisionmaking during the 1982 War.* Pp. ix, 241. New York: Columbia University Press, 1986. $22.50.

KIRP, DONALD L., MARK G. YUDOF, and MARLENE STRONG. *Gender Justice.* Pp. x,

246. Chicago: University of Chicago Press, 1986. $19.95.

KLEINMAN, ARTHUR. *Social Origins of Distress and Disease: Depression, Neurasthenia, and Pain in Modern China.* Pp. xii, 264. New Haven, CT: Yale University Press, 1986. $22.00.

KNOX, P. L. et al. *The United States: A Contemporary Human Geography.* Pp. x, 287. Essex, England: Longman Scientific & Technical; New York: John Wiley, 1988. Paperbound, no price.

KRAFT, MICHAEL E. and NORMAN J. VIG, eds. *Technology and Politics.* Pp. xv, 358. Durham, NC: Duke University Press, 1988. $59.75. Paperbound, $17.95.

LAITIN, DAVID D. and SAID S. SAMATAR. *Somalia: Nation in Search of a State.* Pp. xvii, 198. Boulder, CO: Westview Press, 1987. $28.00.

LAMIS, ALEXANDER P. *The Two-Party South.* Expanded ed. Pp. x, 408. New York: Oxford University Press, 1988. $34.00.

LEVINE, DAVID O. *The American College and the Culture of Aspiration, 1915-1940.* Pp. 281. Ithaca, NY: Cornell University Press, 1986. $29.95.

LEVY, DAVID J. *Political Order: Philosophical Anthropology, Modernity, and the Challenge of Ideology.* Pp. ix, 204. Baton Rouge: Louisiana State University Press, 1987. $22.50.

LEWIS, DONALD M. *Lighten Their Darkness: The Evangelical Mission to Working-Class London, 1828-1860.* Pp. xix, 369. Westport, CT: Greenwood Press, 1986. $35.00.

LI, K. T. *The Evolution of Policy behind Taiwan's Development Success.* Pp. xiii, 189. New Haven, CT: Yale University Press, 1988. $25.00.

LO, WINSTON W. *An Introduction to the Civil Service of Sung China with Emphasis on Its Personnel Administration.* Pp. xii, 297. Honolulu: University of Hawaii, 1987. $36.00.

MANCUSO, JAMES C. and MILDRED L. G. SHAW, eds. *Cognition and Personal Structure: Computer Access and Analysis.* Pp. vi, 341. New York: Praeger, 1988. No price.

MARTIN, EDWIN. *Divided Counsel: The Anglo-American Response to Communist Victory in China.* Pp. xi, 265. Lexington: University of Kentucky Press, 1986. $27.00.

MARX, KARL and FREDERICK ENGELS. *Collected Works.* Vol. 23, *Marx and Engels, 1871-1874.* Pp. xxxv, 808. New York: International, 1988. $15.00.

MASSEY, GARTH. *Subsistence and Change: Lessons of Agropastoralism in Somalia.* Pp. xvii, 238. Boulder, CO: Westview Press, 1987. Paperbound, $34.50

MATSON, CATHY D. and PETER S. ONUF. *A Union of Interests: Political and Economic Thought in Revolutionary America.* Pp. x, 237. Lawrence: University Press of Kansas, 1990. $25.00.

McEVEDY, COLIN. *The Penguin Atlas of North American History to 1870.* Pp. 112. New York: Penguin Books, 1988. $6.95.

McGINNISS, JOE. *The Selling of the President.* Pp. xxii, 253. New York: Penguin, 1988. Paperbound, $7.95.

MELVIN, PATRICIA MOONEY. *The Organic City: Urban Definition and Neighborhood Organization, 1880-1920.* Pp. xii, 227. Lexington: University of Kentucky Press, 1987. $25.00.

MODELSKI, GEORGE and SYLVIA MODELSKI, eds. *Documenting Global Leadership.* Pp. ix, 422. Seattle: University of Washington Press, 1989. $40.00.

MORMINO, GARY R. and GEORGE E. POZZETTA. *The Immigrant World of Ybor City: Italians and Their Latin Neighbors in Tampa, 1885-1985.* Pp. xiii, 368. Champaign: University of Illinois Press, 1987. $24.95.

NARDULLI, PETER F., ed. *Diversity, Conflict, and State Politics.* Pp. xii, 333. Champaign: University of Illinois Press, 1989. $34.95. Paperbound, $19.95.

NELSON, DANIEL N. *Elite-Mass Relations in Communist Systems.* Pp. x, 217. New York: St. Martin's Press, 1988. $37.50.

NELSON, MICHAEL. *A Heartbeat Away: Report of the Task Force on the Vice Presidency.* Pp. ix, 114. Winchester, MA: Unwin Hyman, 1988. $18.95. Paperbound, $9.95.

NIEMI, RICHARD G., JOHN MUELLER, and TOM W. SMITH. *Trends in Public Opinion: A Compendium of Survey Data.* Pp. 344. Westport, CT: Greenwood Press, 1989. $49.95.

NORGREN, JILL and SERENA NANDA. *American Cultural Pluralism and Law.* Pp. xi, 254. New York: Praeger, 1988. $45.00. Paperbound, $16.95.

OAKES, GUY. *Weber and Ricket: Concept Formation in the Cultural Sciences.* Pp. ix, 190. Cambridge: MIT Press, 1989. $22.50.

OWEN, WILFRED. *Transportation and World Development.* Pp. xiv, 156. Baltimore, MD: Johns Hopkins University Press, 1987. $22.50.

PACIFIC FORUM. *Summaries of Three Bilateral Conferences Held in Beijing and Shanghai, the People's Republic of China.* Pp. xv, 72. Honolulu, HI: Pacific Forum, 1988. Distributed by University of Hawaii Press, Honolulu. Paperbound, $9.95.

PIRAGES, DENNIS. *Global Technopolitics: The International Politics of Technology and Resources.* Pp. ix, 220. Pacific Grove, CA: Brooks/Cole, 1989. Paperbound, $17.00.

POSTERMAN, ROY L. and JEFFREY M. RIEDINGER. *Land Reform and Democratic Development.* Pp. xii, 313. Baltimore, MD: Johns Hopkins University Press, 1987. No price.

QUESTER, GEORGE H. *Offense and Defense in the International System.* Pp. xxxiii, 219. New Brunswick, NJ: Transaction Books, 1988. $24.95.

RENFREW, CHARLES B. et al. *Democracy: Its Strengths and Weaknesses.* Pp. 266. Austin: University of Texas Press, 1988. $16.95.

ROBYN, DOROTHY. *Breaking the Special Interests: Trucking Deregulation and the Politics of Policy Reform.* Pp. xii, 295. Chicago: University of Chicago Press, 1987. $24.95.

ROSE, RICHARD. *Politics in England: Change and Persistence.* 5th ed. Pp. xv, 379. Glenview, IL: Scott, Foresman/Little, Brown, 1988. Paperbound, $12.76.

RUGGIERO, KRISTIN HOFFMAN. *And Here the World Ends: The Life of an Argentine Village.* Pp. xvii, 226. Stanford, CA: Stanford University Press, 1988. $32.50.

SANDBERG, NEIL C. *Jewish Life in Los Angeles: A Window to Tomorrow.* Pp. xii, 210. Lanham, MD: University Press of America, 1986. $17.00.

SCHLEIFMAN, NURIT. *Undercover Agents in the Russian Revolutionary Movement: The SR Party, 1902-14.* Pp. xvii, 222. New York: St. Martin's Press, 1988. $29.95.

SCOBIE, JAMES R. *Secondary Cities of Argentina: The Social History of Corrientes, Salta, and Mendoza, 1850-1910.* Pp. xvi, 276. Stanford, CA: Stanford University Press, 1988. $42.50.

SHARKANSKY, IRA. *The Political Economy of Israel.* Pp. xi, 157. New Brunswick, NJ: Transaction Books, 1987. No price.

SHERRY, MICHAEL S. *The Rise of American Air Power: The Creation of Armageddon.* Pp. xiii, 435. New Haven, CT: Yale University Press, 1987. $29.95.

SIMCOX, DAVID E., ed. *U.S. Immigration in the 1980s: Reappraisal and Reform.* Pp. xii, 308. Boulder, CO: Westview Press, 1988. Paperbound, $30.00.

SIMON, JULIAN L. *Theory of Population and Economic Growth.* Pp. xi, 232. New York: Basil Blackwell, 1986. $24.95.

SMITH, JOAN et al., eds. *Racism, Sexism, and the World-System.* Pp. xii, 221. Westport, CT: Greenwood Press, 1988. No price.

SULEIMAN, EZRA N. *Private Power and Centralization in France: The Notaires and the State.* Pp. xxi, 338. Princeton, NJ: Princeton University Press, 1987. Paperbound, $14.95.

TANANBAUM, DUANE. *The Bricker Amendment Controversy: A Test of Eisenhower's Political Leadership.* Pp. xiii, 263. Ithaca, NY: Cornell University Press, 1988. $34.50.

TAYLOR, RICHARD. *Against the Bomb: The British Peace Movement 1958-1965.* Pp. 368. New York: Oxford University Press, 1988. $65.00.

THOMPSON, KENNETH W., ed. *Papers on Presidential Disability and the Twenty-Fifth Amendment.* Pp. xii, 190. Lanham, MD: University Press of America, 1988. $21.50. Paperbound, $9.75.

TICKNER, J. ANN. *Self-Reliance versus Power Politics*. Pp. xi, 282. New York: Columbia University Press, 1987. $35.00.

TIEN HUNG, NGUYEN and JEROLD L. SCHECTER. *The Palace File*. Pp. xvi, 542. New York: Harper & Row, 1986. $22.95.

WACKS, RAYMOND, ed. *Civil Liberties in Hong Kong*. Pp. xiv, 360. New York: Oxford University Press, 1988. Paperbound, $18.95.

WARD, JAMES A. *Railroads and the Character of America, 1820-1887*. Knoxville: University of Tennessee Press, 1986. No price.

WARREN, MARK. *Nietzsche and Political Thought*. Pp. xv, 311. Cambridge: MIT Press, 1988. $25.00.

WRIGHT, DEIL S. *Understanding Intergovernmental Relations*. 3d ed. Pp. xv, 511. Pacific Grove, CA: Brooks/Cole, 1988. Paperbound, $22.00.

INDEX

219